RELIGION IN
TODAY'S WORLD

RELIGION IN TODAY'S WORLD

THE RELIGIOUS SITUATION
OF THE WORLD FROM 1945
TO THE PRESENT DAY

Edited by
FRANK WHALING

T & T CLARK, EDINBURGH

Copyright © T. & T. Clark Ltd, 1987.

Typeset by C. R. Barber & Partners (Highlands) Ltd,
Fort William, Scotland,
printed in the U.K. by Billing & Sons, Worcester,
for
T. & T. Clark Ltd,
59, George Street, Edinburgh EH2 2LQ.

First printed 1987.

British Library Cataloguing in Publication Data

Religion in today's world: the religious
situation of the world from 1945 to the
present day.
1. Religions—History—20th century
I. Whaling, Frank
291'.09'04   BL80.2

ISBN 0-567-09452-9

CONTENTS

v

PREFACE

I am grateful to my distinguished colleagues for their ready collaboration in the writing of this book. This is virtually the only work that attempts to look in breadth and in depth at the religious situation of the world as a whole in the latter part of the twentieth century. Because of this fact, we are aware that this is an important book. We know that there is more to do in order to bring the religious situation in today's world right to the forefront of thought and debate. But we believe that we have made a substantial start. We hope very much that many other writers and scholars will build upon the foundations that we are providing.

Because this is such a significant project, it was important to involve the right people in it. Accordingly eleven experts from ten different universities around the world have pooled their knowledge and insights to write this book. In addition to focusing on the five major religious traditions: the Buddhist, Christian, Hindu, Jewish and Muslim, and the present religious situations in China and Japan, they also look at Civil Religion, Cults and New Religious Movements, Secular World-views, Spirituality, and the Study of Religion in today's world. This provides a comprehensive coverage. It brings into discussion all the crucial issues. It covers the whole world, not just the Western and Christian parts of it.

For some years, I have believed in the notion of a hidden university: that is to say, a community of enlightened hearts and minds scattered around different universities but ready to be brought together at the right time. This is the right time, it is a *kairos*, for this project. *Religion in Today's World* is an idea whose time has come. I like to think that the eleven colleagues who have come together to share their wisdom on *Religion in Today's World* are the visible tip of that invisible university. May our co-operation be important, not just for this particular book, but also for the wider pooling of humane knowledge around our globe.

I am grateful to my colleagues for their diligence and friendship. My thanks are due too to the Carnegie Trust and the Edinburgh University Travel and Research Fund for enabling me to visit India which was helpful for my own writing. I appreciate also the concern and interest of my wife Patricia and my children John and Ruth in the successful completion of another writing project.

Frank Whaling
December 1986

RELIGION IN TODAY'S WORLD: AN INTRODUCTORY SURVEY

Frank Whaling
(Edinburgh)

1(a) Introduction

This work represents a publishing venture of real importance. Much has been written on the past history of religion. A fair amount has been written on the contemporary study of religion. Little has been written upon religiousness itself and the actual life of religious traditions in the present-day world. In this book a team of leading scholars remedy this situation by looking directly at religion in today's world. This is the only book of its kind. As such it is hoped it will be a foundation book for courses on the contemporary religious situation. It will also be vital reading for all students of current affairs, and for all who are concerned for and interested in our global future.

Our present age is one of rapid change in which there is the emerging of a global consciousness. The world has lived through climactic events since 1945, not least in the religious sphere. In this book we chart those events:— the coming of a homeland for the Jews, the renaissance of the Buddhist and Hindu traditions with the coming of independence to South East Asia and India, the rise of a new self-confidence within Islam since the time of the oil crisis, the emergence of new religious currents such as the hundreds of 'new' religions in Japan, the thousands of African Independent Churches, and new cults in the West, the changing fortunes of the quasi-religions of Marxism, Humanism and Nationalism, the spread of

Christianity outside Europe, and the insidious threat to the continuance of the primal religions at a time when their significance is being increasingly recognised.

Eleven scholars from ten universities around the world pool their expertise in a unique team exercise to chart these events, and others of equal importance, in the exuberant religious process that constitutes religion in our time. Although they range back to the seminal date of 1945, they concentrate their main attention on the religious situation today. In so doing, they touch upon many important underlying questions:- What is 'religiousness' in today's world? In what different ways have religious traditions responded to rapid change? What is the significance of the rise of conservative fundamentalism in various traditions? How and why have ecumenical movements begun in different religions? What is the importance of the growing inter-religious stress upon spirituality? What is the relation of nationalism to religion? How do civil religion, the cults, Marxism and Humanism affect our understanding and analysis of religion? Are the newest religions and the oldest ones, the primal religions, passing phenomena? What is the significance for our global future of inter-religious dialogue? What is the process of secularisation and what, if any, are its implications for religious traditions? How can we interpret within the same framework an incipient global religious eirenicism and events in places such as Iran, Northern Ireland, the Lebanon, South Africa and Sri Lanka? Insofar as these and other general matters are, of necessity, merely touched upon in the expert and detailed treatment of particular topics, this introductory survey will attempt a brief overview of underlying motifs.

1(b) Religion and the Study of Religion in Today's World
The subject matter of this book is religion in today's world rather than the study of religion in today's world. With the

exception of one chapter, it is not a study of the study of religion, it is a study of the actuality of religion. It is not a summary of the academic work done on the contemporary Buddhist, Christian, Hindu, Japanese, Jewish, Muslim and Chinese religious traditions, or upon cults and civil religion, the primal religions, secular world-views and spirituality— although it contains reference to such literature. It is a description and analysis of the present state of those traditions and therefore the present state of religiousness in our contemporary situation. Clearly wide reading, exact knowledge and deep scholarship are applied to this investigation. However its aim is not so much to summarise the present state of academic achievement in the study of religion. It is to lay bare the actual religious situation on the face of our globe today.

This is not to suggest that academic analyses of the study of religion since 1945 are unimportant. This is far from being the case, as Jacques Waardenburg points out in his masterly summary of the main trends in the contemporary study of religion. As he shows, the academic study of religion, with its concern for methodology, theory, methods and approaches, and its close investigation of specific topics, is important. Moreover it can have consequences for the living of religion: 'Most politicians have not the faintest idea of the religious forces they may be dealing with. In such a situation experts, scholars of religion, can have a weighty and responsible voice.'[1] Nevertheless the academic study of religion as such is at one stage removed from our endeavour in this book.

As a matter of fact, even had we wanted merely to summarise other studies dealing with recent developments in religious traditions this would not have been easy because such studies are scattered for reasons we will deal with in a moment. Therefore

[1] See page 358.

3

the authors of this book, although variously historians of religion, textual experts, phenomenologists of religion, sociologists of religion, specialists in particular area studies, theologians, anthropologists, or combinations of the above have been challenged to extend the norms of their particular disciplines in order to incorporate insights derived from personal experience, personal contacts, personal visits, long friendships, dialogue situations, inter-colleague discussions, long-distance enquiries by letter and the like. Above all we have been challenged to integrate a vast amount of material, written and otherwise. The fact that we are dealing with the contemporary situation, and the fact of the eminence and wide contacts of the people concerned, have made this process possible. In any case, our concern is to summarise the recent development and present situation of the religious and secular world-views in which we are expert rather than to analyse exhaustively for its own sake the literature on these world-views.

1(c) *The Nature of Religion and the Scope of our Study*

Because the size of this work is finite, and our subject is so complex and wide, limiting choices have had to be made. Our scope is vast, no less than that of the known world. Our religious horizon is far-reaching, stretching as it does from the smallest of the primal religions to the greatest of the major living religions. It seemed clear that the religious traditions at either end of this spectrum, the primal and the major traditions, should be given attention. The case for the inclusion of the primal religions is strong, partly because of what Andrew Walls terms their 'historical anteriority and their basic elemental status in human experience',[2] and partly because of their widespread presence in today's world including as they do the religions of the circumpolar people and of various peoples of the Pacific,

[2] See page 252.

Australasia, the Americas, Inner Asia, South East Asia, India and Africa. The case for the inclusion of the major living religions is also strong, and indeed self-evident. The Buddhist, Christian, Hindu, Jewish and Muslim traditions have been strong religious forces in the past, and they remain so in the present.

We also include the religious traditions of China and Japan. By comparison with the major living religious traditions, their greatness has been territorial rather than universal. They provided the foundation for two important classical civilisations. Their present interest lies in their radical divergence and their mutual significance. At the beginning of our period, China espoused scientific materialism and championed the supremacy of this Marxist ideology over all religious world-views, old or new. At the end of our period, Tu Wei-Ming detects 'a religious revival by any standards of measurement'[3] in the organised religious traditions of China (the Muslim, Buddhist, Taoist, Catholic and Christian-Protestant). Even more importantly he raises the question of what being religious means for the majority of Chinese people, especially intellectuals, who do not belong to an organised religion but have to fashion their life's meaning in a new and potentially more pluralist setting in which Marxist-Leninist socialism, bourgeois capitalism and Confucian humanism are likely to be important factors. The evolving religious consciousness of a quarter of the human race is of crucial relevance not only for the 1,050 million people of China but for the rest of us as well.

The defeat of Japan in the Second World War led her into a religious situation opposite to that of China. Freedom of religion replaced the pre-war state-controlled suppression of religious dissent and originality, with the result that there has been an extraordinary efflorescence of religious expression in

[3] See page 279.

5

Japan since 1945 ranging from varieties of Buddhism, Shinto, Christianity, Confucianism and Folk Religion to what Brian Bocking calls the New Religions and the New New Religions. There is interplay between these different forces, and the Japanese often incorporate aspects from more than one of these religious movements into their lives. Therefore being religious within the confines of this Asian capitalist nation is a complex business. Like China it offers a different religious scenario. As Brian Bocking puts it, Japan offers 'many surprises for those who expected to see a traditional society change, in predictable ways, into a likeness of a modern Western nation.'[4] All societies and all religious traditions are unique. China and Japan are obviously so. Chinese and Japanese religious traditions are included in this book because of their own importance, because of the diverse way in which they have developed a similar cultural background, because they expose as short-sighted simplistic models of religious growth or decline, and because what is happening religiously to almost a third of the world's people in these two Asian giants is of universal significance.

In addition to including eight sets of religious traditions of one sort or another, we also deal with four other topics: civil religion and cults, secular world-views, spirituality, and the study of religion in today's world. We judge them to be of obvious relevance in a global world. Cults and sects are different kinds of new religious movements that are common in many parts of the world. Phillip Hammond provides a definition that brings out their distinctive features: 'a cult is any minority religious group whose primary ideological roots lie not in the religious traditions claimed by the majority religious groups of the society in question but elsewhere. A sect, by contrast, is any minority religious group whose primary ideological roots are shared with the majority religious groups of its society.'[5] Hence

[4] See page 177.
[5] See page 114.

6

the Jehovah's Witnesses are a sect in the USA but a cult in Japan, whereas Nichiren Shōshū is a cult in the USA but a sect in Japan. This is a helpful way of categorising new religious movements which are so widespread today. In addition Phillip Hammond links the notion of cults with the pregnant notion of civil religion, and suggests that when cults proliferate it is likely that the civil religion or 'sacred canopy' of a society is in disrepair. It is our contention that any comprehensive analysis of religion in today's world must take seriously the questions of civil religion and of new religious movements, whether together or in separation.

Jacques Waardenburg's chapter on the study of religion has been mentioned already. It appropriately comes at the end of the book. While not a conclusion in any conventional sense, it does pick up in a different context a number of issues scattered throughout the work and it links them to the study as well as the actuality of religion. Our two remaining chapters deal with seemingly opposed topics, secular world-views and spirituality, that in spite of all appearances may be dialectically linked. Ninian Smart's chapter encompasses the secular world-views of Marxism, Nationalism and Scientific Humanism as substitutes for, rivals of, or allies with traditional religions. Ewert Cousins' chapter reflects upon the recent resurgence of interest in the theory and practice of spirituality, both in the West and globally. The concerns of these two essays present a fascinating contrast. Spirituality has to do with an experiential dimension; the secular world-views engage more with beliefs, practices and social institutions. Spirituality has to do with inwardness and depth; the secular world-views engage more in outward involvement. Spirituality has to do with the spiritual element in human nature; the secular world-views engage with the body and the mind rather than the spirit. Spirituality has to do with intimate awareness of a transcendent reality not confined to human categories; the secular world-views conceptualise

7

transcendence, if at all, in human terms. Spirituality has to do with a material cosmos that points beyond itself; the secular world-views do not recognise that which lies beyond the material cosmos. The issues involved in this contrast are pregnant with possibilities for discussion that require an essay rather than a paragraph. Time and space forbid such philosophical indulgence at this point although we hope they will be followed through at length elsewhere. Suffice it to say that this contrast can be seen in complementary as well as conflict terms; it has a Yin and Yang flavour as well as a confrontational aspect. Secular world-views, insofar as they are functional equivalents of religious traditions (with their own communities, rituals, ethics, social involvement, key texts, doctrines, and aesthetic ideals) find themselves seeking for 'spiritual' values, extolling 'spiritual' champions or even martyrs, and searching for humane transcendence if haply they may find it or be found by it. Discussion of spirituality, while highlighting the deep and the inward, finds itself moving inexorably towards integrating the human world and even the natural world in its multi-layered vision. The striking success of the scientific world-view at the heart of the secular insight in producing a global world has led, due to the very problems of that global world, to a revisioning of that scientific world-view so that it may open up to other aspects of reality, including spirituality. Thus the insightful chapters by Ninian Smart and Ewart Cousins on secular world-views and spirituality are essential ingredients of this work. Religious traditions in today's world contain the secular and the spiritual within themselves; they are in dialogue with nationalism, Marxism, Humanism, and a yearning for spirituality as movements alongside themselves; they are responding, with both failure and success, to elements within human nature itself which craves pattern and meaning and wholeness.

The corollary of the above is that there are some religious

traditions that it has not been possible to include through lack of space. Among these are the Sikh tradition, the Jain tradition, the Parsis, and the Bahā'īs. Their omission is through lack of pages rather than through lack of desire. Although relatively small, they have their own importance. They are of ultimate concern to their own devotees. They are of humane significance to their own local communities. As our primary aim in this book is to describe and interpret religion in today's world in as global and universal a way as is possible, in the interests of our ultimate goal with reluctance we omit them.

2 A New and Exciting Era in Religious History

We live at a key epoch in the global history of religion. This is a bold statement to make. Perhaps all eras have claimed that theirs was the key epoch. Let us be clear first of all what we do not mean by this suggestion. We do not mean that we live in the greatest religious era in history, a kind of golden age fulfilling earlier religious evolution—our age is not greater or lesser than others, it is different. Nor do we live in an age of dramatic change in religious configurations—the early post-war spread of Marxism seemed at one time to be an exception to this notion, and all the religious traditions have changed internally and to some extent in geographical location, but the recognised religious traditions that existed before the Second World War survive now and no one of them has predominance over the others. Nor, so far as we are aware, do we live in a period of convulsively new religious beginnings—there are a plethora of new religious movements around the world with some impressive leaders but the most likely candidates for breakthrough, for example the Bahā'īs, Mormons, and Nichiren Shōshū, have some way to go before they can achieve 'world religion' status.[6] Nor are we witnessing in our time the

[6] However the Bahā'īs, although relatively small in numbers, are quoted as being present in 192 countries. See *World Christian Encyclopedia*, edited by

demise of the religious traditions before the onslaught of the secular world-views and the process of secularisation—debates that suggest this have relied too heavily upon the seeming decline of certain western churches and overtly western models of secularisation, and they have overlooked the significance of new religious movements, the real changes within *both* the traditional religions and secular world-views, and the global context of human religiousness.

In order to examine the real significance of our own age's religiousness, we will look at the historical stages that led up to it, we will examine the background to today's religion in more depth, and we will consider the religious responses to contemporary events made by individual religious traditions, by religious traditions in interplay with each other, and by religious traditions globally.

2(a) Global Religious History Prior to 1945

There are complex hermeneutical problems connected with setting out stages of history, 'secular' or 'religious', not least of them being whether secular and religious history are intertwined or separate. I will set out my stages in the broadest possible framework thereby making the point that the 'newness' of our age, within the widest conceivable context, establishes its difference and its cruciality. My scheme is a modification and an elaboration of the one set out by Ewert Cousins in his chapter.

(i) The first stage, that of Palaeolithic humanity and Palaeolithic religion, is shrouded in the mists of prehistory. It is clear that Palaeolithic humans survived in nature by chipping stone tools, by developing the bow, by domesticating dogs, and by inventing painting as aids in their hunting activity. From Peking Man (c. 500,000 BC) onwards there is evidence of ritual

David Barrett, Nairobi, Oxford, New York: Oxford University Press, 1982, p. 5.

treatment of skulls, from 75,000 BC onwards there is evidence of burial, and from 30,000 BC onwards there is the evidence of cave art to illustrate Palaeolithic religiousness. It is easy to read too much into the relatively sparse evidence that comes from Palaeolithic skeletons, artefacts and caves. We can say however that the Palaeolithic breakthrough to 'humanity' is in itself the greatest leap in the story of humankind, that early evidences of religiousness suggest that from the beginning humans were religious creatures (as well as economic and sexual creatures), and that survival in nature rather than dominance over it was the main Palaeolithic concern.

(ii) The second stage, the Neolithic, starting about 10,000 BC, gave humans a closer relationship with nature and the start of dominance over it by the invention of agriculture and animal husbandry, and also spinning, weaving and pottery-making. For Neolithic humans, the sacred was active in the cyclical rhythms of nature as well as in groups of persons. There was seen to be an interlnking between human beings, the earth they were nurturing, and the transcendent powers (often female) that were felt to reside in both. Again the breakthrough to agriculture was a decisive change in human history. It was lived through religiously by the primal peoples involved. Their religious consciousness remained this-worldly rather than other-worldly, their experience was of groups rather than individuals, and their myths, rituals and symbols held people, nature and the transcendent together rather than separating them out.

(iii) The next stage saw the rise of town civilisations, first of all about 3,500 BC in the Middle East which became the dominant area of the world, (in Mesopotamia and then in Egypt), then by diffusion in the Indus Valley, and then spontaneously in China. The invention of the plough, the use of irrigation, the development of sea travel, the appearance of metallurgy and the rise of writing enabled town-dwellers to develop interests outside agriculture. Contacts were opened up with other areas, by land or by sea, so that trade, knowledge and ideas could be shared with other human groups. It may well have been, as W. H. McNeill suggests,[7] religious groups such as the Sumerian temple community that stimulated agricultural surpluses and then used them to support specialists who developed the skills that built up the towns. Religious specialisms also came into being in the form of separate priesthoods, temples, festivals, and theologies. Religious forms such as sacred kingship made sure that religion kept contact with life. However, although the inter-relationships between nature, human beings and the gods remained, the separation of later town civilisations from nature was prefigured, and disturbing individual questions about suffering, meaning, and life after death were beginning to surface.

(iv) The next main stage (there were other minor ones) found its beginning-point in the Axial Age around the sixth century BC. Great religious leaders arose simultaneously in four different areas of the world: the Middle East, India, China and Europe. During this significant century, the work of the great Hebrew prophets in Israel and the outworkings of Zoroaster's ideas in Persia maintained the Middle East's importance; in India the Buddha and the Jain Mahāvīra were alive and the great Hindu Upanishads emerged; in China Confucius, among others, was offering his message; and in Greece the Ionian philosophers prefigured the wonder of Greek philosophy and the rise of Europe. We can attempt sociological, cultural, economic, and 'spiritual' reasons to account for the Axial Age. For the historian the important point is that it happened. Analysing its outworking from the widest possible canvas, we can look forward to the emergence of four great civilisations

---

[7] W. H. McNeill, *The Rise of the West*, New York: New American Library, 1963, p. 52.

that were to be moulded by religious factors and that were to last for two thousand years on a roughly equal, roughly parallel, and roughly separate basis. They were Europe stemming from Greece and leading into Christian civilisation; India stemming from Hindu roots but also using Buddhist, Jain, Christian, Parsi, Muslim and Jewish sources to build a multi-religious Indian civilisation; China using its Confucian, Taoist and later Buddhist traditions as its *San Chiao*, its three ways, to form Chinese civilisation; and finally the Middle East declining at first from its former eminence but passing, mainly through Jewish and Zoroastrian sources, into the grandeur of later Muslim civilisation. The Middle East, therefore, was no longer dominant. It was one civilisation among four equals. No one religious tradition was dominant. The major ones, the Christian, Muslim, Hindu and Buddhist remained roughly in balance, and they lay at the heart of the European, Middle Eastern, Indian and Chinese civilisations which were essentially religious civilisations.

These four civilisations, and the religious traditions that lay at their core, were very different, and comparisons are fraught with difficulty. We can say, by contrast with former stages, that the following factors were important: a strong sense that our present worldly life was not paramount due to the possibility of continual rebirths, or an afterlife in heaven or hell; a sense of the inwardness of the real self and true faith exemplified in the rise of various monastic systems offering expression to individual religious consciousness; a sense that reason, analysis and intellectual synthesis mattered in affairs of religion whether as constituting the core of religiousness (Greece), the bulwark of civilisation (Chinese exams in the Confucian Classics), or the systematic expression of faith in the classical syntheses around 1250 AD of Aquinas in the Christian world, Maimonides in the Jewish world, al-Ghazzālī in the Muslim world, Chu Hsi in the Chinese world and Rāmānuja in the Hindu world; a sense that

13

religious traditions were not necessarily destined to remain local but could become more universal through mission; a sense that nature was there to be developed whether non-violently through the Buddhist and Jain notion of *ahiṃsā*, or more aggressively through the Judaeo-Christian apprehension that God had given humans dominion over nature; a sense of the social importance of religious traditions, both internally and in their dealings with wider culture, through the growth of a variety of religious movements in each tradition, through the development of many rituals, festivals and sacraments, through the rise of ethical norms, and through the creation of a myriad of aesthetic productions ranging from religious buildings to sculpture to painting to dance and to wider literature; and finally a sense that transcendence and its means of mediation mattered, whether it be seen in terms of God through Christ, Allah through the Koran, Yahweh through the Torah, Brahman through a Hindu personal God or the Ātman, or Nirvāṇa through the Buddha or the Dharma.

(v) The next main stage in global religious history began in the sixteenth century AD when there began a 450 year period centred upon the rise and supremacy of the West. At the beginning of the sixteenth century, one of the four equal civilisations mentioned above, namely Europe, raised the medieval siege wherewith it had been encircled by the Muslim world to the south and Tartar and Mongol hordes to the east. Through brilliant seafarers, it got round the impending bulk of Africa to make contact with the Asia about which it knew little. Through similar seafarers, it also discovered continents that contained important primal religious groups, continents such as the Americas and Australasia, that had as yet been untapped by the great civilisations. There were three main consequences. In the first place, the era of four equal civilisations was over. It so happened that the rapid expansion of a vibrant West coincided with a period of lethargy within the other great civilisations. As at the time of the dawn of town civilisations the Middle East had been dominant, so now from about 1500 to 1945 AD the West was dominant. Secondly, the religious tradition of the West also spread into different parts of the world. The new continents that were discovered, South America, North America, Australasia, and southern Africa, were settled by Europeans and became Christian continents. Christian missionaries went by 1945 to most parts of the world (Stephen Neill mentions as exceptions Nepal, Afghanistan and Tibet)[8] and had good success among the primal religious traditions but only minor success among the great religious traditions. As well as conversions to Christianity (and one or two in the opposite direction), there was greater contact between religious traditions, albeit often in terms of threat and defence, and a stimulation to creative reform among the other religions. Thirdly, the West took not only its religious tradition in a variety of denominational forms to the rest of the world, just as importantly it also took its scientific and industrial revolutions. At one level this provided greater medical facilities and greater material prosperity so that larger cities began to be built, people began to live longer, railways opened up communications, trade expanded, and factories emerged. At another level, it introduced among intellectual élites in other places the western scientific secular world-view, and towards the end of this period an awareness of the force of western nationalism, and the Marxist version of the secular viewpoint.

Again comparisons are difficult. By contrast with the former stage we may suggest the following points: Primal religions which had lived in relative isolation in places such as Siberia, the South Sea islands, the polar regions, and parts of the Americas, Asia, Africa and Australasia underwent dislocation and change; within the major traditions, laymen and vernacular devotion became more important (the great sixteenth century devotional

---

[8] S. Neill, *Christian Missions*, Harmondsworth: Penguin, 1964, p. 253, 461.

reform movements—Protestant Christians, Shī'ite Muslims, the Sikhs, and Hindu *bhakti* movements, as well as Pure Land Buddhists—stressed laymen and vernaculars); more attention came to be placed upon the relevance of religion for matters pertaining to this world such as social reform, material betterment, historical advance, and the like; the West set the agenda for debate with its seeming emphasis upon outward progress which prompted other religions to take it seriously and at the same time to react against its one-sidedness; at the level of scholarship there arose a body of descriptive knowledge about various religions and at the level of believers there arose a greater awareness of other religious traditions, if not yet real dialogue; and human dominion over nature increased apace together with the possibility that a fissure that was emerging within western consciousness between human beings' awareness of nature, of other humans, and of transcendence might be exported around the world.

It is against this analytical background of the past stages in global religious history that we can best understand the cruciality of our own age. We live in a crucial epoch not only because our world is changing so rapidly, including its religious traditions, but also because only now can we look back in time and look around in space and see that the world's religious traditions and humanity itself are part of a global continuum. Since the Second World War we ourselves are living through a new and developing stage in global religious history.

2(b) The Background to Global Religious History since 1945
Let us then look more closely at the background to global religious history since 1945. Our analysis may appropriately be divided into two phases: the immediate aftermath of World War Two, and the emergence of a global vision since about 1970.

(I) The Immediate Aftermath of World War Two

The Second World War itself had traumatic effects upon some religious traditions, as five brief examples demonstrate. Andrew Walls describes the effects of the war in the Pacific upon the Melanesian people who found alien races descending upon them in order to engage in strange conflicts that they interpreted in terms of their own religious world-view. The outcome of the European War delivered eastern Europe at one fell swoop into the political sphere of Soviet Marxism. The Jews were decimated in many parts of Europe and they relocated elsewhere, mainly in Israel and the United States. In the Far East, the outcome of the Pacific War influenced the collapse of the old orders in China and Japan, and resulted in the emergence of new political and religious milieux. More intangibly the horror of the Second World War following after the equal horror of the First World War damaged the credibility of the Christian European civilisations which had fought them. We will look in some detail later at the effects of the aftermath of World War Two upon particular religious traditions. We remain content at the moment with summarising the main factors in the aftermath of war against the background of which religion in today's world lives and moves and has its being.

(i) The first main factor was the end of a number of European empires. The disappearance of colonies and suzerainties of one sort or another was a symbol of the passing of western dominance. A by-product was that Christian missionaries, who had benefited from but not necessarily supported empire, were now restricted in their ability to proselytise abroad. If the *whole* world were to be evangelised for Christ, as the 1910 missionary conference at Edinburgh had urged, it would have to be done by indigenous Christians.

(ii) A second factor was the spread of Marxism, not only into eastern Europe at the close of World War Two, but also into China under the leadership of Mao, into Cuba under Castro, into Asian countries such as North Korea, Vietnam, Laos and Cambodia, and into enclaves in Europe and Africa. What had been a Russian preserve was becoming a universal possibility, the advance of which seemed to rival the breakneck spread of early Islam. However internal quarrels within the Eastern Block, Mao's break with Russian Marxism, and ideological differences as to what constituted Marxism began to show that Marxism was not monolithic and that it was changing rapidly.

(iii) A third factor was the rise of new nation-states in succession to the former empires. Ninian Smart's chapter and various other chapters in this book point out the inter-relationships between nationalism and religion in the post-war period. They have been many and varied. The permutations are endless. New nations with no historical experience of nationalism as a force such as the European nations had long possessed had to cope with the pressures of independence. Religious traditions were variously important in promoting, sustaining and even challenging the nation-states that emerged.

(iv) A fourth factor was the application of models of economic development and modernisation in most countries whereby services such as medicine, education, social welfare and economic matters came more under the aegis of the state, whether the state system was socialist, capitalist, or mixed. According to some secularisation theorists, this transfer of control of formerly religious matters into the care of the state presaged the decline and possibly even the ultimate demise of religion. This is to equate modernisation with a certain form of westernisation. Other states, cultures and religious traditions are modernising in their own way not according to a rigid western model.[9] As William Montgomery Watt points out, part of the

---

[9] This is a complex debate involving on the one side scholars such as Bryan Wilson in, for example, *Encounter*, 45, 'The Secularisation Debate', 1975, pp. 77–83 and Richard Fenn, *Toward a Theory of Secularisation*, Ellington, Connecticut: Society for the Scientific Study of Religion, 1978; and on the

Shah of Iran's mistake was to modernise in too overtly a western fashion. Nations and cultures are coming to terms with the modern world but according to their own propensity.

(v) A fifth factor was the continuing debate between the proponents of science and religion. The natural and allied sciences developed rapidly in the post-war world due in no small part to the rapid stimulus given to scientific innovation by the Second World War itself. The technological revolution, the development of nuclear power, the human achievement in reaching the moon are symbols of the soaring technical successes of modern science. However there is also a growing awareness of the problems engendered by the successes of science through the escalation of nuclear weapons, the growth of population, increasing world poverty, the ecological crisis; philosophers of science have questioned the simplistic scientism of earlier days; there has been the soul-searching agonising of eminent scientists such as Einstein, Polanyi, Bohr and Heisenberg; and there is a dawning sense, enhanced by the failure of secular régimes to stamp out religion, that science has no answer to the basic religious questions of meaning, purpose, awe, transcendence, value and inwardness.[10]

(vi) A sixth factor was the acceleration of the process of industrialisation. In most parts of the world (China under Mao was a partial exception) there was a shift from villages into cities. Cities grew to enormous sizes to cope with the demands of industry. As people moved into cities they were faced with a change of work, a change of environment, a change of life-style, and in effect a change of imaging. For some this could be

other hand scholars such as Rodney Stark and William Bainbridge in, for example, *The Future of Religion*, Berkeley, Los Angeles, London: University of California Press, 1985.

[10] F. Whaling, 'The Philosophy of Science and the Study of Religion', pp. 379–90, see also 'The Study of Religion in a Global Context', pp. 391–443 in F. Whaling (Ed), *Contemporary Approaches to the Study of Religion*, Volume One: The Humanities, Berlin, New York, Amsterdam: Mouton, 1984.

liberating. For others it was not and the ability to make sense of the new experience and to live through it creatively was sometimes provided by a religious tradition, and quite often by a new religious movement.

(vii) A seventh factor was the accelerating exploitation of nature. This had direct consequences for primal peoples in places such as the Amazon and Central Africa. We are beginning to realise that there may also be consequences for the earth itself.

(viii) An eighth factor was the increasing movement of people and information around the world. This had already begun in World War Two when members of various armies visited new areas of the world. Enforced migration, sometimes of religious groups, had both general and religious consequences as in the movements consequent to the Nazi Holocaust whereby the USA, Israel and Russia became the main domiciles of the Jews whose presence in Poland decreased from over three million pre-war to a few thousand today. Elsewhere the Dalai Lama's flight from Tibet took the Tibetan Buddhist tradition into other parts of the world, the migration of Ugandan and other African Asians brought Hindus, Muslims and Sikhs into the West, the Vietnam war resulted in migrations from South East Asia especially into the West, and the Palestinian exodus has had increasing repercussions for Muslims, Jews and others in the Middle East and beyond. Voluntary migration has also been important. Religious movements have accompanied the transfer of various groups of people from the Indian subcontinent so that, for example, there are now a million and a half Muslims in Great Britain, more than the Methodists and Baptists combined. As well as the development of formerly culturally bound traditions into world religions by migration, there has also been the steady conversion of others, including westerners, to those religions as well as the spread of new religious movements originating in one culture into different parts of the world. More important still has been the growth of airline travel, international organisations, computer information services, television and the possibility of immediate information about and almost immediate travel to other parts of the world.

(ix) Finally there is the cumulative effect of all the factors mentioned above. There have been changes in every age. However the miniscule changes of the Palaeolithic and Neolithic stages have developed into a rising curve of cascading change in the post-World War Two era. The fact of change is constant. It is the variety, depth and all-pervading nature of contemporary change that makes our age different.

(II) The Emergence of a Global Vision

The factors of change mentioned above have been responded to, participated in, and sometimes prompted by religious traditions since 1945. Since 1970 there has also emerged a global vision that is increasingly a key element in the religious life of our planet today. We will look briefly at the main facets of this vision.

(i) In the reports associated with the Club of Rome, it emerged initially as a global threat. Insofar as this threat could no longer be met by individual nations or religious traditions acting separately, and insofar as the threat was to the whole of humankind, the need was felt for a global vision that could adequately address the needs of the whole planet.[11]

For the purposes of analysis, the global threat can be seen at three levels. At the physical and ecological level there is the vanishing of various species of wild life in nature due partly to human acts, the decline in the world's tropical forests and the increase of the world's desert areas, the pollution of parts of the global environment due to acid rain and so forth, the running-down of natural resources of minerals and planetary material

---

[11] The Club of Rome study, (see Donella H. Meadows et al, *The Limits to Growth*, New York: Universe Books 1972) is available in about thirty languages with over two million copies in circulation.

assets, the insatiable demand for more energy from the earth's ecosystem, the increasing contamination of the atmosphere and biosphere for nuclear and other reasons, and the sense that the fate of the earth is directly related to the fate of the people who live on the earth. At the human and social level there is the increasing poverty disparity between rich and poor nations, the steeply mounting figures of world population, the need to provide more food for this growing population, a growing concern about sexual and racial discrimination, the economic tension between North and South, the political tension between East and West, and increasing nuclear proliferations and aspirations. At the moral and spiritual level there is concern about the future development of space and the sea which belong in principle to humankind, concern about the global use of genetics and electronics, a sense that the perennial search for meaning and wholeness is the birthright of humanity, and a suspicion that past religious divisions must be transcended in the search for global solutions.

There may be discussion about the organisation of the levels of this analysis. There may also be discussion about whether the correct issues are included in the correct levels. The fact that these are ultimate problems of global concern is hardly in doubt. Religion in today's world is lived against this background of global awareness.

This imperative to global understanding makes our epoch crucial. Over and above the individual adjustments to change that individual believers and religious traditions are called upon to make there is the challenge to a fundamental adjustment of perspective:— to think globally or suffer the consequences.

(ii) By the same token, global threat is also seen as global opportunity. As I write, four sets of events have taken place or are about to take place that symbolise the unfolding of new global possibilities. The Live Aid and Sport Aid and Million Minutes of Peace Appeals are galvanising millions of people at grass-roots around the world on behalf of global concerns. The visit of the British Queen (who also happens to be titular head of the Church of England) to China represents a cultural interchange that was undreamt of when I was in China as recently as 1982. The proposed meeting between the leaders of the United States and the Soviet Union at Reykjavik in Iceland to discuss nuclear arms limitation is being couched in terms of global concern as well as superpower rhetoric. Finally at Assisi in Italy in October 1986 there has been scheduled a meeting between leaders of different religious traditions to discuss how they can work, think and pray together for the peace of the world. Whether some or all of these events are ephemeral or not, the global agenda and climate and expectation are changing.

In brief, some of the parameters within which a global vision is being conceptualised are as follows: particular national and religious concerns, while remaining important, point beyond themselves to a global context; the great cultures and religious traditions of the world are open to each other as never before and they meet, not in the pre-war terms of the supremacy of the West and the Christian tradition, but on the basis of genuine global dialogue; the global threat is real, but so are the global resources—ecological and physical, human and social, and moral and spiritual; our global age inherits unfinished business from the past in regard to an unthinking exploitation of nature, an over-concern for the partial and the outward, and a retreat from sources of inwardness and transcendence; and both the practice and the study of religion have a significant role to play in the creative hermeneutics that will make a vibrant global future more possible.

(iii) There remain parts of the world where religious factors still contribute to global problems rather than global solutions. Two Muslim nations, Iran and Iraq, have lost more than a million dead or wounded in an unfinished six-year conflict. Two

Christian communities, Roman Catholic and Protestant, are facing each other in Northern Ireland; Hindu Tamils and Buddhists face eath other in Sri Lanka; Sikhs and Hindus face each other in the Punjab. In the Middle East an Islamic anti-Semitism relatively new in our period confronts an Israel building a homeland on the ashes of the Holocaust. In South Africa a Dutch Reform Church view of the regional covenant is in conflict with another view of the regional covenant derived at least partly from different Christian values.

The fact remains that the perceived global threat and the motivation to create a new global vision transcend local situations of religious hostility, however acute they may be. The ultimate backdrop to religion in today's world is the global situation itself with its summons to a global vision.

3 Religious Developments in Particular Traditions since 1945

In this section we will briefly survey major developments in particular religious traditions reviewed separately. In a later section we will look at the multiplying interaction between different religions, the place of religion in new global groupings, and religious responses to the new global situation since 1945.

Key Developments in Religious Traditions

(a) The revival of Islamic self-confidence since 1945 lays claim to be one of the crucial religious unfoldings of our time. As Montgomery Watt suggests, 'in order to understand what has been happening religiously in the world of Islam since 1945 it is necessary to have some idea of how Muslims had been responding to the West during the previous two centuries or so.'[12] At her beginnings, Islam had known a time of classical success with the rapid spread of the Muslim tradition at the time

---

[12] See page 232.

of Muhammad and the four early caliphs. On the basis of this 'golden age' of success a great civilisation had been built that had prospered in spite of periodic setbacks such as the fall of Baghdad to the Mongols in 1258 AD. From the sixteenth century onwards, the time of the rise of a confident Christian West had coincided with a time of internal Muslim lethargy which led to various western nations taking control in most of the Muslim heartlands. The Muslim sense of trauma was real. Since 1945, due to a number of factors including the gaining of independence by various Muslim countries and the economic success of OPEC as well as more overtly religious causes, there is a renewal of confidence within the Muslim world that is of major importance.

(b) As far as Jews are concerned, two events right at the beginning of our period were vital. As Louis Jacobs puts its, 'the two events which transformed Jewish thought and life in the period from 1947 to the present day were the destruction of six million Jews—a third of the world population of Jewry—in the Nazi Holocaust, and the establishment of the State of Israel in 1948.'[13] The Holocaust remains a living element within Jewish consciousness (Elie Wiesel is to receive the next Nobel Peace Prize for his writings on the Holocaust) and the State of Israel remains a symbolic focus for virtually all Jews.

(c) The key development within the Christian tradition since 1945 is the fact of, and the symbolic significance of, what Andrew Walls terms the 'end of Christendom.' In his words, 'today over half the Christians in the world live in the southern continents of Africa, Asia, Latin America and Oceania,'[14] and the main diffusion of the Christian Gospel is now within cultures rather than across them from outside sources such as the West. By hindsight we can see that the third phase of the European missionary movement from the late nineteenth

[13] See page 213.
[14] See page 80.

25

century onwards represented, as it were, the swansong of Christendom. The Christian balance has now shifted from the West so that a future Pope and a future headquarters of the World Council of Churches could conceivably come from the Third World. Moreover since the Second World War, other religious traditions have increased in numbers and influence in the West. For example Christian churches in Britain have lost half a million members since 1980, while Muslims in Britain have increased by more than a third.[15] The long-term implications of the end of Christendom are incalculable.

(d) As far as the Hindu tradition is concerned, Indian nationalism was deeply influenced by the Hindu renaissance which in turn was influenced by the West and some Christian ideas. However when India became independent in 1947, she became a secular state by contrast with Pakistan which became a 'Muslim state. One consequence was that the Hindu Marriage Act of 1955 and other legislation downgraded the importance of caste in the sight of the law. Insofar as the caste system has been the lynchpin of Hindu social life since the time of Upanishads as well as being a fundamental religious value with its stress upon purity and pollution, the Hindu reaction to this development is of major importance. The Hindu tradition, while influenced in its renaissance by the West, is modernising in its own way; it is also growing outside India so that Hinduism is being transformed into a world religion.

(e) Concerning the Buddhist tradition, Donald Swearer is also able to comment, 'Buddhism today is truly a world religion.'[16] Like the Hindu tradition it too is influencing the West and has been influenced by it. Within the Buddhist heartlands of Asia, Buddhist fortunes have taken violently different directions. China (including Tibet), Viet Nam, Laos and Cambodia were

---

[15] See the religious figures for Britain quoted in the *UK Christian Handbook*, Marc Europe: Evangelical Alliance and Bible Society, 1986.

[16] See page 55.

taken over by communist régimes; the Theravāda nations of Burma and Sri Lanka were helped to independence by Buddhist nationalism and together with Thailand they maintained the traditional Theravāda links between ruler, monks and laity; in Mahāyāna areas such as Japan, Mahāyāna flexibility remained. (f) The primal religious traditions have been affected severely by the contemporary situation. Their smallness and vulnerability to rapid change have made it less easy for them than for the major religious traditions to survive in recognisable form. Their values, their land, their world-view and sometimes their very existence are threatened by global advance. Either reduction or drastic change are inevitable. As Andrew Walls shows, change can take various forms. One form is by absorption or appropriation into a major tradition sometimes in the form of a new religious movement, a notable example being the growth of the African Independent Churches. In South Africa alone the Zion Christian Church had about a thousand members in 1930 but claims four million today and in 1948 there were eight hundred Independent Churches in South Africa whereas now there are about thirty-three hundred, and in Africa as a whole something like ten thousand.

(g) We looked at the recent religious situation in China at an earlier stage. Following on from our comments about the primal religious traditions, present religious developments in China raise a related issue of the utmost general importance. It is the question of magic. The present Chinese government differentiates between 'religion' and 'superstition'. By religion it means the major religious traditions (the Buddhist, Muslim, Taoist, Catholic and Christian-Protestant) which are tolerated and are undergoing a mini-revival; by superstition it means the Chinese Folk Religions which are frowned upon and whose present influence cannot be assessed. Complicated matters are involved here. To what extent are Chinese Folk Religions primal religions? To what extent is magic part of primal religion? To what extent are magic and/or primal religion part of the major religions? What will happen to Chinese Folk Religions in the new China? The answers will prove to be interesting and significant.

(h) Japanese religious traditions, as we saw earlier, went in a different direction from those of China after 1945. As Brian Bocking puts it, 'with the proclamation of religious freedom, numerous religious cults sprang up almost overnight, and at the same time older minority religions and pre-war "new" religions whose activities had been curtailed by restrictions under State Shinto experienced a dramatic renaissance.'[17] This ties in with Phillip Hammond's notion of the inter-relationship between the proliferation of cults and the decline of civil religion. With the passing of civil religion in the form of State Shinto, new religious movements flowered in Japan. With the loosening of the rigid hold of state civil religion in present-day China it will be interesting to watch the effects.

4(a) The Contemporary Interplay between Religious Traditions
Introduction

So far we have concentrated upon developments in separate religions. A striking feature of the post-war period is the growth of interplay between religious groups in most parts of the world.

Religious interplay has not been completely absent in the past. Since the rise of town civilisation in Mesopotamia, people and religious ideas have travelled along trade routes and religious interplay has resulted. At times religious interchange has been deep. Ready examples come to mind: India just after the Axial Age when Hindu groups, Buddhists and Jains influenced each other; the Mediterranean World at the time of Christian origins when Jews, Graeco-Roman religions,

[17] See page 181.

Mystery religions, Roman civil religion, Zoroastrians and others mingled together; Sassanid Persia where Manichaeans, Christians, Jews, Zoroastrians and oriental groups lived in close proximity; medieval Spain where Muslims, Jews and Christians engaged in a trilogue between each other; medieval China and Japan where the Buddhist, Taoist, Confucian, and (in the case of Japan) Shinto traditions participated in one another; and India in the sixteeth century AD where Sufi Muslims, various Hindu *bhakti* groups and the emerging Sikhs engaged mutually. Since the rise of the West in the sixteenth century, the rate of religious inter-communication has grown due to the increased travel and communications spread by science, but the agenda has often been dictated by the West and the Christian tradition. Since 1945 religious inter-penetration has advanced dramatically. It is no longer merely local, it is also global.

4(b) Religious Blocks as the Background to Interplay

Before we analyse contemporary religious interplay in detail, let us pause to consider the present-day religious blocks within which this interplay takes place. For although religious interaction has increased immeasurably, it has done so not as a frenzied free-for-all but against a background of blocks where religious traditions still remain important. We assume that within these religious blocks, nationalism and secular world-views are present in varying degrees.

One such block is the modern West, North America and Europe, spanning the North Atlantic and having offshoots in Australasia. Despite the demise of Christendom, the background of this block remains Christian, white and democratic. Other religions have a minority presence within the West. Although some state churches still remain nominally intact the prevailing tendency, in spite of the efforts of movements such as the Moral Majority, is towards effective separation of church and state.

Another block is the Marxist one with its heartlands in the Soviet Union and Eastern Europe and having offshoots elsewhere. Although this block has grown dramatically since World War Two, Marxism has also witnessed the functional equivalent of the formation of sects with differing interpretations of orthodoxy being offered by different groups. Emerging mainly in Christian areas in Europe, Cuba and Africa, but also enfolding within its bosom the Muslims of the Steppes and the Buddhists of Viet Nam and its neighbours, the Marxist tradition has exercised state control over religion but has been unable to eclipse it.

A third block is formed by the Muslim tradition. Its original heartlands of North Africa and the Middle East remain central and it has offshoots out as far as Malaysia and Indonesia. Our period has seen a remarkable revival of confidence within the Islamic world as well as a diversion of interest between the Shī'ite Islam of Iran and the Sunni Islam more prevalent elsewhere.

A fourth block centres upon the Hindu tradition within India. Although India is a secular state, and although offshoots of Hinduism have begun to spring up in areas formerly devoid of Hindus, the heart of that tradition remains in India.

A fifth area of importance (it is perhaps too small to be called a block) is Israel as the focal point of post-Holocaust Judaism. Although Jews reside in numbers in the United States and Russia, the new nation of Israel is the emotional heartland of the Jews from the viewpoints of past history and present significance.

A sixth block centres upon the Buddhist heartlands of South East Asia. As we saw earlier, the Buddhist tradition has undergone traumatic experiences in the new Marxist areas of China, North Korea, Viet Nam, Laos and Cambodia, in the heady religious mix of the new Japan and South Korea, and in the new Buddhist nations of Burma, Sri Lanka and Thailand.

Whether supported politically or not it remains an important influence throughout the area.

Potentially a seventh block is the Far Eastern complex of China and Japan. It is too early yet to presume such a development. However they share a similar cultural and religious background in the three ways of the Taoist, Confucian and Mahāyāna Buddhist traditions even though they have diverged economically, religiously and politically in recent times. It remains to be seen whether they come closer together to form a block sharing a Chinese religious inheritance with offshoots in Hong Kong and other places with overseas Chinese.[18]

A final, and much more amorphous, block covers a swathe of societies in the southern world with a background in primal religions and a movement mainly towards new forms of Christianity. Latin America dates its assimilation into the Christian tradition back to the Conquistadores but is now throwing up new indigenous religious forms in the shape of Pentecostal Protestants and Liberation Catholicism. Black Africa and the Pacific peoples of Polynesia and Melanesia have assimilated some of their primal religious expressions into independent churches and other Christian forms, and the process has accelerated during our period.

Before we analyse the religious interplay arising out of these blocks, let us pause to comment that the emergence or re-emergence of these areas where religious world-views are significant is a signal development in global religious history. We saw earlier how at the time of the rise of early town civilisation the Middle East had been dominant; for two thousand years from the sixth century BC to the sixteenth century AD, four areas, the Middle East, India, China and Europe based upon great religious traditions, were equal,

---

[18] Either as a potential block or separately China and Japan are important.

parallel and separate; in the early modern period, up to 1945, the West and the Christian tradition were dominant. Today, no one block of the world, and no one religious tradition, is dominant in the sense that the West and Christianity were dominant up to 1945. We live in a global world—real separation between blocks and religious traditions is no longer a viable possibility—but within that global world sharing and dialogue on a basis of authentic mutuality are more possible than ever before.

4(c) Interplay within Religious Traditions

Since World War Two there has been greater interaction within religious traditions. Various examples appear within the chapters of this book. One facet of this is the rise of ecumenical movements within different traditions. The setting up of the World Council of Churches in 1948 brought together numerous Protestant Churches within the Christian milieu. Since 1948 the World Council of Churches has widened its scope to include Orthodox Churches, some African Independent Churches, and even Roman Catholic observers so that its orbit is wide. The Second Vatican Council of 1962–65 brought the world's Roman Catholics into more intimate contact with each other. The Conference on World Evangelisation held at Lausanne in 1974 did the same for the Evangelical-Fundamentalist Christian groups.

An equivalent development within the Buddhist world was the formation of the World Fellowship of Buddhists in 1952. Added impetus was given to the growing understanding between different branches of Buddhism by the worldwide celebration of the 2,500th anniversary of the *mahāparinirvāṇa* of the Buddha in May 1956.

World Hindu organisations such as the Virat Hindu Samaj led by Karan Singh and the Vishwa Hindu Parishad led by Maharana Bhagwat Singh have performed a similar ecumenical function for Hindus on a worldwide basis.

As Louis Jacobs puts it, 'there has been an advance in ecumenism in this period both within and outside the Jewish ranks.'[19] In spite of the present political differences between Iranian Shīʿite Islam and the less radical Sunnī Islam, there is a similar tendency within contemporary Islam to ask ecumenical questions at a worldwide level.

The different elements within the Christian, Buddhist, Hindu, Jewish and Muslim traditions are in closer contact with each other than ever before, so it is natural that internal ecumenical links should grow.

4(d) Inter-religious Ecumenism

However growing religious inter-connections are not confined to increased contacts *within* religious traditions. Since the Second World War a wider ecumenism *between* religions has become more obvious.

This wider ecumenism happens at the local level in various parts of the world. Sometimes it has been encouraged by the state as in China where both ecumenism within particular religions and closer contact between religions were facilitated by the political situation. More often it has grown naturally as various religious groups have come together within a nation to share social concerns and to engage in dialogue.

Recently there has been increased contact at international level between world representatives of religious traditions through the medium of the Temple of Understanding, the United Nations and other forums. Of necessity such meetings tend to be formal but they are symbolic of a growing feeling towards a wider ecumenism.

4(e) Mutual Religious Participation

In some ways more important than growing formal contacts has been the mounting influence of one religion upon another by

[19] See page 224.

mutual penetration and participation. This has become increasingly possible because since 1945 the major religious traditions have evolved into world religions, that is to say traditions present in many parts of the world not merely within one block. Thus Hindus live not merely in India and contiguous nations such as Nepal, Bangla Desh, Pakistan and Mauritius but also in Bali and Fiji, in Guyana, Suriname and Trinidad, in South Africa, and in every part of the West—in 84 nations in all.[20] Buddhists too have spread from their Asian heartlands into other parts of the world and they also are present in 84 nations. They are growing proportionately very rapidly in India, the land of the Buddha's birth, where they had disappeared during the medieval period. Their influence and presence is clear in various parts of the West. Muslims also have a presence of 162 nations ranging from Middle Africa and the West through their strong Arab heartlands to China, Indonesia and Malaysia in the East. Post-Holocaust Judaism is a partial exception to the rule, having a more particular presence in Israel, the United States and Russia yet Jews still have a scattered presence in 112 nations. Smaller groups such as the Sikhs, Bahā'īs, traditions of Chinese and Japanese origin, and new religious movements are more ubiquitous than ever before. Christianity is more universally present on the face of the globe than at any time in its history, and in fact Christian communities are present in every inhabited nation on earth.

Andrew Walls refers to 'the principal change in primal religions since the Second World War: the search for a universal, not a purely local or ethnic field of reference, a new focus suited to a village all now know to be global.'[21] In other words, from one end of the religious spectrum to the other, not forgetting the complicating factors of nationalism and secular

[20] These and the following figures for the presence of religious traditions in nations are quoted from *World Christian Encyclopedia*, *op. cit.*, p. 5.

[21] See page 278.

world-views, we live in a world of permanent religious inter-connections. All religious traditions are in movement and they are being influenced by each other.

This is especially true of the Christian tradition. Although it remains an important factor in the West, especially in North America, the developing Christian world-view is increasingly being formed within the context of other blocks and other religious traditions. Thus Gandhi's stress upon simplicity over against opulence, truth-as-lived over against truth-as-believed, non-attachment over against acquisitiveness, and active non-violence over against oppression is being filtered by Martin Luther King and his heirs into world Christianity; Kitamori's Japanese theology of the Pain of God is emphasising for the world church the cross and pain as representing the heart of God; Latin American liberation theology is highlighting for other Christians God's freeing concern for social structures and poverty; Indian Christian theology is assimilating and transferring a Hindu concern for a more disciplined interior spirituality; experience of dialogue with Buddhists in Sri Lanka and with members of other traditions elsewhere is being applied at international level; the Chinese Christian experience of House Churches, Koinonia (fellowship) and unity is seen as having a wider relevance; the stress of the African Independent Churches upon healing, dreams, symbols and visions is producing echoes in the world Christian psyche; water-buffalo theology in Thailand is one of a number of prods towards a Christian reinterpretation of ecology and nature; Panikkar is appropriating for global Christian thought the Bhagavad Gītā's stress upon the integral nature of true spirituality; Chinese Christians are pointing to the wider applicability of the Chinese notion of the inter-relationships between God, humanity and nature; the importance of community within the African Church is being heard globally; and the Korean Christian stress upon religious emotion and Christian society (filtered from

Korean shamanism and her Confucian tradition) are not unnoticed in the wider Christian world.[22]

Elsewhere, as Frank Whaling shows, Hindus from Ram Mohan Roy at the end of the eighteenth century to present day have 'Hinduised' western and Christian insights, and Hindus are returning the compliment in the contemporary world as they influence not only Christians (as intimated above) but also other religious traditions in our global planet. Don Swearer's summary of the current Buddhist impact on the West refers to varieties of influence that are relevant at a wider level than Buddhism. He points to Buddhist communities servicing Buddhists who have migrated to the West, Buddhist monastic centres in the West focused on a particular teacher and school of meditation, Buddhist movements attempting to shape western forms of Buddhism, Buddhist scholar-writers such as Suzuki and Watts at work in the academic community, and Christian theologians such as Merton and Cobb engaged in intimate dialogue with Buddhist thought and experience.

The religious interplay involving the primal religions has been very intense. As Andrew Walls suggests it can take four different courses: the creative renewal of a primal tradition, the formation of a new religious movement different from the primal religion and its partner in contact, the formation of independent churches in which the primal religion takes on a Christian form, and the assimilation of the primal religion into a major religious tradition other than Christianity.

As we hinted earlier, the religious inter-connections within Japan since World War Two have been close and complex, and a number of the new religious movements have included elements derived from other religions. It is perhaps not surprising that the Japanese Conference of Religious

[22] These are the chapter headings from my forthcoming book on the influence of non-western Christian theologies on total Christian theology, *Learning from Faith*, Basingstoke: Marshall Pickering, 1987–88.

Representatives has proposed that the day of prayer for peace called by the Pope to Assisi in October 1986 should be succeeded by another in Kyoto in 1987.

Two seeming exceptions to the above religious interplay appear to be the Jewish and Muslim traditions. However the twin movements of assimilation and emancipation had already transformed western European Jewry in the nineteenth century and, as Louis Jacobs shows, although the setting up of the state of Israel and the trauma of the Holocaust have introduced new priorities, the old religious interplay has not ceased, it has merely taken new forms. Equally although mutual religious participation is hardly a priority within Iran, Libya or Afghanistan the global religious situation of Islam ensures that it is not completely absent elsewhere.

5 Global Religious Adjustments

It would be wrong to suggest that there have been no changes in religious allegiance during our period. There has been religious interplay. There has also been religious adjustment and conversion. To give but three examples: since 1945 in the USA alone over 100,000 Jews have become Christians; in India Ambedkar led over a million Hindu outcastes into the Buddhist tradition; and in Marxist states it is often the practice that membership of the communist party is incompatible with active religious observance so that for this and other reasons some believers have become Marxists. What then have been the changes in religious allegiance since 1945?

Raw global figures are hard to come by. When they are available there are problems of source verification and hermeneutics. The *World Christian Encyclopaedia*[23] has no figures for 1945 but it does have figures for 1900, 1970 and 1980 (and projections for 1985 and 2000 which are already slightly off-

[23] *World Christian Encyclopedia, op. cit.*, p. 6.

balance). We will summarise their figures and then comment on them.

Christians numbered 558 million in 1900, 1,217 million in 1970, and 1,433 million in 1980; Muslims numbered 200 million in 1900, 551 million in 1970, and 723 million in 1980; Hindus numbered 203 million in 1900, 466 million in 1970, and 583 million in 1980; Buddhists numbered 127 million in 1900, 232 million in 1970, and 274 million in 1980; Jews numbered 12 million in both 1900 and 1945 (having lost 6 million in the Holocaust), 15 million in 1970, and 17 million in 1980. Among a mass of other figures, the following are also relevant. Chinese folk-religionists numbered 380 million in 1900, 215 million in 1970, and 198 million in 1980; tribal religionists numbered 106 million in 1900, 88 million in 1970, and 90 million in 1980; 'new religionists' numbered 6 million in 1900, 76 million in 1970, and 96 million in 1980; 'non-religious' (agnostics of various sorts) numbered 3 million in 1900, 543 million in 1970, and 716 million in 1980; and 'atheists' (including Marxists) numbered less than a million in 1900, 165 million in 1970, and 195 million in 1980. To round off the statistics, the authors quote the following figures for 1980: 14 million Shamanists, 14 million Sikhs, 5 million Confucians, 4 million Shintoists, 4 million Bahā'īs, 3 million Jains, 3 million Afro-American Spiritists, 2 million Spiritists, 154,000 Parsis, 31,000 Mandaeans, and a million 'other religionists.'

Bearing in mind the inherent drawbacks in such statistics—problems of definition, the fact that some figures involve inspired guesswork, and the fact that they reflect the mindset of the people who sought them—certain trends are clear. Due to the rapid rise in world population since 1945, the larger major religious traditions, the Christian, Muslim, Hindu and Buddhist, have increased in numbers. However although Muslims and Hindus increased proportionately to 16.5 per cent and 13.3 per cent of the world's population, Christians and

Buddhists decreased proportionately to 32.8 per cent and 6.3 per cent. More striking has been the decrease of Chinese folk-religionists from 23.5 per cent in 1900 to 4.5 per cent in 1980, and of primal/tribal religionists from 6.6 per cent in 1900 to 2.1 per cent in 1980. The most striking increases are among the 'non-religious' from 0.2 per cent in 1900 to 16.4 per cent in 1980, the 'atheists' from no rating in 1900 to 4.5 per cent in 1980, and the 'new religionists' from 0.4 per cent in 1900 to 2.2 per cent in 1980.

These trends confirm that, apart from local changes in religious allegiance too numerous to mention here, and apart from biological evangelism due to population growth, the major religious transferences have been from Christianity to secular world-views in the western and Marxist worlds, from Chinese folk-religions to secular world-views in China, from primal religions to the major traditions especially Christianity in the Third World, and to new religions in every part of the world. The last point is important because the figure of 96 million cited for the new religions masks the tremendous growth of new movements *within* each tradition. As Barrett puts it concerning Christianity's 20,800 denominations, 'the number of denominations was found to be four times as numerous as the estimates made in 1968.'[24] Hints are also given throughout this book of the exuberance of new religious movements within other religious traditions.

6 Religious Traditions and a Global Vision

We saw earlier how the contemporary epoch is crucial because it has witnessed the emergence of a global vision designed to meet a global need. This development is at the opposite end of the religious spectrum from the one mentioned above, for new religious movements tend to be absorbed in their own

[24] *Op. cit.*, see Preface.

expansion, their own vibrant experience and their own particular vision, although we may notice in passing that some of the new religious movements are able to leap from their local concerns to a global vision.

During our era, the major religious traditions have become increasingly aware that they share together in a common and transcending destiny involving the fate of the earth and its inhabitants. Religious parochialism is still the pervading order of the day yet, year by year, global awakenings are conspiring to transcend it. We remain content to give four examples.

The first has been intimated already, and it is the move towards dialogue and inter-religious understanding. Up to 1945 there was the tendency to judge other religious traditions through the spectacles of the convictions of one's own, so that other traditions were false, or mundane, or due to wither away, or destined to be fulfilled, or were vehicles for one's own advance. Through dialogue there is the desire to understand others for their own sake. Contemporary dialogue takes many forms: international ecumenical meetings, local ecumenical meetings, freelance exchanges, grassroots co-operation and the aim is to achieve a deeper mutual understanding.

A second level of interchange is inter-religious meetings to address wider global issues. The topics of concern vary and may include secular global issues such as meaningful social involvement, the role of women, bio-medical ethics, the desire to avoid nuclear war, and ecological renewal. Again these exchanges may take place at international and local level, and they may also include carefully staged mutual prayer for the issues concerned.

A third and more far-reaching development is the move to see one's own religious tradition as part of a wider whole, namely the planet earth. Attention is then diverted from one's own tradition as the centre of concern from which one may move in the direction of the globe to the globe as the centre of concern from which one may move in the direction of one's own tradition. An instance of this is to be found in the work of Wilfred Cantwell Smith and John Hick[25] who talk about all religious traditions as being vehicles whereby one may move from self-centredness to God-centredness, with attention being centred upon God and the globe rather than religious traditions as such. Another instance is the school of perennial philosophy which contends that all religions are different outwardly in their practices and beliefs but contain at their inmost core a perennial philosophy which gives them a transcendent unity and holds them together.[26] Whether there is agreement in detail about these two formulations is not the point, they are examples of a growing number of attempts to globalise religious thought.

A fourth development is articulated in this book in Ewert Cousins' chapter. He concentrates upon spirituality, defined in an integral fashion, and he suggests that in the contemporary world a global spirituality is emerging that uses the insights of the world's religious traditions to uncover the spiritual significance of the total fabric of human life—its rootedness in nature, its relation to other humans, and its openness to transcendence. In other words, religion in today's world is central to the evolution of a planetary global vision.

7 Different Responses to Religious Change in Religious Traditions

Most devotees at grassroots level are dimly aware of the global challenge that faces humankind and their own religious tradition. Their immediate awareness, since World War Two, has been of rapid change. Their immediate concern has been to

[25] Wilfred Cantwell Smith, *Towards a World Theology*, Philadelphia: Westminster, 1981; John Hick, *Problems of Religious Pluralism*, Basingstoke, London: Macmillan, 1985.

[26] Huston Smith, 'Perennial Philosophy, Primordial Tradition' in Huston Smith, *Beyond the Post-Modern Mind*, New York: Crossroad, 1982.

make sense of a changing universe through the medium of faith articulated through their own tradition. In order to serve as effective vehicles for the mediation of transcendence to their devotees, religious traditions have responded to change in structurally similar ways.

(a) The first option is not to respond to change, to retreat into a shell, and to react passively to the mysterious turmoil happening around. The probable consequence of this is recession or reduction. The old symbols and rituals lose their effective meaning. All religious traditions in one part of the world or another, and at one time or another, have been prone to this ineffective passivity since World War Two. This is especially true of some of the primal religions. It was also true of the Roman Catholic Church before Vatican II, of Tibetan Buddhism before the Dalai Lama's flight, and of elements within the Hindu tradition denounced by Hindu secularists such as Nehru. It represents not so much traditionalism as an unwillingness to admit that change is necessary.

(b) The second response is to work for a creative restoration of tradition. Although this type of response may tend to be conservative and right-wing, it can also be revitalising. Thus some American Indians and Australian Aborigines have managed to revitalise their religion by attempting to restore their traditional roots. Louis Jacobs points to the revitalising work of Jewish Orthodoxy since 1945 through the work of the Yeshivah World, the Hasidim, and the Modern Orthodox branches of contemporary Judaism. Donald Swearer illustrates the importance within the Buddhist tradition of the restoration of classical Buddhist sites, of monastic organisation and educational institutions, and of meditation practices. Within the Christian Church, the resurgence of conservative evangelicalism denotes by its very name the desire to creatively conserve tradition, and every denomination has its traditional wing. As Montgomery Watt points out, the revitalisation of

Islam in a mainly conservative direction was probably due mainly to 'the fear of a loss of identity'.[27] Within the Hindu tradition also there is a traditional branch that is anxious to ensure that Hindu identity is not erased within the secular state of India.

The temptation is for creative restoration to sink back into passivity or to become obstructive to necessary change as happened with Mao's Cultural Revolution and is happening in parts of the Muslim world. Another tendency is for conservative traditionalism in religion to align itself with a similar outlook in politics. The conservative fundamentalism of the Moral Majority in the United States, the Muslim Brotherhood in the Islamic world, the Arya Samaj, Hindu Mahasabha and RSS in India, the outlook represented in an extreme form by Rabbi Kahane in Israel, and certain Buddhist elements in Sri Lanka and Burma come to mind. However such an alignment between conservatism in religion and politics is not universal, and such a retrenchment, where it occurs, may be part of the process of re-establishment of roots which is a necessary precursor of any advance into globalism.

(c) Another response to change is that of reform and adjustment and appropriation. This response takes many different forms according to context and cultural background but it acknowledges the need to make changes in the religious tradition to respond to changes in the surrounding world. A common element in this response is social reform. Prior to 1945, the West was often a catalyst in this respect. Since 1945 more potent influences have been the push of Marxism, with its social and economic priorities, in South East Asia; the rise of new nation-states dedicated to various forms of modernisation; and the prophetic work of religious leaders such as Gandhi with his stimulus to hasten reform of the Hindu caste system, his

[27] See page 237.

43

inspiration is to set up Sarvodaya movements under Vinoba Bhave in India and Ariyaratna in Sri Lanka, and his influence upon Martin Luther King.

Reform can also be addressed to the fabric of religious traditions in their own internal workings. Various examples are offered in these pages. One of the most striking is the switch from Latin to the vernacular enacted by Vatican II within the Roman Catholic Church. Universally there have been reforms within religious movements, in rituals and festivals, in ethical interpretation, in scriptural exegesis, in doctrinal formulation, in aesthetic expressions, and in spiritual disciplines. Sometimes reform movements find particular expression as in Conservative and Reform Judaism, liberal Protestantism, neo-Hinduism, the work of Mawlana Abul-Kalam Azad, and the promptings of the Dalai Lama. More often they happen spontaneously in local situations.

Reform can also take the shape of appropriation of elements from other traditions. We looked at this earlier in connection with our discussion of religious interplay. This appropriation can be interpreted as returning to elements already present within a tradition that have been overlaid or neglected. Thus modern Rabbis can evoke the medieval Jewish responsa tradition while appropriating help from others in their discussion of just wars, the right to strike, sabbath observance, religious compromise, bio-ethics and the like. Christians can rediscover, by appropriation from others, an ecological concern already present in Jesus and St Francis, or a depth of spirituality already there in the Christian Classics of Western Spirituality. Neo-Hindu reformers can find a concern for history, matter, this-worldy issues, progress, and the role of women, appropriated from dialogue with the Christian West, in lesser-used parts of the Hindu sacred corpus such as the Ṛg Veda and the Tantra, and by analogy the same applies to neo-Buddhist reformers.

(d) A fourth response to change is that of radical restatement and reinterpretation. This involves the willingness to accept that some issues thrown up by our global situation are radically new and they cannot be met by creative restoration of tradition or reforming adjustment within the tradition. Something deeper is needed in order to speak to new conditions of technological sophistication, medical ethics, ecological disaster, nuclear threat and global perspective than a restoration of tradition or reformation supported by a backward appeal to tradition. Radical newness demands radical reinterpretation. In practice reinterpretation often shades back into reform, yet in principle it goes beyond it. It implies a universalism that, in some measure, transcends past particularism. Two traditions, for understandable reasons, have found it less easy to engage in reinterpretation: the Jews because of their concern to rebuild roots after the trauma of the Holocaust, and the Muslims because of their concern to rebuild roots after the trauma of western dominance of their heartlands. The passing of symbolic 'restoration' figures such as the Jewish leaders surviving from the Holocaust and Ayatollah Khomeini may be prerequisites for a more thoroughgoing reinterpretation. However within these two traditions, and also within primal religion which has similar difficulties with reinterpretation, the seeds of creative invention to meet contemporary problems are clearly present. Reinterpretative fruits are already emerging within the Christian, Hindu, Buddhist and Japanese religious traditions as has been seen and will be seen in this book.

(e) A fifth response to change is to abandon the religious tradition one knows, as being incapable of meaningful adjustment, in order to form a new religious movement. We may add that it may also increasingly involve abandoning the unsatisfying secular world-view one knows in order to form or join a new (or old) religious movement. We have already mentioned the more obvious examples of new religious movements: the ten thousand African Independent Churches, the hundreds of Japanese New Religions, the 20,800 Christian denominations (many of them new), and the new Asiatic religious movements present in the West. Some of them are break-aways from a primal religion, from a major Japanese religious tradition, from an older Christian church, or from a major Asian religion; some of them are spontaneous creations.

Throughout recorded history new religious movements have come into being.[28] As religious traditions have become hide-bound reforming movements have arisen within them, and in situations of unusual change and perplexity religious movements have arisen outside the established religious traditions. It is not surprising that in our age of unprecedented change new religious movements should be so plentiful.

8 Continuity and Change in Today's Religion

In spite of the importance of change in today's religion, it is necessary to emphasise that change and continuity go hand in hand. Brian Bocking illustrates this in relation to Japan. Of all the areas of the world, Japan appears to have undergone a religious metamorphosis in 1945 with the disestablishment of Shinto, the mushrooming of New Religions, and the effervescence of religious pluralism. Yet as Bocking rightly states 'looked at another way, Japanese religion seems hardly to have changed at all.'[29] When I was in China in 1982, everyone I spoke to stressed the continuity that existed between the old and the new China when the situation of 1982 seemed to be vastly different from that of 1945, and today the continuity seems to be even more apparent.

---

[28] An attempt to analyse this according to a global theory is offered in R. Stark and W. S. Bainbridge, *The Future of Religion: Secularisation, Revival and Cult Formation*, Berkeley, Los Angeles, London: University of California Press, 1985.

[29] See page 175.

It is, of course, possible to imagine continuities that are not there. Indeed throughout this introduction I have stressed the fact that we live in a new epoch of global religious history. Nevertheless, within this new epoch, change and continuity accompany one another.

The human capacity to live through change is extraordinary. In spite of the incredible flux of our time, many humans are born into an ongoing religious tradition, they exercise faith through it, they have an impact actively or passively upon it, and when they die their successors inherit a religious tradition minutely changed because of their influence upon it.

To be sure, some of the people mentioned in this book have had a more than minute impact upon a religious tradition. Creative persons such as Mawlana Abul-Kalam Azad, Mawlana al-Mawdudi, Ayatollah Khomeini, Pope John, Mother Teresa, Teilhard de Chardin, the Dalai Lama, U Nu, D. T. Suzuki, Bandaranaike, Ariyaratna, Mao, Black Elk, Vinoba Bhave, Radhakrishnan, Sri Aurobindo, Sathya Sai Baba, Rabbi Gelberman, Carl Jung, Bertrand Russell, Josei Toda, Daisaku Ikeda, Nikkyo Niwano, Emil Fackenheim, the Rebbes of Sotmar and Lubavitch, Mr Moon, Maharishi Mahesh Yogi, and Pope John Paul II (to name but a handful) have had a deep influence upon religious traditions and the wider world. Nevertheless most ordinary people have experienced and coped with religious change rather than directed it. They have done so within a wider framework of continuity.

How wide is this framework of continuity? This perhaps is the crucial question. For some people it remains local and fairly narrow. However static enclaves of religious traditions are becoming more rare. Durkheimian elementary forms of the religious life are becoming hard to find. There are various circles of religious continuity—narrow, intermediate, and wide—and the ultimate circle is that of our global world *in toto*.

8(a) Circles of Religious Change and Continuity
(i) The Local Circle

Devotees of religious traditions exercise their religiousness, in the first instance, within a local circle of continuity. They inherit a local sacred geography. They have access to transcendence through local mediating foci: in the case of the major traditions God through Christ, Allah through the Koran, Yahweh through the Torah, Brahman through a personal Lord or the Ātman, and Nirvāṇa through the Buddha or the Dharma. To practise their religiousness, they inherit local religious movements, local rituals, local ethical norms, local spheres of social involvement, local myths or sacred texts, local presuppositions of belief, local aesthetic symbols, and local modes of prayer. In a village setting these elements may be interlinked and self-contained. Since 1945, according to context, they will have changed to some degree depending upon the amount of dislocation within the context and the religious creativity of the local personnel concerned.

(ii) Wider circles

Since the Second World War relatively few settings, even village settings, have remained self-contained. Many people have moved into towns or cities in various parts of the world. Here they are exposed to more varieties of their own tradition, and to other religious forms. Even those who remain in villages often have a complex system of marriage relationships with people in other settings, and therefore access to wider religious forms. There is inter-borrowing, or at any rate inter-knowledge, between the local circle and the wider circle. The folk tradition and the greater tradition are in symbiosis.

In the wider circle there is also interaction between the various responses to change we analysed earlier. Passive resignation, creative restoration of tradition, adjusting reform, reinterpretation and new religious movements do not operate in complete separation. There is dialogue and tension between

48

them. They interact and provide a fluid context within which devotees can exercise faith.

Furthermore the wider circle invites, and sometimes encourages, the complex forms of interplay with other religious traditions we looked at previously. So transcendent reality and the avenue of mediation remain. But there is increased fluidity in the religious movements, the rituals, the ethical systems, the modes of social involvement, the beliefs, the sacred texts, the artistic forms, and the spirituality that are the dynamic continuum of religiousness for any particular person in the wider circle.

(iii) *The Global Circle*

The widest framework of continuity of all is the global circle. Through personal contacts, television, city life and increasing awareness a devotee comes to existential realisation that he belongs to a tradition that is worldwide. He becomes aware of the ecumenical vastness of his or her own tradition. The innocence of local parameters is dispelled.

There is also an awareness of the ecumenical vastness of other traditions, and a sense that all traditions have their joint place within a global milieu. In practice there is dialogue and tension between a devotee's apprehension of, and loyalty to, the local circle, the wider circle and the global circle. The devotee's faith may, in fact, be simple, but the context in which it is exercised and the religiousness which it entails is complex indeed.

Religious change and continuity go hand in hand—the uniqueness of our age lies in the growing complexity of frameworks of continuity and the global ultimacy of the most comprehensive framework of continuity beyond which it is impossible to advance further.

(iv) *New Religious Movements*

What, it may be asked, about new religious movements? Is not change, by definition, central to them? Are they not, in the nature of the case, local rather than global?

Clearly change is central to new religious movements, but so are patterns of continuity. The 20,800 Christian denominations mentioned by Barrett affirm in one way or another the centrality of God in Christ while altering the local pattern of apprehending that reality, so by analogy do similar religious movements within the other major religious traditions. Primal religious movements that relocate within a major tradition enjoy a double framework of continuity. The primal world-view is continued within the new framework while, at the same time, there is interaction between the relocated primal tradition and the wider circle. The Japanese new religions likewise are in continuity with the traditions they synthesise or claim to transcend.

Although new religious movements are usually intent upon local considerations, since 1970 there is evidence that a significant minority of them are anxious to be involved in global concerns. For example Raja-Yoga with 250,000 members is affiliated to the United Nations. As Brian Bocking comments, Japanese Religions, including New Religions 'overwhelmingly proclaim world peace and human co-operation as their goal, and strive to attain a global rather than a narrowly national perspective on human affairs.'[30] It appears, therefore, that a number of new religions are able to combine a local circle and a global circle in their practice of religiousness.

(v) *Secular World-Views and Spirituality*

As we saw earlier, two of the most significant changes in religious allegiance since 1945 are the advance of secular world-views in the western world and Marxist Europe and in China, at the expense of Christianity and Chinese Folk-Religions. The lapses in continuity in the former western Christendom and in Chinese Folk-Religions are probably two of the most serious religious developments of our time. Change is far more

[30] See page 175.

apparent here than continuity. Especially so in the case of China where the threat to Folk-Religion is accompanied by moral persuasion to limit families to only one child.

Three comments are in order. There is evidence to suggest that the high-watermark of Marxist world-views has been reached. Although they exhibit most of the elements of religion, they are weak on transcendence and spirituality and therefore cannot realistically offer eternal life. Their confident promise of lesser compensations such as social justice and material betterment has been only partly fulfilled. The major religious traditions are at least holding their own and are likely to grow within Marxist states.

The deeper query relates to Folk Religions. Such evidence as we have suggests that they have seriously declined in China. Together with the worldwide decrease in Primal Religions, this points to the possibility that if Folk Religions and Primal Religions are to survive it is likely that their survival will mainly be within the framework of other traditions than as entities in their own right.

Our third comment is that the secular world-views have presented a double challenge to religions. On the one hand, the challenge to take the secular world and its concerns of poverty, social justice, and reasonable comfort seriously; and on the other hand, to rediscover springs of spirituality that open up resources of love, joy, peace, eternity, awe and imagination unavailable to secular world-views. Ewert Cousins suggests that the contemporary resurgence of spirituality integrates secular, humane and spiritual concerns into a new global consciousness. If this is so, the contemporary framework of continuity for religious traditions contains the secular-scientific world, including the world of nature which finds itself in peril, and the resources of spirituality that are already present in religions waiting to be revalorised.

9 *Apparent Lack of Interest in our Contemporary Religious Situation*

If the contemporary period in global religious history is as important as we have intimated, why is so little written about it? As Jacques Waardenburg puts it 'there is a cruel lack of factual studies treating recent developments of various religions at the same time.'[31] Many studies of religions peter out just after the Second World War, and in this book we find ourselves stepping out onto almost virgin soil. Why should this be? Let us glance briefly at some possible reasons in order to establish the crucial significance of our endeavour.

Some may reason that change has been so rapid since World War Two that any attempt to chart that change must be in vain. Others may argue that we cannot do justice to the contemporary global religious situation because we are part of the drama; we cannot stand aside from it in order to assess it because we ourselves are involved in it and phenomenological distancing from our material becomes impossible. Others may suggest that scholarly objectivity and value-free assessment is difficult to apply because our sources of information are not historical texts or static data but scattered documents relating to dynamic movements and living persons. Others may opine that a study of contemporary religiousness should not be so bound up with a consideration of secular events—or alternatively that it should be more bound up with secular events! Others may consider that to involve religion in contemporary global problems is to renege on the academic dispassion that may be taken to be the hallmark of the objective study of religion. Yet others may intimate that twenty volumes and a hundred scholars are needed to do full justice to the theme.

We may readily admit an element of truth in some of these suggestions but to combat them fully would require another

[31] See page 340.

volume—and what an important volume that would be! Many of the authors of this work have written on past historical questions and will doubtless do so again, and we recognise that excellent writing on the past history of all religious traditions is central to the task of Religious Studies.

In short compass, Jacques Waardenburg deals with some of the above matters in his chapter on the study of religion. They raise again the question of theory and method, what is the study of religion all about? Without pre-empting his chapter, let me end with two comments.

The religious history of the period from 1945 to present day is part of the total religious history of humankind. As such it is important anyway, and it deserves as much attention as any other era in religious history. For reasons outlined in this book, it seems evident that we live at a crucial time in global religious history. Because this is so, it is doubly necessary to give due attention to our contemporary religious situation even though we ourselves are part of it.

If the study of religion is to play a full part in present-day intellectual life and the contemporary university it can hardly avoid the path of creative hermeneutics.[32] Creative hermeneutics can and should be applied to the past history of religion, and it is equally relevant to the study of contemporary religion. As I have written elsewhere 'the study of religion should play a creative role in contemporary scholarship not only for the sake of the study of religion itself but also for the sake of the world of learning in general, especially during this period when we are confronted with global issues affecting the whole planet earth.'[33]

---

[32] From a different standpoint, Mircea Eliade pleads for creative hermeneutics. See for example *The Quest: History and Meaning in Religion*, Chicago, London: University of Chicago Press, 1969.

[33] Frank Whaling (Ed.), *Contemporary Approaches to the Study of Religion*, Volume One: The Humanities, Berlin, New York, Amsterdam, 1984, p. 443.

We offer this work as a pioneering venture, and we trust that its insights will be closely explored and its issues comprehensively followed through. For what is happening to humankind religiously in the latter part of the twentieth century is of basic significance not only for the study of religion but also for the living of life in our world today.

2

THE BUDDHIST TRADITION IN TODAY'S WORLD

Donald Swearer

(Swarthmore)

The stereotypical picture many Westerners had of Buddhism as a religion of saffron-robed recluses meditating in a peaceful forest hermitage was shattered by television coverage of Vietnamese monks protesting against the Diem regime on the streets of Saigon in the 1960s. What is Buddhism? A retreat from the world of everyday activities in pursuit of a goal of wisdom and equanimity known as Nirvāṇa, or a powerful force within the cultures and social and political fabric of the countries where it has taken root and developed in Southeast, Central and East Asia?

Buddhism, like all the great historic religions has been many things to many people. The teachings and cultural expressions of Theravāda Buddhism in Southeast Asia differ dramatically from the Tantric Buddhism of Central Asia and the various forms of Mahāyāna Buddhism in East Asia. The variegated nature of the Buddhist tradition has become even more complex in the modern period as it has spread to Europe and America, and as it has been challenged by political revolution and Western modes of thought in its own homelands. Buddhism today is truly a world religion, a religion whose light may burn as bright in the modern West as in the countries of its birth and early development.

The variety and complexity of Buddhism make

generalization about its nature in today's world exceedingly difficult. Within the compass of a few pages a country by country analysis of Buddhism from Sri Lanka north and east to Japan, and in Western countries is not possible. Consequently we shall explore the face of contemporary Buddhism in terms of four varied and significant themes: the magical and syncretic nature of popular Buddhism; Buddhism, politics and the nation-state; the impact of the modern West on Buddhism; and the development of Buddhism in Europe and America. These themes do not exhaust even the most significant directions being taken by contemporary Buddhism throughout the world, but their exploration serves to emphasize both the staying power of this tradition as well as the problematic of its future.

Popular Buddhism. Magical and Syncretic
Throughout its history and into the present popular Buddhism has been fundamentally syncretic. In particular, it interacted with indigenous spirit belief and cult producing what might well be seen as a type of Buddhist animism. This animism operated on many levels—personal, communal, agricultural. On the personal level Buddhism in most cultures absorbed indigenous ideas of a spirit or soul power within each individual. Popular Buddhist cults evolved rituals to 'call' the spirit(s) into the body of the subject at a time of illness, crisis or transition, e.g. adolescent rites of passage, marriage, and to propitiate the spirits of the deceased. On the communal level Buddhism adapted itself to indigenous beliefs in guardian spirits of various kinds—household, village, province, and even of kingdom or nation. In some cases it was believed that these spirits resided in or entered into shrines at auspicious ritual occasions, e.g. the city pillar of Bangkok.

In others, they were thought to be present in particularly awesome or dominating sacred places, e.g. Mt. Popa in Burma,

Mt. Fuji in Japan. Animist beliefs and practices also permeated all aspects of food production, in particular planting and harvest times. For example, guardian spirits of the rice paddies, the spirit of the rice itself, of the threshing floor and granary all had to be supplicated and propitiated. Buddhism sometimes existed side by side with such autochthonous magical-religion, satisfying a different set of religious needs and aspirations, but at others absorbed it in a process of mutual transformation. Indeed, while doctrinal Buddhism developed distinctive schools and sects, at the cultural level an even greater diversity arose as a result of the process of interaction with indigenous religio-magical traditions.

Our analysis of Buddhism in today's world begins with its popular or folk aspects for several reasons. Westerners are often prone to think of religion in modern scientific or rational terms, rejecting that which smacks of 'magic' and 'superstition'. This point of view necessarily ignores much of the popular Buddhist tradition. Furthermore, Westerners who are personally attracted to Buddhism are interested primarily in meditation and the highest spiritual ideals attendant with this practice. This attitude leads them to reject the magical-animistic aspects of Buddhism as either unnecessary or harmful. A more holistic understanding of Buddhism in today's world, however, provides us with a fairer assessment of its varied nature. What then, are some of the expressions of popular Buddhism in Buddhist Asia today?

The character of Buddhist animistic beliefs and practices naturally depends on the nature and vocabulary of particular autochthonous traditions. In some cases, as in Sri Lanka for example, a synthesized pantheon of divine beings and spiritual powers emerged. Today the Buddha reigns at the apex of a pyramidal structure flanked by the Hindu god Indra known in the Theravāda Buddhist tradition as Sakka. Of more practical significance are pan-national gods the likes of Kataragama or

Skanda, second son of Śiva, whose annual festival nearly rivals the yearly procession celebrating Sri Lanka's most famous Buddhist shrine, the Temple of the Tooth. The hierarchy of deities descends through various ranks from regional gods to local guardian spirits. Formally, the entire pantheon is subject to the power and authority of the Buddha, a position expressed in the nature and type of ritual offerings as well as differentiations among types of ritual practitioners. Distinctions between specifically Buddhist and non-Buddhist elements frequently disappear in the eye of the beholder, however. I remember a surprising conversation with a well-educated business man in Kandy, Sri Lanka, who cited as an example of the Buddhist resurgence in the 1960s a secular friend of his who sought the counsel of the Brahmin priest at the Kataragama Temple. He seemed oblivious to the fact that the Kataragama priest spoke for the Śaivite tradition, not Sinhalese Buddhism.

In other countries the amalgam between Buddhist and magical animism seems to defy a hierarchical structure. While in a formal sense the superiority of the Buddha to Hindu gods or local spirits prevails, the relationship between Buddhist and non-Buddhist elements is often informal and relatively imprecise. Burmese folk religion, for example, centers on *nats*, a miscellaneous class of powerful beings ranging from national or regional gods to local-personal spirits of notable citizens and departed relatives. While a distinctive tradition in its own right, the worship of *nats* complements rather than competes with Buddhism. It has been said that Burmese appeal to the Buddha for ultimate salvation and even some miracles, but to the *nats* for health, safety, good crops, fertility and prosperity—a convenient division of labour.

Myth and legend often establish the superiority of Buddhism over local traditions. In Tibet, for example, Padmasambhava's success in bringing Buddhism to that country was a consequence of his conquest of the indigenous shamans with a superior magic. This legend not only points to the ascendence of Buddhism in Tibet as the dominant religion, but of the wizardry that has traditionally characterized at least the 'Old School' (rNying-ma-pa) of Tibetan Buddhism to the present day. Other Buddhist myths and legends tell of visits of the Buddha, his disciples and later saints to various parts of Buddhist Asia where, in a similar manner, they contest with autochthonous forces. As we observe much local Buddhist practice today, however, in such countries as Sri Lanka, Burma, Thailand and Nepal the 'victories' of the Buddha and his followers may have been more 'mythic' than actual, for many forms of Buddhist practice reflect non-Buddhist beliefs and attitudes.

In China popular piety toward Kuan Yin (Jap: Kwannon) as a granter of boons points to an assimilation between a local Chinese wish-fulfilling, protective deity and the bodhisattva, Avalokiteśvara. In Japan the omnipresence of Jizo stones evidences a similar amalgam between the bodhisattva, Kṣtigarbha, and an indigenous Japanese kami (spirit). In Thailand and Laos nearly all Buddhists wear amulets around their necks not to signify their religious faith, but for protection against accident and ill-fortune. These amulets may contain relics of monks famed for their feats in meditation or magical powers and have been consecrated in special ceremonies. Buddha images on temple altars have been similarly consecrated, a ritual in which various ritual objects, viz. images and amulets, will be charged with a sacred power symbolically unleashed by chanting monks.

The syncretism which characterizes traditional Buddhism throughout Asia has also infused new religious movements and sectarian developments. In some cases, as for example Tenrikyo in Japan, elements of Shinto, Buddhism and a Christian Science type of faith-healing blend to make a distinctive sub-tradition. Others of the so-called New Religions in Japan have brought together various aspects of Buddhism, Shinto, Christianity, shamanistic folk traditions, and humanistic psychology. Like many of these new religious groups the Risshō Kōseikai begun in 1938 was founded by a shaman-type figure, in this case a woman (Myōkō Naganuma), but its use of discussion groups for the purposes of personality development seems reminiscent of psychological encounter groups. In Korea, Won Buddhism founded by Soe-Tae San in the early part of the twentieth century is much like a modern folk religion combining elements of Buddhism, Confucianism and an emphasis on social service, and before the Vietnam war, the new syncretistic religions of Cao Dai and Hoa-Hao together claimed over four million adherents in that country. In short, popular Buddhism in Asia today, whether in traditional or more modern guises, is fundamentally syncretistic.

Buddhism, Politics, and the Nation-State

From its outset Buddhism has been closely associated with political rulers. At Siddhartha Gotama's birth his greatness as either a Buddha or a world ruler was predicted, and Buddhist chronicles delight in relating stories of monarchs who supported the monastic order which in turn helped to legitimate their rule. In the modern period this close relationship between religion and the state has continued unabated albeit in somewhat altered forms. In particular, Buddhism contributed decisively to the development of the new Asian nation-states at the end of the colonial period. It has, however, also attempted to resist the pressures put on the tradition by these new governments and their policies. Finally, in some cases, the state has done its best to restrict or repress Buddhism and the cultural values it represents. We shall examine each of these dimensions of the relationship between Buddhism and the modern nation-state.

In the former colonies of Great Britain, Sri Lanka (Ceylon) and Burma, the early nationalist movement was fed by strong

Buddhist sentiments. Buddhists in both countries felt that British attitudes toward their religion were demeaning, and that British policies undermined the traditionally close relationship between Buddhism and the state. In Sri Lanka aggressive monks began speaking out against Christianity and British rule toward the end of the nineteenth century. Their efforts gained momentum with the support of the American theosophist, Henry Steel Olcott, and the leadership of the Anagārika Dharmapāla and such groups as the Mahābodhi Society (founded 1891) and the Young Men's Buddhist Association of Colombo (founded 1898). The forces of Buddhist revivalism and Sinhalese nationalism continued unabated through the first half of the twentieth century abetted, as in the rest of colonial Asia, by the interregnum of World War II. Finally, spurred on by the celebration of the 2,500th anniversary of the birth of the Buddha in 1956, and the simultaneous publication of the Report of the Buddhist Committee of Inquiry with strong anti-British sentiment, S. W. R. D. Bandaranaike and the Sri Lanka Freedom Party (S.L.F.P.) were swept into power backed by Buddhist and Sinhalese nationalistic fervor.

Bandaranaike had been part of the first wave of Sinhalese nationalism, and as the leader of the Sinhala Maha Sabbha represented Sinhalese and Buddhist interests. He broke from the ruling United National Party (U.N.P.) which had governed Sri Lanka since its independence in 1948, attacking what he considered to be its residual imperialism. Along with other Buddhist leaders of former British and French colonies, Bandaranaike espoused what has come to be known as 'Buddhist socialism'. He supported the adoption of Buddhism as a state religion in order to promote a religious–democratic socialism. In a speech delivered in 1950 he justified his belief in democracy on the grounds of Buddhist doctrine of *karma*, that people are measured by their own merit and not extraneous circumstances. Furthermore, he justified his socialism on the grounds of the Buddhist doctrine of love and compassion (*mettā*) toward all beings, especially those condemned to poverty, ignorance and disease. Unfortunately, Bandaranaike was assassinated in 1962, although the close relationship between Buddhism and politics, and the political activism of Buddhist monks continues to characterize Sri Lanka.

The year 1962 was equally important in Burma for it coincided with the demise of U Nu, Burma's prime minister since 1948 and a strong advocate of a Buddhist socialist state. As in Sri Lanka, Buddhism represented the only widely accepted symbol able to focus the accumulated economic, social and psychological grievances of the people. In the early decades of the twentieth century the nationalist cause was led by such politically active monks as U Ottama and U Wisara. U Nu along with Ne Win and Aung San had been part of the Thakin movement at the University of Rangoon before World War II and a member of the Anti-Fascist People's Freedom League (A.F.P.F.L.) which was to win independence from Great Britain in 1948. When Aung San, the greatest hero of the independence movement, was assassinated on the eve of the declaration of Burma's freedom from British colonial rule, U Nu was called upon to form the new government. Under his leadership Buddhism because one of the foundations of the modern Burmese nation-state.

U Nu tried to create a Buddhist socialist state in which the government would provide sufficient material needs for everyone, class and property distinctions would be minimized, and government policy would inspire all to strive for moral and mental perfection. The state would, in short, meet the material needs of the people, and Buddhism their spiritual needs. Unfortunately, U Nu's commitment in 1960 to make Buddhism the state religion proved to be an unpopular move with minorities like the Christian Karens. The promulgation of Buddhism as the state religion became one of the reasons given by General Ne Win for deposing U Nu as Prime Minister in 1962. Although Ne Win declared Burma a secular state, his policies have increasingly reflected the central and pervasive importance of Buddhism throughout most of the country.

Buddhism has taken an active role in the modern nation-state in ways other than supporting movements for national independence against Western colonial powers. In Japan Soka Gakkai (Value Creating Society) founded in 1937 as a lay wing of the Nichiren Shōshū has become one of the most powerful popular movements in the history of Japan. It has developed a political party known as the Kōmeito or Clean Government Party which since the mid-60s has been a major political force. Daisaku Ikeda, the current leader of Soka Gakkai, has enunciated a type of Buddhist democratic socialism which he characterizes as a middle way between capitalism and communism based on respect for humanity and the realization of a true public welfare in a warless world.

Thailand provides still another kind of example of the relationship between Buddhism and the State. There Buddhism and the monarchy continue to function as the most visible symbols of national unity. In addition, the government has carefully designed a number of national development programs utilizing Buddhist monks. Two of these, the Dhammadhūta and Dhammacarika organized during the 1960s, train monks to work in politically sensitive areas in the northeast bordering Laos and Cambodia, and among the animistic hill tribe peoples in northern Thailand. Both programs aim to encourage national loyalty among people whose affiliation rests more strongly with a regional ethnic group or tribe. More recent government programs have encouraged monks to take leadership roles in rural economic development such as rice and buffalo banks, and vocational training in non-agricultural jobs such as electrical repair, sewing and weaving to supplement family and village income.

There are, of course, numerous instances during the past fifty years when Buddhism and the state have not been mutually supportive. One of the most dramatic was the protest of Vietnamese monks against the Diem regime in the 1960s which included several instances of self-immolation. In Thailand today, while the national monastic order strongly supports the state, there have been instances of charismatic monks in the north and northeast regions of the country who have resisted pressures by the state toward standardization of monastic education and practice. One of the best known was the northern Thai monk, Khrūbā Sīvijāya, of Chiangmai who ran into problems with the national monastic hierarchy because he ordained monks and novices according to the northern Thai custom without having been recognized as a preceptor by the national order. On the other side, there have also been instances where the state has discouraged Buddhism or has taken active steps to disestablish it. The best known cases are those where communist regimes have come into power—China, Tibet, Vietnam, Laos and Cambodia. It must be kept in mind, however, that in these countries anti-religious efforts on the part of the government have varied greatly. The most devastating anti-Buddhist periods were the time of the Cultural Revolution in China and the reign of Pol Pot in Kampuchea (Cambodia).

The Impact of the West: Restoration, Reform, Reinterpretation
Anyone who has travelled to Asia, especially its urban areas, has undoubtably been impressed with the pervasiveness of Western influence. Countries like Thailand and Japan where modernization has proceeded nearly unchecked during the past twenty to thirty years have been subjected to what one of my Buddhist friends has referred to as 'TV cultural homogenization'. To be sure, Bhutan and Ladak are not Thailand or Japan, and have remained relatively immune to Western influence. Despite such exceptions, however, the

colonial period, World War II, the post-war influence of America, communist revolutions, and the continuing pervasive economic and political influence of the West have forever challenged and changed the face of Buddhism.

Confronting this onslaught, Buddhism has shown a great deal of tenacity and adaptability. To be sure, it has been subject to the eroding influences of secularism, as has Western religion, and in various ways reflects the breakdown of a traditional worldview. There have been efforts to shore up the tradition, however, to restore its institutions, scriptural integrity, monastic and meditational disciplines, and moral values. Renewal and reform have taken place; in particular, there is a new activism on the part of Buddhist laity; and, Buddhist apologists are also reinterpreting their tradition to appeal to modern, educated élites.

It goes without saying that the impact of modern scientific and secular thought on Buddhism has been enormous. It must be kept in mind, furthermore, that Buddhist Asia has had much less time to absorb the changes associated with modernity than has the West. Perhaps the most dramatic examples are those countries where forms of Marxism have become the dominant political philosophy of the ruling élites. In China (and Tibet), Laos, Cambodia and Vietnam accommodation has been reached with traditional institutional Buddhism. It is tolerated, but not encouraged. Monastic education and practice continue, however, and public rituals and worship are permitted. The material wealth once owned by Buddhist monasteries or donated to them has been confiscated or greatly restricted, but the destructive excesses of the Red Guards in China and Pol Pot in Kampuchea (Cambodia) were exceptions, not the rule. Marxist revolution has not led to the end of Buddhism in Asia any more than to the end of Christianity in Communist Europe, although lack of government support has certainly affected the nature of Buddhism as an institution.

It has been argued, however, that the impact of Western materialism has had an equally eroding effect on the basic health of Buddhism in non-communist Asia. I remember a conversation with a Japanese friend in Kyoto who asked me why I was studying Buddhism there since the Japanese people of today were basically non-religious. One can argue about what my friend meant by religion, but his opinion is one shared by many (if not most) modern Japanese. A 1984 BBC documentary on Buddhism in Thailand and Laos attempts to show that in some respects Thai Buddhism is suffering more under the excesses of materialism than Laotian Buddhism under the restrictions of a communist government. While the documentary reflects an obvious bias, the point cannot be ignored. Indeed, my Thai acquaintances, both lay and monastic, are deeply concerned about the state of Buddhism in the country even though it seems to be prospering and receives the official support of the government. A well-known Buddhist layman and medical educator recently gave a talk where he caustically observed that Thailand may have more than a quarter of a million men wearing the saffron robes of the Buddhist monk, but that there are twice as many prostitutes.

The underlying issue in the cases of Laos and Thailand or both communist and non-communist Buddhist countries is the fundamentally secular materialistic challenge to a traditional religious worldview, the institutional structures and practices associated with it, and the attitudes and values towards life embedded in it. The problem is a universal one and not unique to Buddhist Asia. In such a situation religion might survive as a cultural relic, preserving institutions and rites associated with the tradition. Although the significance of religion at this level cannot be denied, some would argue that religion must adapt and change if it is to remain an integral part of peoples' beliefs and attitudes. In the twentieth century Buddhism has attempted renewal in various ways which we shall examine in terms of restoration, reform, and reinterpretation.

One of the foremost efforts to restore the place of Buddhism during the twentieth century was by a Sinhalese layman, the Anagārika Dharmapāla. Born David Hewavitarane (d. 1933) but better known by his ordained title, Dharmapāla was the founder of the Mahābodhi Society in 1891 with the primary aim of restoring Buddhist sites in India, especially Bodhgaya, and establishing an international Buddhist college there. The Society had a broader missionary outreach, however, especially through its English language journal. While the Society made few Indian converts, it helped to restore the prestige of Buddhism in Sri Lanka and Southeast Asia, and was one of the instruments responsible for propagating Buddhism in the West. Dharmapāla, himself, made a significant impact on the World Parliament of Religions in 1894 in Chicago where he delivered stirring speeches in defense of Buddhist teaching and values. These early attempts to restore the prestige of Buddhism foreshadowed the formation of the World Fellowship of Buddhists (1952), an ecumenical Buddhist organization which has not only sought cooperation among Buddhists but has helped Buddhism to take its place internationally with such Christian organizations as the World Council of Churches.

The restoration of Buddhist sites as part of an effort to stimulate pride in the Buddhist tradition has continued to be an integral part of the renewal of Buddhism. In its own way, tourism has been a part of this picture for it has not only brought in tourist dollars, but the admiration of foreigners for the great Zen monasteries in Kyoto, the classical sites of Pagan in Burma and Sukhothai in Thailand, and so on, has served to give Asian peoples a pride in their own Buddhist traditions.

The restoration of Buddhism in this century has, of course, been much more than rebuilding monuments. In Thailand monastic education was completely restructured throughout the entire country as a means of regularizing monastic training and enhancing the place of the monk in Thai society. The key figure in reorganizing the monastic order and the education of monks was the Prince Patriarch Vajirañāṇa-vororosa, one of the greatest Asian religious leaders of the twentieth century. Vajirañāṇa, furthermore, made a major contribution to Pāli scholarship and textual study. Buddhist scholarship has been advanced in many other countries as well, for example, the École Supérieure de Pāli in Cambodia, the assiduous study of Tibetan texts in Tibet before the revolution and now in India, Europe and America, the seminaries founded by T'ai-hsü (d. 1947) in China beginning with Wuchang in 1922, Vidyalaṅkara and Vidyōdaya Buddhist universities in Sri Lanka, Hanazona and Ōtani Universities in Kyoto, etc. Westerners have contributed greatly to Buddhist scholarship, as well, not only in the West, but in Asia too. Notable among them are Caroline and W. D. Rhys Davids, founders of the Pāli Text Society, and Westerners who became monks, e.g. Lama Anagārika Govinda and Nyanaponika Thera from Germany, Soma Thera from England.

Buddhism is associated in the minds of many with the practice of meditation, and the past few decades have seen a renewed interested in meditation in many Asian Buddhist countries. Burma has led the way with such eminent monks as Ledi Sayadaw (d. 1923), and Mahāsi Sayadaw who has students all over the world. Of particular interest is the spread of meditation practice among the laity. U Ba Khin founded the International Meditation Center in Rangoon, and the fastest growing Buddhist group in Thailand, Wat Dhra Dhammakāya outside of Bangkok, stresses a visualization form of meditation for all adherents. *Zazen* has also become popularized in Japan, not simply as a monastic discipline or part of the samurai tradition but more generally. A recent BBC documentary on Buddhism in Japan, for example, opens with a scene of waiters and waitresses in a Japanese restaurant beginning their work day with *zazen* meditation!

Restoration of classical Buddhist sites, of monastic organization and educational institutions, and a resurgence of interest in meditation have, to be sure, often been part of attempts to change and reform Buddhism. The Buddhist universities in Sri Lanka and Thailand teach not only traditional courses in sacred texts and Buddhist doctrine but 'secular' subjects as well, and the educational reforms of T'ai-Hsü in China reflected modern currents of thought. In recent years the Dalai Lama living in exile in India has spoken of the need to reform Tibetan Buddhism, and throughout Buddhist Asia there have been a variety of voices calling for change. Bhikkhu Buddhadāsa in Thailand is critical of the preoccupation of Thai Buddhism with merit-making, ritualistic activities which he sees as a form of religious materialism. From Sri Lanka to Japan, Buddhists are demanding that their tradition be more involved in social service and address problems of imminent need. Buddhist laity have taken particularly important leadership roles, and the emergence of lay persons in the forefront of various Buddhist movements including, as we have seen, meditation, is a preeminent characteristic of contemporary Buddhism.

From a national standpoint, one of the most impressive lay leaders in the area of social service or economic and social development has been A. T. Ariyaratna. 'Ari', as he is known, founded the Sarvodaya Sharmadana Movement which, for the past twenty years, has been actively engaged in trying to revitalize the lives of poor villagers throughout Sri Lanka. Inspired by the example of Gandhi and his disciple, Vinoba Bhave, Ariyaratna began taking his students from an élite Colombo high school to work in villages outside of the capital to help give the villagers a sense of pride, to show them that the educated élites cared for them, and to be of practical assistance.

He gradually evolved a philosophy of service deeply rooted in Buddhism, but with a universalistic perspective. The Sarvodaya Movement has now worked in over 3,000 villages in Sri Lanka and has involved over 300,000 people in its projects. It has attracted considerable international attention and financial support.

In Thailand, Sulak Sivaraksa, a prominent Buddhist lay activist, has helped to found a vital human rights group, and the Asian Cultural Forum For Development, an organization which seeks to guide the development of third-world countries according to principles rooted in their spiritual cultures. Sulak argues that only religion can bring out the true value of human development. From a Buddhist perspective he believes that development should reduce craving, avoid violence, and enhance the spiritual and moral dimensions of life as well as the material. He actively promotes social uplift activities in Thailand, is involved in various international organizations working for non-violent social change, and is a critic of the materialism of both Western capitalism and communism. Along with many lay reformers, Sulak attempts to interpret the universal values of the Buddhist tradition in terms of contemporary needs and courses of action.

Sulak's essays on religion and development point to one of the major directions taken today by Buddhist apologists attempting to reinterpret the Buddhadharma (teachings of the Buddha), namely, an insistence on its relevance to the human situation in all of its complexity. In Japan one finds this emphasis not only among the New Religions, but the traditional sects as well. For example, the slogan of the 21st General Buddhist Congress in Japan (1973) was, 'Buddhism resolves the crises of humankind'.

Among some apologists the Buddha is depicted primarily as a social reformer within the context of a completely demythologized narrative of his life. Other have sought to harmonize Buddhism with modern scientific thought, for example, U Chan Htoon, a former chief justice of the Supreme Court of Burma sees Buddhism as consistent with all modern scientific theories from evolution to relativity, and Daisaku Ikeda, the head of Soka Gakkai, sees field theory in modern physics as a confirmation of the Buddhist teaching of the inseparability of matter and space. Other areas of modern Western thought Buddhist apologists find particularly compatible with Buddhism include humanistic and developmental psychology which stress the dynamic nature of the person or psyche, pragmatic and empirical traditions in philosophy, e.g. David Hume, and process theology, e.g. A. N. Whitehead. D. T. Suzuki, for example, one of the great interpreters of Zen Buddhism to the West, finds similarities between Zen and the humanistic psychology of Eric Fromm, as well as between Zen and Christian mysticism.

Buddhism and the West
The time is long past when Buddhism in America and Europe can be considered esoteric or exotic. Westerners have studied Buddhism academically and pursued its practice personally for decades, and in recent years Asian Buddhists have settled in the West in ever increasing numbers.

In the latter part of the nineteenth century Caroline and T. W. Rhys Davids founded the Pāli Text Society (1881) together with Friedrich Max Müller, the general editor of the monumental *Sacred Books of the East*. In the first decades of this century the Buddhist Society of Great Britain and Ireland (1907) sought to propagate an interest in Buddhism through its journal, *The Middle Way*, and books by Christmas Humphreys, one of its leading exponents. This story was repeated on the continent and later in America. The names of Burnouf, Poussin, Oldenberg, Kern, Geiger, Stcherbatsky and so on recall a generation of scholars who not only opened up the field of modern Buddhist studies, but for whom Buddhism often had a strong personal appeal as well. Buddhism, furthermore, was discovered by philosophers and writers the likes of Schopenhauer, Nietzsche, Thoreau and Herman Hesse. Buddhist societies on the continent included Les Amis du Bouddisme (1929), co-founded by G. Constant Lounsberry, and the Altbuddistische Gemeinde (1921) founded by Grimm and Seidenstücher. In the United States the Buddhist Society of America was begun in New York City (1930) by the Venerable Sokei-an and is now known as the First Zen Institute of America with an outstanding meditation facility in western New York State.

With the end of World War II western interest in Buddhism burgeoned, abetted by extensive contact between Asia and the West, and an ever increasing quest for personal meaning in life among a generation emerging from a period of rapid social change and disruption. Zen Buddhism, in particular, had a strong appeal. In America the 'beat' generation and the poets of the 'San Francisco Renaissance', e.g. Jack Kerouac, Alan Ginsberg, Gary Snyder, helped to foster an interest in Buddhism. D. T. Suzuki's interpretation of Zen became so influential that some students of Buddhism referred to Zen in the West as 'Suzuki Zen'. Alan Watts, attracted to Buddhism through the Buddhist Society of Great Britain, emigrated to America where he helped to popularize a perennial philosophy type of Zen Buddhism.

International events were to play a major role in an even more extensive Buddhist presence in Europe and America. Chinese military forces occupied Tibet forcing the Dalai Lama into exile in India, and groups of Tibetan monks found their way to Switzerland, England, Canada, and the United States. In America two major centers emerged. The Tibetan Nyingma Meditation Center organized by Tarthang Tulku Rimpoche in Berkeley in the late 1960s, and the Vajradhātu Foundation organized by Chögyam Trungpa Rimpoche in the early 1970s and headquartered in Boulder, Colorado. Groups of Theravāda Buddhists came in large numbers at the end of the Vietnam War through the 1970s, in particular Lao and Cambodian refugees. This has led to the development of Theravāda centers in France, England, America and elsewhere, greatly augmenting the few Sri Lankan monasteries founded earlier in America, England and Germany. In America there are now over fifteen Thai monasteries whose principal role at the moment is that of Buddhist cultural centers and mediators for first generation Thai and Lao communities adjusting to the West. Theravāda Vipassanā meditation centers are also being founded in ever increasing numbers, as well, led by American and European monks and lay persons who have returned from years of practice with such Buddhist masters as Acharn Cha in northeast Thailand and U Ba Khin in India.

Currently Buddhism is making an impact on the West in a variety of ways. These might be summarized as follows: (1) communities focusing on a meditation discipline usually built around a reputed teacher representing a particular monastic tradition or lineage, e.g. the Shasta Abbey Zen Center, the Vipassanā Center in Barre, Massachusetts, (2) Buddhist communities whose outreach extends primarily although not exclusively to Asians, e.g. Japanese, Thai, Cambodian, Lao, Vietnamese, (3) Buddhist movements shaped specifically to develop a distinctive American or European form of Buddhism, e.g. the Vajradhātu Foundation, (4) Western and Asian interpreters who have sought to popularize Buddhism in the West primarily through their writing, e.g. D. T. Suzuki, Alan Watts, (5) Christian theologians and spokespersons whose study of Buddhism and contact with Buddhist masters have influenced their thought and religious practice, e.g. the Trappist monk, Thomas Merton and the protestant theologian John Cobb. Although this list is not exhaustive, it suggests the types or modes of Buddhism impacting on the West today.

The long-standing but relatively small and élite interest in Buddhism in the West beginning in the late nineteenth century is now becoming an important religious force in its own right. Many Tibetan, Japanese, and Thai Buddhist masters see the West as the place where the 'light of the Dharma will burn the brightest in future years'. That, of course, remains to be seen. It cannot be denied, however, that Buddhism as a world religion has taken on an international scope unprecedented in the first 2,500 years of its existence. As a consequence of its growth in Europe and America it will be changed, and will, in turn, affect the religious ethos of the West.

Bibliography

Anthropological Studies of Theravada Buddhism (*Southeast Asia*) (Asia Studies Cultural Report Series No. 13). New Haven, Conn: Yale University Press, 1968.

Bstan-'dzin-rgya-mtsho, XIV, Dalai Lama, *My Land and My People*. New York: McGraw-Hill, 1962.

Buddhism. A Modern Perspective, ed. Charles S. Prebish. University Park, Pa.: Pennsylvania State University Press, 1975.

Buddhism in the Modern World, eds. Heinrich Dumoulin and John C. Marldo, New York & London: Collier Macmillan Publishers, 1976.

Bush, Richard D., *Religion in Communist China*. Nashville: Abingdon, 1970.

Nanh, Nhat, Thich. *Vietnam. Lotus in a Sea of Fire*. London: SCM Press, 1967.

King, Winston L., *A Thousand Lives Away. Buddhism in Contemporary Burma*. Cambridge, Mass.: Harvard University Press, 1964.

Merton, Thomas. *Zen and the Birds of Appetite*. Philadelphia: New Directions, 1968.

McFarland, H Neill, *The Rush Hour of the Gods*. New York: Macmillan and Co., 1967.

Prebish, Charles S., *American Buddhism*. North Scituate, Mass.: Duxbury Press, 1979.

Religion and Change in Contemporary Asia, ed. Robert Spencer. Minneapolis: University of Minnesota Press, 1971.

Schecter, Jerrold, *The New Face of Buddha: Buddhism and Political Power in Southeast Asia*. Tokyo: Weatherhill, 1967.

Swearer, Donald K., *Buddhism in Transition*. Philadelphia: Westminster Press, 1970.

Tarthang, Tulku, *Gesture of Balance*. Emeryville, Calif.: Dharma Publishing, 1977.

Trungpa, Chögyam, *Born in Tibet*. London: Allen & Unwin, 1966.

Welch, Holmes, *Buddhist Revival in China*. Cambridge, Mass.: Harvard University Press, 1968.

Welch, Holmes, *Buddhism Under Mao*. Cambridge, Mass.: Harvard University Press, 1972.

Tradition and Change in Theravada Buddhism. Essays on Ceylon and Thailand in the 19th and 20th Centuries, ed. Bardwell Smith. (Contributions to Asian Studies, No. 4). Leiden: E. J. Brill, 1973.

3

CHRISTIAN TRADITION IN TODAY'S WORLD

Andrew Walls

(Aberdeen and Edinburgh)

A Fundamental Shift

Christianity has always been universal in principle; it is of the nature of Christian claims that the God of all creation redeemed that creation (and specifically humanity) in the person of the God-Man Jesus Christ. But it is only in recent Christian history that Christianity can be said to have become universal in practice. The period since 1945 has seen a culmination and acceleration of a process of diffusion which had begun considerably earlier, but did not become noticeable before the nineteenth century. Christians form a substantial presence in every continent, and according to one recent survey are to be found in every one of the world's 223 nations.[1] This is not only unique among the world's religions; it is a new feature for the Christian faith itself. Classical Christian theology has long used the words 'catholic' and 'ecumenical' with their sense of universality, to designate an essential aspect of the Church. In their literal sense they have now become more applicable than ever before.

But the process of diffusion has not been a simple story of direct expansion, such as has characterized Islam in the same period. In fact, professing Christians probably represent a

[1] D. B. Barrett, (ed.) *World Christian Encyclopedia: a comparative study of churches and religions in the modern world AD 1900–2000*. Nairobi: Oxford University Press 1982, 6 (Global table 4). The statement presumably takes account of foreign residents in certain countries.

marginally *smaller* proportion of the world's population now than they did in 1900.[2]

In other words, the process of diffusion has been accompanied by a process of contraction. The convergence of the effects of these two processes imply a transformation of many aspects of Christianity that appear to have been a fixed part of its expression for centuries past.

If we take the process of expansion during the nineteenth century, this was most considerable (and significant for the future) in North America;[3] in the period since 1945 it has been most considerable in sub-Saharan Africa.[4] This may be thought surprising in view of the fact that the period has coincided with the decolonization of Africa with its marked rejection of Western hegemony and uninhibited assertion of traditional African values; but in fact Christian adhesion has gone on within Africa at a remarkable rate since the middle of the last century— in other words, throughout the pre-colonial, colonial and post-colonial processes. Christian profession in Africa is currently estimated at 236 millions, representing more than 15% of the world's Christians, and still rising.[5] Melanesia, where the Christian movement had made little impact by 1900, has also seen a substantial adhesion of Christians; in Papua New Guinea

[2] Barrett's figure, *ibid.*, is 34.4% in 1900, 32.4% in 1985.

[3] Cf. K. S. Latourette, *A history of the expansion of Christianity volume IV: The Great Century AD 1800–AD 1914*; London: Eyre & Spottiswoode 1941, chapters 6–12.

[4] Barrett estimates that the number of urban Christians in Africa increased by an average of 5.71% per annum between 1970 and 1985 and rural Christians by an average of 2.38% per annum. His total figure of professing Christians in Africa by the year 2000 AD (arrived at by projection of present trends) is over 393 millions. This estimate for 1900 is just under 10 million (Barrett p. 780, from Global Table 21).

[5] Barrett p. 4 (Global Table 2). The basis of computation of these and other figures quoted from this source, and the definition used to deduce Christian profession, are set out pp. 39–72. It is not necessary to accept without question either the statistics or the method of compilation to agree with the *directions* which they indicate.

and Irian Jaya for instance, this has notably accelerated since the Second World War.[6] On the major Asian culture blocks, India, China, Japan, which saw the greatest concentration of the nineteenth century missionary movement, the Christian impact (as measured in numbers of adherents), has been much less, and in the major Islamic theatres, barely noticeable. Nevertheless even some of these areas have received a new Christian presence. Many Indian tribal groups, for instance, have seen mass movements towards Christianity, and Christians form over 11% of the population of Indonesia, where, even with the large Dutch establishment, they made up less than $1\frac{1}{2}$% of the population of the Dutch East Indies.[7] Only one Asian country, the Philippines, has a Christian majority; in another, South Korea, Christians form the largest single religious group. Nonetheless, the Christian minorities of Asia have been substantial enough, and distinctive enough, to affect the general shape and direction of the world Christian community as a whole.

Similarly Latin America, where Christianity has been the majority profession of faith for three hundred years, has diversified its European Christian inheritance and developed new Christian forms and structures which have begun to have an effect on the older Christian centres that could not have been visualized in 1945. It is not only the relative numbers of Christians in the southern continents which has increased since the Second World War, but their relative significance.

This process has been enhanced by the rapid decline in Christian profession and observance in the traditional Christian lands in Europe. This again is the fruit of a long process which was masked by the degree of recovery in European Christianity in the earlier nineteenth century, (a recovery which formed the

[6] Cf. C. W. Forman, *The Island Churches of the South Pacific. Emergence in the twentieth century*. Maryknoll, N.Y.: Orbis 1982, 144ff.

[7] Barrett p. 382.

78

springboard for the missionary movement which was essential to much of the recent diffusion). In 1945, the most obvious aspect of numerical decline was the transformation of Holy Russia, successor to the Christian Empire of the East, into an atheistic state. By the 1980s, the decline in the Western European countries had become steady and prolonged. Indeed, after a period of renewed religious observance in the decade following the Second World War, it was the liberal, open societies of the West, rather than the officially atheistic regimes of Eastern Europe, which saw the most marked Christian decline. (Christian profession in the Soviet Union seems to have been fairly steady, perhaps even shows a modest increase, during the period, and Poland is perhaps the most demonstrably Catholic country in Europe. In both countries the degree of participation in Christian worship is notably higher than in, say, the United Kingdom).

We have already spoken of North America as the most obvious scene of Christian expansion during the nineteenth century. It was particularly remarkable in that it reversed the situation of Europe, where Christian observance took little root in the cities which were to form such a crucial new element in Western society. Urban America, which produced industrial and technological developments of global significance, achieved a remarkably high degree of Church attachment. The United States became not only much the largest national grouping of professing Christians but an unparalleled source of manpower and resources for its diffusion.[8]

There are signs of very similar processes of decline to those which have affected Western Europe, but, with the immense

---

[8] See W. R. Hogg, 'The role of American Protestantism in world mission, in R. P. Beaver (ed.) *American missions in bicentennial perspective*, South Pasadena, Calif.: William Carey Library 1977, 354–402. On the United States as source of missions manpower see V. H. Rabe, *The home base of American China missions 1880–1920*, Cambridge, Harvard University Press 1978.

base of the nineteenth century expansion they have been much slower to take effect.[9] Statistics of Christian profession as between Western Europe and North America are particularly misleading in that the latter has a considerably higher degree of observance and active participation.

The emergence of North America as the arsenal of Western Christianity itself represented a transformation of the configuration of the Christian world that had obtained for centuries. But developments since 1900, becoming far more noticeable in the past forty years, have produced a far more radical change. In 1900 Europe (including Russia) and North America together accounted for 83% of the world's Christians. The continent of Africa accounted for less than 2%. Today over half the Christians in the world live in the southern continents of Africa, Asia, Latin America and Oceania.[10]

The change has much more than demographic significance. Within a very short period of time the conditions which have produced the phenomena characteristic of Christianity for almost a millennium have largely disappeared. After centuries in which the norms by which Christian expression have been tested have arisen from the history and conditions of the Mediterranean world and of the lands north and east of it, the process has been transferred into a new and infinitely more varied theatre of activity. The conditions of African and Melanesian life, the intellectual climate of India, the political battlegrounds of Latin America, increasingly provide the context within which the Christian mind is being formed. The process is already beginning to produce changes in Christian priorities, and in the structure of Christian thought, practice and government. Indeed, most of the discernible changes in

[9] See Barrett's table for USA, p. 711. Cf. Clyde Curry Smith, 'Demographic factors in American Christianity', *Bulletin of the Scottish Institute of Missionary Studies* NS 3, 1986.
[10] Cf. Barrett p. 4, figures in Global Table 2.

Christianity since 1945 come from this fundamental southward shift.

The End of Christendom

In 1945 the shape of Christian thought and life was still largely determined by two long distant events—the conversion of the Roman Empire and the virtually total response of the peoples of northern and Eastern Europe to the faith of the converted Empire, expressed in terms of a single all-embracing spiritual organization, 'the Church', outside of which no religious organization had legitimacy. The Christian Empire of Constantine's successors when translated into Northern European terms became the concourse of Christian princes with their peoples and led in turn to the idea of the Christian nation. The Church acts upon all who are born into the Christian nation. A notional partnership of throne and altar is thus established, and Christianity is given a quasi-territorial and a quasi-political significance. It becomes Christendom. There are nations which belong within this Christian society and there are those beyond it.

The idea outlasted schisms and ruptures of the 'one' Church; it was easily adapted to the idea of 'national' churches established in each Christian state. It even outlasted the power or desire of the state to enforce conformity to a national church. It outlasted the enhanced position of the individual within Western society which was to lead to the recognition of religion as belonging within the sphere of personal decision, though such a concept is ultimately inconsistent with the idea of Christendom. Individualism is the parent of secularism.

The earliest expansion of Christianity from Europe was a simple extension of Christendom. The Iberian conquests which later became the Latin American nations have substantially broken with that framework only in the last fifty years. The United States represents a later development; in conscious breach of the European pattern it eschewed recognition of any single church and yet long retained the self-consciousness of being a Christian nation. The last flourish of the Christendom idea was perhaps displayed within the missionary movement itself. Even in 1945, amid the deepest conviction that 'heathenism' had descended on the West, it was natural to distinguish between the Christian lands of old Christendom (now minus Russia, but with the accession of the Americas and the emigration-based nations of Australia and New Zealand), and 'the mission field' where 'younger churches' were emerging. The territorial connotation of Christianity had remained even when the political connotation had been eroded.

But the shift of the balance of Christianity towards the southern continents has not produced a new Christendom. The new Christian communities cannot be plotted on a map; they form no natural block as did the new Christian communities of early medieval Europe. In Asia, as we have seen, with the rarest exceptions, even the largest are minority communities. In most African states, even those with vast Christian populations, there are also many who are Muslims or who adhere to the old religions of Africa.[11] Moreover, in hardly any country does any one church predominate so conspicuously that the nation can regard it as the sole voice of the Christian community, still less adopt it as a 'national' church. Even Latin America has seen a drastic modification of its traditionally understood relationships of state and church. Many of the republics now have substantial communities that are not only Protestant but Pentecostal, where once the Catholic Church had a monopoly of education, medicine and social services. Whereas in 1945 it would have been natural to identify the Roman Catholic Church as an

[11] Cf. Adrian Hastings, *A history of African Christianity, 1950–1975*, Cambridge: Cambridge University Press 1979; and E. W. Fasholé-Luke, R. Gray, A. Hastings and G. Tasie (eds.) *Christianity in independent Africa*, London: Collings 1978, part 1.

essentially conservative force in Latin American soci
often provides the most devastating critique of
modes of government. The alliance of throne and
splintered where it was apparently triumphant.

In Western Europe the apparatus of established churches has
(on the whole) survived; but it no longer reflects any
partnership of throne and altar, and in nations such as Britain,
Germany and the Netherlands the state is increasingly having to
take account of the fact that it has communities which profess
faiths other than Christianity. Paradoxically, the ghost of
Christendom has survived in a more substantial form in certain
Eastern European countries, where continuation of traditional
State-Church relationships at hierarchical level has enabled the
state to maintain a degree of control of the Church life; but
equally the strength of Christian communities in Eastern
Europe has sometimes come from the fact that they offered an
alternative community to that prescribed by the state.

It seems then that Christendom—the territorial idea of
Christianity, with an implied official relationship with the
state—has been eroded in the lands of its birth, and that its re-
emergence elsewhere is not at the moment possible nor likely in
future. A much more diffused Christian presence
geographically, a much more diverse Christian presence
culturally, has emerged since 1945. Life in plural churches and
amid a plurality of faiths within the secular state is the likely
condition of Christian existence.[12] The new religious states in
the modern world are not Christian ones.

The Transformation of the Missionary Movement
The new geographical position of Christianity is the fruit of the
missionary movement from Europe. This movement had
several phases; the first associated with re-invigorated Iberian

[12] Cf. A. T. van Leeuwen, *Christianity in world history. The meeting of the
faiths of East and West.* London: Edinburgh House Press 1964.

Catholicism in the sixteenth century and after, the next with Evangelical Protestantism from Western Europe and New England in the eighteenth and early nineteenth century, the third with almost all branches of Western Christianity from the late nineteenth century on. Seen in the context of the total history of Christianity, it is one of a series of cross-cultural initiatives which have altered the whole form and expression of Christianity at certain crucial periods. The recurrence of these transforming initiatives is one of the most marked characteristics of historic Christianity. Seen in its own immediate historical context, however, the missionary movement is associated with a particular phase of Western political, economic and social development.[13]

It was in many respects the last flourish of Christendom. It was based on a geographical concentration of Christians in one area, a natural division of the world into 'fully missionized' and 'not yet fully missionized' lands, as the World Missionary Conference of 1910 explained. It was associated with a particular form of civilization and advanced theology, the generally beneficent tendency of which was widely acknowledged, and by Christians linked both historically and essentially to the nature of Christian faith itself. And it implied both political systems which permitted free association for voluntary action and economic structures which produced surpluses and permitted their export.

Demographic change, the contraction of Christianity in Europe and the general Western insistence on the individual nature of religious choice have now undermined the whole concept of 'fully missionized' lands, and Christians are infinitely more diffused than they were a century ago. The link between Christianity and technology is much less obvious. High

[13] See, e.g. Max Warren, *The missionary movement from Britain in modern history*, London: SCM 1965 and *Social history and Christian mission* London: SCM 1967.

technology is not longer necessarily associated with countries also associated with Christianity, and most Christians now live in areas relatively low in technological capacity. Further, the confident assertions of Christians about the power of technology have given place to awareness of its limitations, consciousness of its power for demonic destruction and desire for its control. And Europe at least, the principal source of the missionary movement until into the twentieth century, no longer has the economic capacity to maintain overseas expensive operations of voluntary societies, ecclesiastical formations and missionary orders.

New missionary societies have been founded in Asia and other parts of the new 'Southern' Christianity, which now have numbers of missionaries serving in countries other than their own. A number of older, Western-originated mission societies have diversified their structure to include nationals of countries of 'new Christianity'. But it is significant that the countries most prominent in sending 'overseas' missionaries are those which have a prospering Western-type economy, such as South Korea. For the greater part of the Third World the economic basis simply does not exist for an overseas missionary movement based on personnel maintained by voluntary religious societies.

In other words, the model of Christian transmission has changed since 1945. Its classic expression is increasingly becoming diffusion *within* culture areas, rather than across them. Southern Christianity still relies on Western manpower, and sometimes Western finance, for some of its medical, educational and administrative institutions; but the vast mass of congregational life has no such dependence. In the continuing Christian histories of Africa, Asia and the Pacific, the missionary period is already an episode.

Having said this, it remains true that there are still large numbers of Western missionaries abroad; and in some poorly resourced or broken-backed states the combined presence of the mission agencies represents a formidable technological capacity. The great majority of missionaries are from North America, where the economic capability for missionary societies remains, at least in residual form; where cultural factors still favour the idea of expansion; and where some sections of Christian activity have adapted more quickly to changed technology than to changed perceptions of the world. Inasfar as the missionary movement continues as a separate identifiable phenomenon in the world it is likely to be seen, for good or ill, as part of the United States presence overseas.

The Diversification of Christianity
Christianity has commonly been divided by its own historians into three branches, Orthodox, (Roman) Catholic and Protestant. Inasfar as these diverse branches were culture-shaped and culture-bearing entities, they reflected the history and values of Eastern, of Southern and of Northern Europe respectively. Inasfar as they embodied doctrinal distinctions, these arose from conflicts among Christians of the lands surrounding the Mediterranean, or of the European heartlands.

The extension of Christianity to the Americas at first appeared to produce no major modification of its expression. The European heritage was so strong among those who settled in North America and dominated Central and South America, that it appeared that they had simply transplanted the Northern and Southern European forms of Christianity, Protestantism and Catholicism. There was no need to change the threefold model of Christianity. (It is arguable that there was one important exception to this. In North America a special version of Protestantism, with essentially American norms, developed an Evangelical Fundamentalism, and increasingly distanced itself from the older Evangelical Protestantism.)

The special form which the Christianization of Europe took, produced an assumed identity of community and church. This encouraged a self-consciousness within each of the branches that it was itself the authentic expression of Christian faith, the sole or at any rate the principal contemporary representation of the teaching and fellowship of the apostles. The official teaching of Roman Catholicism and (Eastern) Orthodoxy claimed that this teaching and fellowship was embodied in institutional form—the Church *was* Christianity.

By 1945, though the threefold division of Christianity into Orthodox, Catholic and Protestant was still axiomatic, the assumption that any one of these should be identified as the sole 'authentic' version was becoming less common. Since 1945 the claim of any one communion or tradition to exclusive representation of authentic Christianity has virtually disappeared from the official teaching of the major Christian bodies. In practice, seminal Christian thinkers exercise an influence no longer bounded by their own confessions. The central affirmations and emphases of each tradition now often find echoes in the others. A liturgical movement among Western Protestants emphasised God's action in the sacraments as in traditional Catholic theology; one among Western Catholics emphasized the simplicity of common participation in the Lord's Supper, as Protestant Reformers had done. Institutional union of formerly distinct bodies has occurred only within Protestantism, but it has been more widely discussed. Catholic and Protestant consultation and co-operation take place in countless ways which would have been unthinkable even in the 1940s; and in such bodies as the World Council of Churches Protestant and Orthodox share without inhibition.

The wider Christian diffusion is itself one cause of the greater openness of the Christian communities to each other. So many of the adherents of the Roman Catholic Church, and of many of the larger Protestant communions, now belong to the Southern Continents that issues and events that loom large in European history no longer have the same power, while issues never prominent in Europe may be primary concerns. This was evident within the missionary movement itself; there is a direct historical link between the international conferences convened to discuss the better prosecution of missionary operations and the establishment of the 'ecumenical' movement and the World Council of Churches concerned with all aspects of the mission of the Church and with its faith and order.[14] The first great (and in many ways the most striking) example of actual union, the Church of South India, occurred through the realization by Indian Christians of the irrelevance and danger in the Indian situation of Christian divisions shaped in Europe.[15] The outlook of even believers of European origin has been transformed by transfer to a new setting; the vision of Christianity of Russian Orthodox believers living in the United States or Australia was inevitably different from that to be gained in Eastern Europe.

In fact the threefold division into Orthodox, Catholic and Protestant is becoming progressively less useful. Its value is now greatest at the purely organizational level, and has its limitations even there. It is not only that the traditions are seeing interchange and commingling to an unprecedented degree; it is not even that new 'Southern' priorities are becoming quite as important as those arising from Western history that have produced the 'classical' and 'traditional' models. It is that Christianity is developing new local forms shaped by the priorities and conditions of the cultures in which it has more recently taken root; and that these new forms growing out of the soil of Africa and Asia and Latin America seem to be producing configurations of Christianity as distinct as the Catholicism shaped by southern and the Protestantism shaped by northern Europe.

[14] See R. Rouse, S. C. Neill and H. E. Fey, *A history of the ecumenical movement*. London: SPCK 2 vols.

[15] B. Sundkler, *Church of South India: the movement towards church union 1900–1947*, London: Lutterworth 1954.

Christian faith has always depended on translation. At its heart is not the prophetic Word (God speaks to man), but the incarnate Word (God as man among men). This implies the expression of the divine under the conditions of *particular* human societies, which in turn implies diversity.

In the course of Christian history certain counterbalancing factors have limited this innate tendency to diversity. Some of these were inherent in the original Christian tradition, notably the acceptance of a single body of Scriptures of essentially Jewish origin, and the acceptance of a view of history in which the Christian community, the Church, has an essential continuity with the early history of Israel. Other limits on diversity were fortuitous. The change of the Christian movement from one shaped by Palestinian Judaism to one based within Hellenistic civilization led to a substantial act of translation within the first Christian century. The passage of Christian faith from its Hellenistic-Roman form to the northern peoples of Europe involved a less radical, or at least a much slower, process of translation, since those peoples were simultaneously absorbing much of the cultural mass in which Christianity was embedded. In particular, the use of a single language for Scripture reading, worship and theological writing, combined with a strong central organization which nevertheless allowed enough local flexibility to avoid rupture, gave a high degree of apparent uniformity to the Christian faith. The sixteenth century rupture known as the Protestant reformation produced northern vernacular forms of Christianity, but elsewhere it if anything strengthened the idea of a 'universal' Christian form based on Southern Europe and expressed in Latin. And Latin Christianity was the nursery of a substantial part of the missionary movement.

Today the Roman Catholic Church represents well over half the total Christian population of the world. It is by far the largest organized body of Christians—indeed, it is probably the largest organized unitary religious body of any kind. It is unique in religious history for its durability and cohesiveness, and it would be wrong to underestimate its capacity to maintain those features.[16] But since 1945 the Roman Church has undergone a series of changes as fundamental as anything that happened to it in the sixteenth century. Many of these changes were given voice in the Second Vatican Council which met between 1962 and 1965. While maintaining the unique character of the Catholic Church, the Council stressed that all the Christian communions are instruments of salvation, and that the divine initiative for the salvation of all men is not restricted to the Christian revelation. It produced a new emphasis on the value of secular life, a new stress on the importance of the laity in Christian witness and worship and on the mission of the Church as that of the whole people of God. In the sphere of theology, the Word of God made available in the Scriptures plays a major role; the teaching authority and the preaching of the Church is subjected to it, it is linked with the eucharist as the sign of God's present activity among his people. And in all sorts of ways a stress appears on the importance of the *local* church. Centuries of uniformity in areas such as liturgy and clergy training are abandoned. The title 'Vicar of Christ', long arrogated to the Pope alone, is referred by the Council to all the bishops, the representatives of the teaching function of the Church.[17]

The emphases can increasingly create diversity within the Roman Church by the way in which they point to local factors and local relevance. But of all the important changes within

[16] Cf. J. L. McKenzie, *The Roman Catholic Church*, London: Weidenfeld and Nicolson 1969.

[17] Texts in W. M. Abbott (ed.) *The documents of Vatican II*. New York: Associated Press and Herder 1966. Succinct analysis and commentary by Adrian Hastings, *A concise guide to the documents of the See and Vatican Council* London: Denton, Longman and Todd, 2 volumes, 1968.

Roman Catholicism in the past half century, none has greater potential for change than one within the sphere of language. The general abandonment of Latin as the language of liturgy and theology has coincided with the widespread encouragement of Scripture reading in the vernacular. There are already signs that this is leading to theology, liturgy and practice that is markedly local in colour. Not surprisingly, by reaction there are attempts at the organizational level to maintain universality of the traditional type. It is too early to attempt to predict the outcome, but it is not sufficient to see here a simple tension between centre and periphery or between progressives and conservatives. Catholicism has frequently known tensions of these kinds. What is new is the recognition accorded to the Word of God in the vernacular, which implies the legitimation of differences of expression as wide as the differences among vernaculars. But this is a new factor only in terms of this, the largest strand in Western Christian history. In terms of total Christian history, this stress on the vernacular factor, with its implications for the interpretation of Christianity in terms of particular local societies, may be seen as a reversion to the norm. It is the long persistence of Latinity which has been the anomaly.

The work of vernacular translation of the Christian Scriptures generally has if anything intensified since World War II. By 1980 parts of the Bible were available in more than 1,700 living languages, and the entire Bible in 275.[18] There has certainly been much more stress on revision and new translation in languages where vernacular versions have long existed. Both in primary translation and in revision, modern linguistic practice has tended to seek cultural equivalence where older versions were content with literal renderings of the ancient text, even if these could have little meaning in the receptor

[18] *United Bible Societies Annual Report* 1981.

language.[19] These factors have tended to sharpen local identities and given an impetus to local theologizing.

African Christianity—a new mode
The result of a number of developments is a freer inter-action between the Christian tradition as expressed in Church and Scriptures and the cultural patterns of the southern continents, and a consequent development of new modes and expressions of Christianity.

The development is particularly clear in Africa. The proportion of African Christians belonging to the so-called African Independent Churches, especially those of the 'prophet-healing' or 'spiritual' type, has greatly increased since 1945, and the appreciation by others of their significance has changed completely. Forty years ago they seemed to belong to the margins of Christianity. Polemical Catholic commentators declared them the logical outcome of Protestant divisiveness and unfettered Biblicism; embarrassed Protestants described them as 'cults' or 'syncretistic movements'. They are now recognized as representing an attempt to express Christian faith and Biblical symbols amid the stark realities of African life; as wrestling with elements in African experience left untouched by Christianity in its Western form, whether Catholic or Protestant, because the West had no recent equivalent to that experience. As such the spiritual churches speak powerfully to countless people of the most diverse religious background. Leaving aside questions of historical origins, it makes little sense to describe, say, the Sacred Order of Cherubim and Seraphim, or the Church of the Lord (Aladura) as either Protestant or Catholic. Each represents an indigenous reading of Scripture, an

---

[19] Cf. E. A. Nida, *Bible translating. An analysis of principles and procedures, with special reference to aboriginal languages*, New York: American Bible Society 1947; and more recently E. A. Nida and C. R. Taber, *The theory and practice of translation*, Leiden: Brill 1982.

inter-action of the Biblical tradition with African life. When the Government of Zaire, in the interests of national unity, sought to reduce the number of separate religious structures, it acknowledged the right of the huge Kimbanguist Church (EJCSK) to stand alongside the Roman Catholic Church and a newly amalgamated Protestantism.[20]

The African Independent churches are only part of African Christianity, and statistically they are a minority. But it is becoming clear that their concerns are the concerns of vast numbers of Christians organizationally classified as Catholics or Protestants. Perhaps the Independent churches are best seen not so much as representing a division within African Christianity—that division is likely to matter less and less—than as providing an index to the characteristic features of an African Christianity underlying the faith and practice of countless African Catholics, Protestants and Independents alike.

At the conceptual level, a major concern of African Christianity is the nature of the African past, the conviction that the God of the Bible is also the God of Africa and the God of our fathers. It is no accident that current academic African theology is so concerned with the interpretation of traditional African religion. By reaction from the utter rejection which earlier African Christians made of the African past as dark, savage and 'primitive', a new African generation is establishing its identity, the human and religious values of African tradition; and a new

[20] A review of the massive literature on African Independent churches and related phenomena up to a decade ago is provided by H. W. Turner, *Bibliography of new religious movements Volume I Black Africa*, Boston: G. K. Hall 1977. See also H. W. Turner, *Religious innovation in Africa: collected essays on new religious movements*, Boston: G. K. Hall 1979. See also D. B. Barrett, *Schism and renewal: an analysis of six thousand contemporary religious movements*, Nairobi: Oxford University Press 1968. B. G. M. Sundkler, *Zulu Zion and some Swazi Zionists*, London: Oxford University Press 1976. For the Cherubim and Seraphim cf. J. D. Y. Peel, *Aladura: a religious movement among the Yoruba*, London: Oxford University Press 1968, and for Kimbanguism, M. L. Martin, *Kimbangu: an African Prophet and his church*, Oxford: Blackwell 1976.

Christian generation is viewing that tradition in the light of its Christian faith and symbols. In Africa the name of the God of the Bible is commonly the vernacular name of the Supreme God recognized in pre-Christian times. The continuity of the activity of God in Africa is thus an underlying concern in the establishment of African Christian identity. In many ways the debates of African theologians and the energy with which they analyse and interpret traditional religion, recall the debates within Hellenistic Christianity about the nature of the Greek past and the relationship to Christ of pre-Christian philosophers who pointed to the true wisdom. Outside the academic field similar issues constantly arise for African Christianity moved both by Christian Scripture and liturgy and by the wisdom of the fathers.[21]

The application of the categories of conventional Western philosophy of religion to African primal religions has given endless trouble. Should they be described, as early writers took for granted, as polytheistic? How then to explain the place of the Supreme Being? Neither 'monotheistic' nor 'pantheistic' seemed any more adequate, and new categories like 'diffused monotheism', or theories of oscillation of perception were introduced.[22] In fact, while African worshippers were often ready to recognize many divinities, they had no doubt who was God. Of the rivalry and knock-out competition among

[21] This theme is well illustrated and documented by Kwame Bediako, *Identity and integration: an enquiry into the natural problems of theological indigenization in selected early Hellenistic and modern African writers*, (Ph.D. thesis University of Aberdeen 1984. A published version of this important thesis is expected shortly.) See also L. O. Sanneh, *West African Christianity: the religious aspect*. London: C. Hurst 1983 and 'Christian mission in the pluralist milieu: the African experience,' *Missiology* 12(4) 1984, 421–433.

[22] Cf. E. B. Idowu, *Olódùmare: God in Yoruba belief*, London: Longmans 1962; J. S. Ukpong 'The problem of God and sacrifice in African traditional religion', *Journal of Religion in Africa* 14(3) 1983, 187–203. For a fierce attack on European approaches and assumptions, see Okot p'Bitek, *African religions in Western scholarship*, Kampala: East Africa Literature Bureau, nd [c1971].

divinities common in the Semitic World they knew little.[23] Recognition of the God of the Bible created no problem; the choice of the One or the Many that early Europe knew was avoided. But abolition of the focus of communal worship provided by the other divinities (especially where these had strong local or festal significance), and by the ancestral spirits, was another matter. Many communities have not fully settled whether local or ancestral cult can be combined with Christian commitment and a Christian world-view. Much African Christianity at local level is directed to the clarification of this issue. At the level of proclamation, African Christianity[24] has to take account of perceptions of a universe of spiritual forces whose influence can be traced in disease and misfortune and deprivation and alienation; with fears of the baleful effects of witchcraft or sorcery; with the concretized consciousness of envy or malice that induces witchcraft confessions. Christian proclamation thus becomes a demonstration of the direct activity of God in the local society, the power of Christ or the Holy Spirit in conflict with evil or disabling powers. The Independent churches exemplify that conflict dramatically with their healings and revelations, their uninhibited recognition of the fact of witchcraft, their use against evil forces of Christian symbols like Bible or water consecrated by Christian prayer, their challenge to those seeking their assistance to abandon the diviner and the herbalist and the magical apparatus often maintained as a 'fail-safe' device.[25]

[23] Cf. P. J. Ryan, 'Arise O God!' The problem of 'gods' in West Africa, *Journal of Religion in Africa* 11(3) 1980, 161–171.

[24] A portrait is attempted by Adrian Hastings, *African Christianity: an essay in interpretation*, London: Chapman 1976.

[25] As examples among many, see H. W. Turner, *African Independent Church*, Oxford: Clarendon Press 1967, especially volume 2, *African Independent Church: the life and faith of the Church of the Lord (Aladura)*; and C. M. Dillon-Malone, The 'Mutumwa' churches of Zambia: an indigenous African religious healing movement, *Journal of Religion in Africa* 14(3) 1983, 204–222.

African Christian worship combines order and hierarchy on the one hand, with spontaneity and ebullience on the other. In the West, these features, at least until recently, were regarded as belonging to different ends of the Christian spectrum, but both have deep roots in traditional Africa. The Independents are notable for a multitude of ranks and offices, so that every member fits into an assured place and position. Though often the spheres of activity of dominant charismatic leaders, they are equally notable for their vigorous congregational participation in worship and in the conflict with evil the singing and praying and striving of the congregation are as indispensable as the leader's special gifts. Women have often a special place in maintaining this vigorous congregational life.

In the field of praxis, Christianity has often to contend with the disturbance of values, hierarchy and focus brought about by the processes of modernization. It has to cope with the confusion felt by people experiencing both the traditional claims of custom and kin and the claims of modern society and state, not to mention ethical codes of Christian origin shaped partly by Western social experience. Some of the areas of greatest confusion are the most pressing and immediate, such as marriage and family. The most urgent need of many people is to regain wholeness of perception, to be free from confusion, to make *assured* moral choices.

All these factors may be more important in understanding the African Independent churches than their more spectacular phenomena of trance, dance and ecstatic utterance. But exactly the same factors face countless African Catholics and Protestants and shape their practical devotion. African Christianity is finding new readings of the Christian Scriptures and new adaptations of the Christian tradition, especially in the areas with which the Western form in which Christianity was first transmitted to Africa was not equipped to deal. An engagement with African perceptions of reality, once thought of as 'syncretism', is not a sign of the insecurity of Christianity in Africa but of the thoroughness of its acceptance.

Latin America—Christendom transformed

The Hispanic-speaking mestizo complex of Latin America is now the largest Christian culture area in the world. For centuries it appeared to be an extension of European Christendom, and unequivocally part of its Latin expression. In 1900 there was no reason to question this view, and even in 1945 there was little to indicate the coming impact of the Continent upon Christian faith and practice.

In fact the Latin American situation differed from old Christendom in several respects. In the first place, and most importantly, it represented a long period of symbiosis between Iberian Catholic Christianity and the traditional cultures of the Native American peoples, (with in many areas a strong African infusion also). Second, the Church had a special part in the colonization process. Third, many of the republics had to make late concessions to pluralism in order to secure sufficient non-Iberian immigrants to develop their economies.[26]

In the period since 1945 Latin American Christianity has been developing traditions quite distinct from those of the West. The period has seen a burgeoning of Protestantism, so that in several of the republics evangelical Christianity is now a significant minority.[27] Europe has seen no parallel movement from Latin

[26] Latin American Church history is being rewritten through the labours of the Commission for Latin American Church History (CEHILA) with an ambitious revisionist programme. For the intellectual background, see E. Dussel, *A history of the Church in Latin America. From colonialism to liberation (c1492–1979).* Grand Rapids: Eerdmans 1981. It may be noted that the Philippines, the only Asian country with a Christian majority, has a Christian history in many respects parallel with that of Latin America. In the events leading up to the revolt of 1986, the effect of 'praxis theology' characteristic of Latin America, and of the basic communities, was evident.

[27] See W. R. Read, V. M. Monterroso and H. A. Johnson, *Latin American Church growth,* Grand Rapids, Eerdmans 1969; and W. M. Nelson,

Christianity since the sixteenth century. Further, the evangelicals have frequently developed charismatic features: enthusiastic worship marked by glossolalia and a spirituality stressing 'the filling of the Holy Spirit'. This was often quite contrary to the desires of the North American missionaries who first introduced evangelical Christianity, and has helped give Latin American Protestantism a certain distinctiveness.

In 1945 Pentecostalism[28] appeared to be on the fringes of Christianity, an eccentric feature of some forms of (principally American) Protestantism. Latin America has drawn it towards the Christian centre, a frequent (and evidently liberating) element in Protestant life shared by many Catholics also. The steady development of Pentecostal churches elsewhere in the world (including areas where older churches have declined); the ecstatic features in African Christianity; and the presence of a 'charismatic movement' within Western Catholicism and the older churches of Western Protestantism, all suggest that the associated phenomena are becoming more widely associated with Christianity than at any time since its first century.

Still more dramatic in the effects have been the changes within Latin American Catholicism. The evangelical and Pentecostal developments were themselves signs of a pastoral crisis; in the revolutionary climate of post–war Latin America, Churchmen saw the growing gap between rich and poor in states that were theoretically and constitutionally Christian. They reflected on the part the Church had played historically in producing the subjugation of the Indians and their culture and in maintaining the framework of an unjust society. The Christian vocation was to be a 'Church of the poor'. Official recognition of this is associated with successive Latin American

Protestantism in Central America, Grand Rapids: Eerdmans 1984, chapter 5 and 6.

[28] The most comprehensive study is that of W. J. Hollenweger, *The Pentecostals: the charismatic movement in the churches.* London: SCM 1972.

Bishops' Conferences at Medellin, and later at Puebla (attended by the Pope in person) in 1978.[29] The reformulation of Christian teaching has, however, gone further. Instead of isolated acts of identification by priests with revolutionary movements a whole 'theology of liberation' has developed. This aims at the creation of an alternative Christian society marked by justice and equity in relationships. Its protagonists insist on praxis as the critical area for theology, and this produces involvement in the movements of society; they frequently adopt the tools of Marxist economic analysis.[30] And the result of the 'Church of the poor' has been the emergence of 'Base Ecclesial Communities' or groups of committed lay people, frequently poor, who read and reflect on the Bible and apply it to their own situation, and act accordingly. In a measure, the Base Ecclesial Communities actualize the alternative Christian society sought by liberation theologians; and they implicitly and explicitly challenge the power structures of the nations.[31]

Western Christendom perhaps never produced such a sustained social critique from its Church as Latin America has known in the past generation; and in Europe the types of organism reflected in the Base Ecclesial Communities have been more characteristic of radical Protestantism than of established

[29] J. Eagleson and P. Scharper (eds.) *Puebla and beyond: documentation and commentary*, Maryknoll, N.Y.: Orbis 1974.

[30] The literature is now immense. The best starting point in English is probably still G. Guttierez, *A theology of liberation*, London: SCM first published in Spanish in Peru in 1971. One of several selection volumes is R. Gibellini, *Frontiers of theology in Latin America*, Maryknoll, N.Y.: Orbis 1979. The journal *Puebla* (Petropolis: Editorial Vozes) reflects many of the concerns and productions of socially active Catholic theologians all over Latin America.

[31] Again the literature is growing monthly. See, e.g. S. Torres and J. Eagleson (eds.), *The challenge of Basic Christian Communities*, Maryknoll, N.Y.: Orbis 1981. For the attempt to relate the Basic Ecclesial Communities to Protestant situations see G. A. Guillermo Cook, *The expectation of the poor. Latin American Base Ecclesial Communities in Protestant perspective*, Maryknoll, N.Y.: Orbis 1985.

Catholicism. There are signs of Latin American Christianity having a direct effect on contemporary Western Christian theology and practice.[32] The headiness of religious and social ferment in Latin America since 1945, the emergence of different types of radical change in the church, the development of local, vernacular styles of Christianity all recall the turmoil which reshaped European religion and society in the sixteenth century.

Asia and the potential for change

Christianity has made no such impression on Asian cultures as it has in Africa and Latin America, and consequently has taken no such impression from them. Nevertheless the Asian Christian minorities are both substantial enough and distinctive enough to have an effect on the world Christian community. It has already been mentioned that India took the lead in promoting the union of diverse churches in the Church of South India in 1947.[33] A parallel development in North India (where Christians are far fewer) followed. India has also been the scene of some of the most searching examination of the nature and content of Christian faith. India has in many ways provided Christianity with its most challenging environment, since so many Christian affirmations about God and Christ can be readily accepted without any change of basically Hindu positions.[34] Christians have thus faced on the one hand the danger of foreignness, on the other, that of absorption. The post-war independence and partition of India, have reduced the perceived threat to Hindu solidarity which complicated the relations of Christians with the national movement in the time of the British Raj; though the

[32] Latin American theologies have been made widely accessible in the West and have been widely read. The Maryknoll Society's publishing house Orbis has been particularly active in this. The themes have also been related to other 'Third World' situations.

[33] See note 15.

[34] M. M. Thomas, *The acknowledged Christ of the Indian Renaissance* London: SCM 1969.

attractiveness of Christianity to many Indian tribal peoples continues to alarm conservative Hindus. The same years have seen profound social, industrial and technological change in India, and Indian Christians have been prominent in efforts to understand and cope humanely with these changes. The Christian Institute for the Study of Religion and Society in Bangalore has been a prolific source of studies in this area.[35] India has also produced a series of theologians, (such as M. M. Thomas, long Director of the Institute) who, while using language intelligible in terms of Western theological discourse, have provided theology with different perspectives drawn from the setting of Indian society in change.[36] In particular they have organically related the themes of personal and societal salvation, which have frequently shown an awkward disjunction in Western theology.[37] There are Indian evangelists who have adopted the ancient tradition of the wandering *Sannyasi*, and a variety of Christian ashrams, and there are evangelistic groups who practise self-help low-technology crafts of the sort favoured by Gandhi himself.[38]

Whatever may be true within India itself, a good deal of Christian thought elsewhere in the past forty years has been influenced by Gandhi's life and teaching. It was popularized in the West by the evangelical American missionary, E. Stanley Jones.[39] It was critical to the way in which Martin Luther King

[35] The journal *Religion and Society* published by the Institute reflects this activity.

[36] A conspectus of approaches to politics and society, religion and culture, and Indian Christian theology in R. W. Taylor (ed.), *Society and religion: essays in honour cf. M. M. Thomas*, Madras: Christian Literature Society 1976.

[37] Cf. M. M. Thomas, *Salvation and humanization. Some crucial issues of the theology of mission in contemporary India*, Madras: Christian Literature Society 1971.

[38] A reflection of some of these activities coming from the *TRACI Journal* (New Delhi).

[39] Jones became well known through his pre-war books *The Christ of the Indian road* and *Along the Indian road*. His final salute to Gandhiji was *Mahatma*

formulated his Christian rationale for the civil rights movement for American Blacks.[40] Resistance to evil should be active and deliberate but not violent, suffering patiently accepted as a means of liberation. This stream of thought can be detected in many subsequent Christian settings, often with explicit reference to Gandhi.[41]

Asia has provided many modes and foci for dialogue between Christians and those of other faiths. Besides direct encounter on the nature of truth claims, and comparison of attitudes on urgent practical matters such as environment, industrialization, social change, war and peace, there have been mutual explorations of the devotional and religious life, especially involving Christians of the Catholic mystical or monastic traditions. These have occurred not only in India, but also in Buddhist-influenced cultures, notably Japan.[42] Post-war Japanese Christianity has not produced the new shapes and developments which might have been predicted from the existence of such striking pre-war figures as Kanzo Uchimura and Toyohiko Kagawa; but despite the apparent replication in Japan of Western (and especially American) styles of church life, their theologies sometimes break into areas inconceivable in the

Gandhi: an interpretation (1948) recently republished as Gandhi: portrayal of a friend, Nashville: Abingdon 1983.

[40] See J. J. Ansbro, Martin Luther King, Jr.: the making of a mind. Maryknoll, N.Y.: Orbis 1982.

[41] Cf. I. Jesudason, A Gandhian theology of Liberation, Maryknoll, N.Y.: Orbis 1984.

[42] The World Council of Churches Sub-Unit on Dialogue has initiated various encounters and discussions. See S. J. Samartha (ed.) Dialogue between men of living truths, Geneva: WCC 1971. Faith in the midst of faiths: reflections on dialogue in community, Geneva: WCC 1977. A journal actively reflecting 'dialogue' concerns in East Asia, in which the exploration of the religious life takes a prominent part is Inter-Religio (Nanzan Institute for Inter-Religious Research, Nagoya, Japan). An influential Roman Catholic explorer of the mystical traditions in Christianity and Hinduism was Abhishiktananda (Henri Le Saux) cf. his Hindu-Christian meeting point within the cave of the heart, Bombay: Institute of Indian Culture 1969.

classical Western tradition.[43] (A striking example is Kitamori's theology of the pain of God).[44] Korea, with its very substantial Christian community, has been notable for the use of local narrative modes for theological discourse and other developments of 'Minjung' theology, in form rooted in popular culture and in content reflecting the concerns of ordinary people.[45]

In any survey of human affairs, China, a quarter of humanity, can hardly be omitted. In the 1960s and early 1970s it looked as though the Christian presence in China had been reduced almost to negligibility. It now appears that it is lively and far from negligible, though both Catholics and Protestants have been deeply divided over co-operation with the State and the proper response to the charge of foreignness. The facts of survival and transmission in an environment so long hostile, the effects of the period of effective isolation, the uncertain future relations with the considerable numbers of Christian overseas Chinese, and the long term effect of the eventual absorption of Hong Kong all point to special developments in Chinese Christianity which are as yet indefinable.[46]

[43] Cf. J. M. Phillips, *From the rising of the sun. Christians and society in contemporary Japan*, Maryknoll, N.Y.: Orbis 1981.

[44] K. Kitamori, *Theology of the pain of God*. Richmond, Va.: John Knox Press 1965.

[45] A good collection in J. Moltmann (ed.) *Minjung. Theologie des Volkes Gottes in Südkorea*, Neukirchen: Neukirchener Verlag 1984. The word 'Minjung' has recently been more widely applied to movements in various parts of the world for a 'theology of the people' not dominated by a clerically directed scholastic tradition. See, e.g. *Ministerial Formation* (Geneva) 31, 1985.

[46] It is too early for a definitive study, and both the history of the past forty years and the present situation are interpreted differently by different authors. The best resources are in the periodical literature: *Ching Feng* (Tao Fong Shan Institute, Hong Kong), *Research Papers* published by Christian Communications, Hong Kong, and Father Spae's *China Update* reflect different standpoints and interests as between the Three Self Patriotic Movement, the evangelical House Churches and the Vatican-orientated Roman Catholics. The *Chinese Theological Review* (Distributed Foundation for Theological Education in Southeast Asia, Holland, Michigan) presents Chinese theological writing (mainly from TSPM sources) in English.

The Pacific

Polynesia now has a long Christian history. In Melanesia the most publicized aspect of the encounter with Christianity, the so-called 'cargo cults', have been less noticable or at least less dramatic, in recent decades. However, one observer says 'Cargo is the Melanesian word for salvation', and certainly Melanesian Christianity recalls some of the solidly material, this-worldly aspects of divine blessing characteristic of the Old Testament.[47] The Pacific populations are small as a proportion of the world population; but in view of the size of their Christian communities they can be expected, like the other southern continents, to produce a markedly local form of Christian expression.[48]

The New Conciliarism

The post-war period has thus witnessed a substantial variegation of Christianity as the new local forms have developed with the southwards shift in centre of gravity. It may be significant that where local forms have *not* developed on a large scale, Christianity has remained weak. In this category belong some of the oldest encounter stories of the missionary movement, such as the Native American peoples and the Australian Aborigines, both groups who have lost out in the longstanding relationship with the Whites who represented and transmitted Christianity. By contrast, in South Africa the widespread adoption of Christian faith enabled Blacks to engage

[47] J. G. Strelan, *Search for salvation: studies in the history and theology of cargo cults*. Adelaide: Lutheran Publishing House 1977.

[48] Cf. Forman, *op. cit.* p. 73 'An examination of the village churches will show that indeed they did constitute a distinctive type of church, indigenous to the Pacific'; *ibid.* p. 125 '. . . the Pacific churches had their own character and a distinctive life, which they themselves had created. They had their own understanding of the Christian faith and their own moral codes, which though they were derived from missionary reading were much influenced by local attitudes in the way they were carried out'.

dominating Whites in their own terms. The period since 1960 has seen dramatic actions by the various Black churches and of mixed churches conscious of Black aspirations, the development of a Black Theology drawing from the same Scriptures but consciously rejecting white theological criteria, and the emergence of church bodies and black churchmen as the only effective legal opposition to the government. South Africa is perhaps the most theologically active country in the world.[49]

That the diversification of Christianity described here has not yet produced fragmentation is due to another tendency which has been at work to a degree unpredictable fifty years ago. This is the re-emergence of a process of consultation and consensus involving Christians of different areas. This was characteristic of early Hellenistic and Roman Christianity and embodied in 'councils', usually of bishops, either local or 'ecumenical' i.e. 'worldwide'. Early conciliarism suffered from the fact that even at 'ecumenical' councils there was little or no representation from outside the Roman Empire, thus setting bounds in practice to most ideas of 'oikumene'. As the Eastern, Oriental and Latin traditions separated, councils became less important and more circumscribed geographically. In Latin Christianity the central importance of the Papal office militated against the calling of general councils; the Vatican Council convened in 1870 was the first since the Council of Trent in the wake of the sixteenth century Reformation.

[49] The work of the Afro-American James H. Cone (cf. *A Black theology of liberation*, 1970) sparked off the Black Theology movement in South Africa (cf. B. Moore (ed.) *Black Theology: the South African voice*, London: Hurst 1973). A special local form of Reformed theology developed in South Africa; the critique of this from within and from outside (cf. *Met de moed der hoop opstellen aangeboden aan Dr. C. F. Beyers Naudé*, Baarn: Ten Have 1985) has produced a new literature. A stream of English-speaking theological thought has drawn heavily on the experience of the Confessing Church in Nazi Germany (cf. J. W. de Gruchy, *Bonhoeffer and South Africa: theology in dialogue*, Grand Rapids: Eerdmans 1984. The *Journal of Theology for Southern Africa* (Johannesburg) reflects this tradition).

The Second Vatican Council, 1962–1965, was not only remarkable in itself, an assembly of bishops from all over the world in which those from the traditional centres of power were in the minority; nor for what it achieved in articulating a new spirit and fresh attitudes. It was remarkable in that it inaugurated the use of the conciliar method as central to the Church's future deliberations. Bishops have met regularly in synod ever since the Council.[50] Conferences of bishops, such as those of Latin America and Eastern Africa, have presented special perspectives and priorities. The conciliar structure has not visibly diminished the personal importance of the Pope. Indeed, the Pope has become far more visible than before. It is significant that in 1978 the centuries long tradition of Italian popes was broken with the election of the Cardinal Archbishop of Cracow as John Paul II. It is equally significant that his vigorous programme of travel has concentrated on Latin America, Africa and Asia.

New Protestant conciliar developments had begun, as we have seen, well before our period, with international conferences on missionary questions (and national Christian councils in 'mission' countries).[51] A new era began with the World Council of Churches established in 1948. Through successive international meetings, a stream of consultations and special studies and the work of permanent commissions, it has brought together representatives of churches from many traditions and from all of the world. Its composition reflects the fundamental shift in Christianity during this century. As its membership has increasingly leaned to the southern continents, priorities and viewpoints characteristic of those continents have prevailed, sometimes to the discomfiture of conservative

---

[50] Cf. McKenzie *op. cit.* p. 110.

[51] See W. R. Hogg, Ecumenical foundations. *A history of the International Missionary Council and its nineteenth century background.* New York: Harper 1952.

Western Christians. The Council, which has no power to bind the actions of its member churches, nevertheless provides a forum in which Christians of varied background and location together consider matters of faith and church order, Christian proclamation, relationship to environment and society and to other faiths.[52]

Originally a Protestant concept, the Council has been changed in recent years by the increasing participation of Orthodox churches;[53] but it is likely that the increased African, Asian and Latin American participation have changed it far more.

The Roman Catholic Church has not joined the Council, though observers are exchanged; and many churches of the Evangelical-Fundamentalist tradition have viewed it with hostility.[54] The special association of Evangelical-Fundamentalism with North America,[55] and the uneasiness about America natural to a body increasingly dominated by non-Western members, has introduced political and cultural complications into the relationship.

However, evangelicals have also embraced a conciliar system. The Conference on World Evangelization held at Lausanne in

[52] The series *Internationale Ökumenische Bibliographie* published at irregular intervals since 1962 (Munich: Kaiser and Mainz: Matthias-Grunewald Verlag) gives multilingual coverage of works on the ecumenical movement. For the WCC see W. A. Visser 't Hooft, *The genesis and formation of the World Council of Churches*, Geneva: WCC 1982. N. Goodall, *The Ecumenical Movement* London: Oxford University Press 1961 and *Ecumenical progress: a decade of change in the ecumenical movement 1961–1971*, London: Oxford University Press 1972.

[53] See C. G. Patelos (ed.) *The Orthodox Church in the Ecumenical Movement. Documents and statements 1902–1975*. Geneva: World Council of Churches 1978.

[54] See e.g. H. T. Hoekstra, *The World Council of Churches and the demise of evangelism*, Wheaton, Ill.: Tyndale House 1979.

[55] See G. M. Marsden, *Fundamentalism and American culture: the shaping of twentieth century evangelicalism, 1870–1925*, New York: Oxford University Press 1980.

1974 was a vast international meeting representing much of the Evangelical-Fundamentalist spectrum together with others of the older Evangelical Protestant tradition. Lausanne has developed its successor conferences, its consultations and study groups, and its permanent organization. Its activities have brought the voices of Evangelicals from Latin America and the southern continents to bear, and to their influence the heightened concern among Evangelicals about matters of social and racial justice must at least in part be attributed.[56]

The new conciliarism, working in different ways in different Christian communities, has tended to make Christians of one area more aware than could otherwise have been possible of the concerns and priorities of those of another. It has naturally tended to emphasize those of the new heartlands. It is perhaps inevitable that unease should be displayed in older heartlands, especially the United States, with a different set of priorities and values.

The Christianity expressed in the southern continents has shown no special desire to abandon or even revise the credal and confessional statements which have been the landmarks of western Christian history. It is simply that these statements have little direct to say about the matters that most concern the Christians of the new heartlands. Western Christian views of the place of the Church in society have been formed by the special history of Christendom. The Western division between material and spiritual realms was influenced by the prevalence at a formative period of views of matter as inherently evil. More recently, Western religion has been radically affected by Western perceptions of the autonomous individual. The new

[56] These concerns are reflected in many of the Occasional Papers series published by The Lausanne Committee for World Evangelization (Wheaton, Illinois). For the original Lausanne conference itself see J. D. Douglas (ed.) *Let the earth hear His voice: official reference volume*. Minneapolis: World Wide Publications 1975.

heartlands are shaped or influenced by the political consciousness of Latin America, by the exaltation of life and the reproduction of life dear to African and Pacific societies, by the Asian ascetic and meditational and discipleship traditions, and by different forms of corporate consciousness. They are also marked, more or less, by the geopolitical divide of the northern and southern world, with the economic consequences and historical memories. And they have their own specifically local Christian histories, local reproductions and reworkings of a tradition originally received from the West. All these things will mark the new forms of Christianity.

The new conciliarism is a recurrence of a well-established feature of historic Christianity: the consciousness of belonging to a community, a people of God, transcending the local one. The new regional Christianities show no signs at present of abandoning the other recurrent features of all previous Christian history: the worship of the God of Israel, the attribution of the ultimate significance to Jesus Christ, the recognition of the activity of God where the believers are, the reading of the common scriptures, or the special use of bread and wine and water.[57]

[57] For these as marks of historic Christianity, cf. the article 'Christianity' in J. R. Hinnells (ed.), *A handbook of living religions*, Harmondsworth: Penguin 1984, 56–122.

4

CULTS AND CIVIL RELIGION IN TODAY'S WORLD

Phillip Hammond
(*Santa Barbara*)

Introduction

One might suppose that in a volume such as this—in which most chapters focus on one or another of the major religious traditions to be found in today's world—a chapter on 'cults and civil religion' is a catchment for residual material. And so it is. In recent years, while both of these subjects have attracted enormous attention, most of that attention is found outside traditional religious scholarship. Both topics, for example, have been explored more by social scientists than by persons trained in language, philosophy, or phenomenology. Both, moreover, require attention to unorthodox religious currents as well as, if not instead of, the ordinary religious currents. And finally, because in neither the cult nor the civil religion is 'text' likely to dominate, the 'contexts' of these phenomena are featured in their analysis.

But there are reasons—beyond the reaons for attending to both cults and civil religion in a volume such as this—for attending *jointly* to these two topics in a single essay. That is what I propose to do here, emphasizing not just the work done on cults *or* civil religion in recent years but also the implications for religious studies of treating these subjects *together*.

The first and most obvious reason for treating cults and civil religion together is that they emerged at the same time as subjects of scholarly interest. Hardly any but descriptive attention was paid to cultic phenomena prior to the 1960s, and—until Robert Bellah's seminal essay (1967) on the American civil religion—Rousseau's notion of civil religion had essentially been forgotten. (Some few exceptions are detailed in Richey and Jones, 1974 and/or Hammond, 1976). Just as religious studies has been vulnerable to getting bogged down in the study of text without context, so has sociology of religion been vulnerable to treating the church as the limit of its focus. Both cults and civil religion required of scholars that they transcend those limitations.

Even when cults gained currency as a scholarly topic, the bulk of the early research simply carried over into these exotic arenas the same questions that had been asked of church members: What do they believe? How did they convert? What is the hierarchy of membership? etc. Later, however, prompted in part by the growth of an anti-cult movement (Shupe and Bromley, 1980; Beckford, 1985) the larger setting of these questions became apparent, and thus so did their larger social ramifications. For example, the fact that cults were converting young adults almost exclusively forced revision of the question of why Cult X attracts young people into the question of why society was losing some of its youthful generation to unconventional religious perspectives. Similarly, whereas much of the earlier social psychological study had to do with people's religious 'commitment'—and endless debate occurred over how to measure, with how many dimensions, this commitment—the appearance of cults on the scene required a parallel look at cult members' 'commitment' to their society. And this, in turn, led to the question of how and to what degree church commitment in the traditional sense reflects basic agreement with society's values and institutions. In other words, the social psychological investigation led to inquiry into fundamental issues of social organization and cultural analysis.

The second and less obvious reason for treating cults and civil religion together is that, as I shall soon propose, unless 'cult' is just another pejorative label for an unusual religious viewpoint, it necessarily implies an 'alien' or 'foreign' character relative to the society in which it is found. But therefore it further implies a rupture in the sacred canopy of that society, and insofar as sacred canopy = civil religion (an issue to which I return later), cults and civil religion are intimately linked. As Ninian Smart says of cults in India and China: '. . . it is important that we should see new religions in the wider context of challenges to cultural identity' (1982: 140). In other words, the popularity of cults says something about the legitimacy of the state and culture in which they are popular. It is therefore not just coincidence that the widespread appearance of cults in many parts of the world has been accompanied by a rush of interest in civil religion.

While the analytic literature on cults is vast, as we shall soon see, little such literature on civil religion exists, most being studies of single societies or—even less helpful—polemical tracts about the very existence of the civil religion phenomenon. Bryan Wilson called for an understanding of this imbalance in his recent lectures in Japan:

> If our study of new religions produces no unified theory to explain, under one set of theoretical propositions, all such phenomena, wherever they are found, we need not regard such a conclusion with alarm. . . . Such a conclusion can be produced only by ignoring the importance of empirical evidence and the historical diversity of societies and their cultures, and *only by subsuming factually diverse contents under highly abstract summary propositions* which obscure by their abstraction as much as they illuminate about social reality (1982: 147; emphasis added).

Unfortunately, relative to the literature on cults, the literature on civil religion is 'highly abstract'. If we are to benefit from juxtaposing these two topics—which juxtaposition, I have been arguing, is entirely justified on theoretical grounds—we must nonetheless come to our subject matter in piecemeal fashion. I shall first say something about cults, then something about civil religion, and in concluding return to their joint discussion.

Cults

The word 'cult' derives from the Latin word meaning to care for (i.e., cultivate), and in scholarly parlance it thus came to refer to ritual activities a religious group performed by and for itself. It was in this sense that Joachim Wach spoke of 'cultus' (or religious practice) as distinct from: (a) doctrine and (b) 'communion' or the social expression of religion (1944: Chap. 2). From such an understanding, the distance was short to applying the label to religious groups whose 'practices' seemed bizarre and maybe predominant over other aspects of the religion. In the extreme, indeed, organizations that Stark and Bainbridge (1985) call 'audience cults' may not be groups at all but only a set of practices that unconnected individuals perform for their own benefit. This feature, with its attendant lack of concern for society's ills, is what led to the pejorative character the word cult still may connote.

Yet another consideration enters into the special meaning we are about to assign this word cult, and that derives from the popularity of Ernst Troeltsch's typology of church-and-sect (1931). Sensing readily the idea of a *church* that affirmed the world and a *sect* that rejected the world, scholars were nonetheless aware of religious groups that were neither church nor sect. 'Cult' thus became a residual category for many of these groups. Moreover, because this terminological development occurred in the West—where religious groups qualifying as churches or sects were chiefly inner-worldly ascetic and thus attentive to the world, if only to 'reject' it—this residual category tended to be filled with religious groups influenced by the East—where other-worldly mystical concerns, thus ritual or 'cultus', were thought to predominate.

The upshot is a fortuitous alien or foreign character to the cult, a character that I, following Stark and Bainbridge (1985), propose be made explicit here: A *cult* is any minority religious group whose primary ideological roots lie not in the religious traditions claimed by the majority religious groups of the society in question but elsewhere. A *sect*, by contrast, is any minority religious group whose primary ideological roots are shared with the majority of religious groups of its society. Thus Nichiren Shoshu is a cult in America but a sect in Japan; Jehovah's Witnesses are a cult in Japan but a sect in America.

Thus also, many of the new religious movements that burst forth in recent decades are cults by this definition. As Bryan Wilson puts it: 'Many of the new movements in the West are cultural imports which offer a redevelopment of the traditional wisdom of some society other than those in which these movements are active' (1982: 137).

As I said above, most of the scholarly attention paid to cults before the 1960s had been descriptive, often of a single group. Some of this work was good (e.g., Dohrman, 1958) but typically it was not accumulative and thus tended to be atheoretical. Vittorio Lanternari's *Religions of the Oppressed* (1963) represents a worldwide compendium of such case studies, though many of his cases are, by the definition here, sects and not cults.

Perhaps Japan, whose immediate post-World War II experience seemed to encourage the proliferation of religious groups, was the first to draw a new kind of attention from scholars. Instead of isolated exotic movements, each attractive only to a few alienated individuals, new religious movements in Japan were obviously saying something not just about those few individuals who joined but about the entire Japanese society. Thus books summarizing these movements (e.g., McFarland, 1967; Earhart, 1970; 1982) explicitly deal with why Japan would experience a 'rush-hour of the gods', as McFarland felicitously put it. In other words, given sufficient density or frequency, cults evoke questions about their host societies as well as about the persons attracted to them.

This increasing theoretical sophistication came rather quickly, helping make sociology of religion one of the more exciting specialities within sociology and drawing to it the attention of some scholars who would not otherwise have any concern for 'religion'. Questions of who converts to a cult, and why, began the inquiry but soon broadened. In America, two influential volumes (Zaretsky and Leone, 1974; Glock and Bellah, 1976) raised basic questions of social—not just psychological—processes. Bryan Wilson's *Magic and Millenium* (1973) did the same for third-world religious movements, as did Biezas' *New Religions* (1975) for Scandinavia primarily. By now it is common for the contextual setting of cults to be included in their analysis (e.g., Nordquist [1982] in the case of Sweden, Chagnon [1985] in the case of Quebec, Jules-Rosette [1979] in the case of Africa). And by now also some very good analytic collections are available (e.g., Robbins and Anthony, 1981; Barker, 1982; 1984; Wilson, 1981; Bromley and Shupe, 1981; Ellwood, 1979; Needleman and Baker, 1979; Tipton, 1982). There continue to be numerous treatments of single cults, many of which transcend theoretically the narrowness of the earlier single-cult descriptions (e.g., Wallis, 1976; Lofland, 1977; Bainbridge, 1978; Bromley and Shupe, 1979; Downton, 1979; Barker, 1984). And there is the complementary literature arising as a spin-off from the existence of cults, largely dealing with anti-cult activities and attendant legal issues (e.g., Shupe and Bromley, 1980; Kelley, 1982; Beckford, 1985; Robbins, Shepherd, and McBride, 1985).

Generalizations about Cults
From the abundant literature, samples of which have just been cited, come a number of generalizations about cults, ranging

from empirical propensities to abstract theoretical propositions. Since space permits discussion of only a few of these propositions, and extensive discussion of none, it is perhaps appropriate to regard what follows as but one person's 'hypotheses', to be further tested by evidence.

1. The first generalization is put very well by Bryan Wilson (1982: 114):

> The new sectarian movements in western countries, and particularly those that have originated in the East, or which purvey some variant of an eastern religious tradition, appear to have one distinctive feature which distinguishes them from at least most of the established sects of Christian history, and this is their conspicuous appeal to a specific generational group—the young ...

Just *why* the appeal is age-specific raises other issues, of course, including the link between cults and civil religion which is to be addressed presently. Suffice for now to say that the overwhelming evidence—at least in the West—points to a largely young adult membership. Since young adulthood is a time of developing identities distinct from parents', there is reason to think that cult attraction is intimately bound up in this process of identity-formation.

2. A second generalization has to do with the speeded-up development of many modern-day cults. Some have been born, developed, and died within a few years, but even those that have survived appear to have progressed rather quickly along the path of 'domestication'. Thus the Unification Church in America, for example, has gone from a miniscule cell of 'misfits' (Lofland, 1977) to a beleaguered collection of suspects, to a sponsor of many cultural and commercial activities, to a victimized group joined by friends and foes on left and right to protest their leader's tax discrimination, to a 'church' that, in all probability, would like nothing more than to take its place as

but another denomination in the various councils of churches.

Even the followers of Bhagwan Shree Rajneesh, who seemed to be flourishing some years after other cults had peaked in growth, have fallen into some sort of disarray. From 575 meditation centers in 32 countries in 1982, the Rajneesh Foundation International now lists only 19 centers in 10 countries, including seven in West Germany. In the United States, besides the headquarters in rural Oregon, only Laguna Beach, California, survives (The Portland *Oregonian*, June 30, 1985: 2M). The defection of Anand Sheela and other trusted lieutenants, accompanied by charges of fraud and mismanagement—all this in the face of continuing legal challenge by state and federal authorities—suggests that, once again, a cult is undergoing a quick change-about.

What has been learned in this 'abbreviated' organizational growth/decline cycle is the importance not just of leadership (something known for a long time) but of the delegation of authority and—to use the new terminology—the importance of 'resource mobilization'. ISKCON (the Hare Krishnas) in America, for example, seems to have solved the problem of leadership succession, and the Unification Church (Moonies) seem everywhere to deploy their resources in an efficient manner. Whether the calculated risks taken by the former—to give up aggressive public evangelizing in favor of becoming 'home' to increased numbers of East Indian immigrants—and whether the latter can survive the probable Korean vs. American 'successor fight' upon Sun Myung Moon's death, remains to be seen.

3. A third generalization based on research into cults was already in process among mainline denominations (e.g., Roof, 1978), but the proliferation of new religious movements with their often-times 'incredible' belief systems provided a hothouse situation for researchers. The issue—which is uniquely posed in the pluralistic modern world—is how anybody can believe 'that

stuff'. What became clear with regard to belief in bizarre cultic doctrines is that people are not 'believers' at the initial stages of involvement with a cult. Perhaps many are predisposed toward breaking with conventional beliefs, but their final choice of beliefs appears to have more to do with social contacts than with the substance of the doctrines. Religious believing, at least in the modern world where knowledge of religious pluralism is widespread, is therefore not simply a matter of aligning personal predilection with the appropriate offering on the religious belief cafeteria line. Rather it is a multi-step process of social involvement with a community of like-minded persons whose commitment to their beliefs rises and falls with their commitment to each other. Just as Roof found among Episcopalians, then, individual background reveals something of what makes for credibility, but so too does the individual's embeddedness in a social group. If your friends believe 'that stuff', then probably you will too, irrespective of what it is.

4. A final generalization has to do with the relative frequency of cults vs. sects. Minority religions have appeared in most parts of the modern world, but some—such as the Cargo Cults, so-called, of the South Pacific region—have been nativistic responses to alien cultural forces and thus not cults but sects, by the definitions here. An interesting question can therefore be asked about the societal conditions giving rise to cults, as distinct from those giving rise to sects. Stark (1981) has made a convincing theoretical and empirical case for why the two are inversely related, but more can be learned about why sects might thrive in one place, cults in another.

Leaving aside the sticky issue of exactly what *is* a cult or a sect (for, in actuality, some religious movements have elements of both), one might suppose that cults, because they drawn upon alien traditions, are more likely to appear in settings where the indigenous traditions are losing their hold—where the culture, so to speak, has lost legitimacy. Sects, by contrast, would seem more likely in settings where the culture is unchallenged but the traditional religious structures are seen as inadequate. Thus, until or unless they become majority religion, both sects and cults, as minorities, attract persons unhappy with the status quo, but sectarians accept the majority view of ultimate reality and seek a purer means to it, while cultists replace the majority view with one drawn from elsewhere.

If true, this fourth generalization suggests that the appearance of a significant number of cults in a society indicates turmoil in the legitimacy of that society's culture. Insofar as cultural legitimacy is oftentimes religiously cloaked, it might be said that a society's 'civil' religion is thus challenged by cults. In order to pursue this analytic possibility we must now turn attention to the notion of civil religion.

Civil Religion

Several years ago I tried to make the following point about the analysis of civil religion (1980: 138):

> While Rousseau is generally credited with coining the term 'civil religion', analysis of civil religion in sociology has been influenced more by Durkheim. Durkheim was, of course, an intellectual heir of Rousseau, but nevertheless a gap of great proportions separates them: For Rousseau civil religion is a sensible thing for leaders to create and encourage; for Durkheim it is an emergent property of social life itself.
>
> On this rather simple difference hangs a conceptual issue obscuring almost all contemporary analyses of modern-day civil religion. Those influenced by Rousseau often begin with a bias against civil religion on the grounds that it is or easily can be an idolatrous fraud preperated on naive believers. Those influenced by Durkheim, by contrast, often begin with a bias in favor of civil religion on the grounds it is inevitable in any case. . . .

Since those words were penned I have read a number of works dealing with civil religion, but with the exception of

Michael Hughey's *Civil Religion and Moral Order* (1983), little has caused me to change my earlier diagnosis. Some scholars— still drawn largely, I believe, from the humanities—continue to doubt the reality of the civil religion phenomenon and therefore evidence discomfort in analyzing it. Others—still found largely in sociology—seem so comfortable with the concept that they make use of it without subjecting it to critical analysis. The upshot, unlike the situation with respect to cults, is a dearth of *analytic* literature about civil religion. Instead, we have assorted monographs dealing with specific instances (e.g., Moodie [1975] on the civil religion of South Africa, Liebman and Don-Yehiya [1983] on that of Israel, or Burkett [1978] on the civil religious impetus of the Garveyite movement), all of which demonstrate at least the heuristic value of the concept but are not particularly analytic about it. And we also have literature (e.g., Kelly, 1984) so wary of granting ontological status to the concept that it never gets past the prolegomena stage. (See Gehrig, 1979, for a review of the American case).

Robert Bellah can take part of the blame for this situation inasmuch as he has contributed to the erroneous view that 'every' society must have an identifiable civil religion. He writes (1975: ix):

> . . . any coherent and viable society rests upon a common set of moral understandings about good and bad, right and wrong, in the realm of individual and social action. . . . [T]hese common moral understandings must also rest in turn upon a common set of religious understandings. . . .

Such an assertion, in my view, is misleading. Any society may have all the necessary *ingredients* for a civil religion, but whether those ingredients cohere into something deserving the label 'civil religion' depends upon more. Durkheim, who is usually invoked by those who believe a civil religion is inevitable, actually appears to imply that civil religion is by no means common in modern societies (Hughey, 1983: 17).

We still face, then, a murky theoretical situation when it comes to civil religion. The question can be asked whether the scholarly attention to cults in recent years adds clarity to this situation. The answer, I think, is 'Yes, but not much'. To this issue we turn in conclusion.

Cults and Civil Religion

In one of the earlier popular commentaries on Robert Bellah's provocative essay on the American civil religion (Bellah, 1967) Martin Marty claimed that the idea of a civil religion 'remains chiefly the product of the scholar's world; the man on the street would be surprised to learn of its existence' (1974: 141). What makes this comment less than helpful is its failure to recognize that, for most of human history, most people did not know of the existence of any religion; religion was precisely part of the taken-for-granted world and therefore not the object of widespread speculation.

In the modern world, at least in those sectors subject to the condition of religious pluralism, most people now are aware that they, in some sense, 'choose' their religion and, hypothetically at least, are free to change it. Anyway that is the case with 'ordinary' religions.

But suppose there still exist religions—or views of ultimate reality—so unquestioned as yet to be unacknowledged? What would be their shape? Their vehicles for doctrine and ritual? Their membership? Much as the fish, living in water, is likely to be oblivious to water and 'be surprised to learn of its existence', so might the citizen, surrounded by an ideology seemingly universal, not readily 'know' he holds to a religion in which his 'nation' or his 'people' or his 'group' is the decisive agent.

Now, whether this agent *is* decisive, and whether its purposes are judged *sacred*, and whether those sacred purposes are cast in *transcendent terms*, and whether the transcendent terms are expressed in *ritual and doctrine* are matters of fact. In this sense, every society has only the potential for a civil religion, with many conditions to be met before the potential becomes actual—at least actual enough to convince skeptical scholars. The point is, the possibility exists, the more so, it seems to me, to the degree people conceive of their politics as sacred and their religion as political. Hence the U.S. has long had an intrusive, palpable—though waxing and waning—civil religion. Bellah has correctly insisted on describing and interpreting it.

It is in this sense—given the fact that citizens may become aware of their civil religion and question the sacredness of their politics—that they become potential recruits to cults. Stated in reverse, when cults proliferate, we have reason to suspect some disruption in the civil religion (or its ingredients), some tear in that society's sacred canopy. Of course, we can still recognize other 'causes' of cults as well. Once more, Bryan Wilson states the case (1982: 29):

> ... civil religion [is] the more or less explicit symbolic celebration by its members of their society and often indeed of the state. Yet, today, states have tarnished reputations in the eyes of many of their citizens; and society becomes too amorphous in many ways, too similar, in its basic deficiencies, to other societies, and too bound up with them economically for 'our society' to be much of a focus of identity, much less of pride. . . . The old religions . . . lose all influence on social and political structures. . . . The emergent new religions provide new focal points of commitment.

Wilson no doubt has in mind chiefly western, industrialized nations. Compare, therefore, his analysis with McFarland's (1967: 65) of Japan: 'With the collapse of the old authoritarianism and the granting of unprecedented religious freedom at the end of World War II, the New Religions rose like mushrooms.' One need only query whether 'collapse of the old authoritarianism' and 'unprecedented religious freedom' are tantamount to a disruption in Japanese civil religion to see the parallel.

For yet another, radically different example, compare Barrett's *Schism and Renewal in Africa* (1968), where cultic movements (granted, the definitional problems are particularly awkward here) are tied to events in *national* life.

We are left, then, with a rather powerful theoretical proposition, apparently believed to be true by many who have analyzed cults at the societal (as distinct from the personal or social psychological) level. This proposition states, in effect, that cults tend to flourish in societies where significant numbers of citizens do not regard their indigenous religious traditions as adequate to express their relationship (whether favorable or unfavorable) with the society. The corollary is that, ordinarily, religious traditions may adequately express citizens' relationship with the society—with involvement in the church (so-called) indicative of a favorable relationship, and sectarian involvement indicative of an unfavorable relationship; thus, again, cults represent a movement 'outside' of both church and sect.

The problem arises over documentation. The appearance and popularity of cults in one or another society present no particular difficulty (at least conceptually; the collection of adequate facts may be another matter). Likewise, the uniform observation that cults have been primarily attractive to young adults *from the middle classes* suggests that alienation from the homeland and its institutions is a major factor, since middle class youth typically are most in line to inherit the conventions of their societies. But what about the 'civil religion' end of the proposition? Who is to say when alienation means loss of faith in the civil religion?

This part of the proposition, it must be admitted, is not just weak in evidence but hardly explored conceptually. The few exceptions, with their almost complete lack of data (Wuthnow, 1980; Johnson, 1981; Hunter, 1981; Martin, 1981; Anthony and Robbins, 1981 and 1982; Hammond and Gordon-McCutchan, 1982), merely demonstrate this lacuna. Roy Wallis (1984: 64–9) is correct in his recent challenge to those who would link cults with civil religion; we have yet to learn enough about people's sacred ties to their societies to use such a notion sensitively in analyzing their behavior.

One possible exception to the above dreary diagnosis is the work of Hans Mol (1976, 1982a, 1982b) on 'religion and identity'. Ironically, Mol has not paid particular attention to either cults (as that word is used here) or civil religion, though he has certainly attended to minority religious responses in New Zealand, Australia, Canada, and elsewhere, and he acknowledges the similarity of his concern to Bellah's concern with civil religion. Religion, for Mol, is the sacralization of identity, which may be personal, group, tribal, social, and/or national. Religion is seen as that which 'fixes' or 'firms' the identity, in which case investigations into personal and group identities could include instances of why people join cults. By contrast, investigations into tribal, social, and national identities, obviously bear on civil religion, at least potentially. Now, if one were observing the erosion of the latter type of identity, and simultaneously observing the increased use of 'alien' religion to solidify the former type of identity, then one would be harvesting in the field of this essay—cults and civil religion.

While Mol has undertaken systematic investigation of his theoretical model, however, he has not, as I said above, paid particular attention to cults, as discussed here. His theory remains an interesting possibility, therefore, and the fascinating proposition informing this chapter lingers. . . .

Bibliography

Anthony, Dick and Thomas Robbins, 1981, 'Culture Crisis and Contemporary Religion.' Thomas Robbins and Dick Anthony (eds.), *In Gods We Trust*. New Brunswick, NJ: Transaction Books.

——, 1982, 'Spiritual Innovation and the Crisis of American Civil Religion.' *Daedalus* (Winter).

Bainbridge, W. S., 1978, *Satan's Power*. Berkeley and Los Angeles: University of California Press.

Barker, Eileen, 1982, *New Religious Movements*. (ed.) New York: Edwin Mellen Press.

——, 1984a, *Of Gods and Men: New Religious Movements in the West*. (ed.) Macon, GA: Mercer University Press.

——, 1984b, *The Making of a Moonie*. Oxford: Basil Blackwell.

Barrett, David B., 1968, *Schism and Renewal in Africa*. Nairobi: Oxford University Press.

Beckford, James A., 1985, *Cult Controversies*. London: Tavistock Publications.

Bellah, Robert, 1967, 'Civil Religion in America.' *Daedalus* (Winter).

——, 1975, *The Broken Covenant*. New York: Seabury Press.

Biezas, Haralds, ed., 1975, *New Religions*. Stockholm: Almquist and Wiksell International.

Bromley, D. G. and A. D. Shupe, Jr., 1979, *'Moonies' in America*. Beverly Hills, CA: Sage Publications.

——, 1981, *Strange Gods*. Boston: Beacon Press.

Burkett, Randall K., 1978, *Garveyism as a Religious Movement*. Metuchen, NJ: The Scarecrow Press, Inc. and the American Theological Library Association.

Chagnon, Roland, 1985, 'Les Nouvelles Religions Au Quebec.' Paper presented to the International Association for the History of Religions, Sydney, Australia.

Dohrman, H. T., 1958, *California Cult*. Boston: Beacon Press.

Downtown, J. V., Jr., 1979, *Sacred Journeys*. New York: Columbia University Press.

Earhart, H. Byron, 1970, *The New Religions of Japan*. Tokyo: Sophia University Press.

——, 1982, *Japanese Religion: Unity and Diversity*. Belmont, CA: Wadsworth Publications.

Ellwood, Robert S., Jr., 1979, *Alternative Altars*. Chicago: University of Chicago Press.

Gehrig, Gail, 1979, *American Civil Religion: An Assessment*. Society for the Scientific Study of Religion Monograph Series, Number 3.

Glock, C. Y. and R. N. Bellah, eds., 1976, *The New Religious Consciousness*. Berkeley and Los Angeles: University of California Press.

Hammond, Phillip E., 1976, 'The Sociology of American Civil Religion: A Bibliographic Essay.' *Sociological Analysis* 37 (Summer).

——, 1980, 'Pluralism and Law in the Formation of American Civil Religion.' Robert N. Bellah and Phillip E. Hammond, *Varieties of Civil Religion*. New York: Harper and Row.

Hammond, Phillip E. and R. Gordon-McCutchan, 1981, 'Cults and the Civil Religion.' *Revue Francais d'Etudes Americaines* 12 (October).

Hughey, Michael W., 1983, *Civil Religion and Moral Order*. Westport, CT: Greenwood Press.

Hunter, James D., 1981, 'The New Religions: Demodernization and the Protest Against Modernity.' Bryan Wilson (ed.), *The Social Impact of New Religious Movements*. New York: The Rose of Sharon Press.

Johnson, Benton, 1981, 'A Sociological Perspective on the New Religions.' Thomas Robbins and Dick Anthony (eds.), *In Gods We Trust*. New Brunswick, NJ: Transaction Books.

Jules-Rosette, Bennetta, ed., 1979, *The New Religions of Africa*. Norwood, NJ: Ablex Publishing.

Kelley, Dean M., ed., 1982, *Government Intervention in Religious Affairs*. New York: Pilgrim Press.

Kelly, George Armstrong, 1984, *Politics and Religious Consciousness in America*. New Brunswick, NJ: Transaction Books.

Lanternari, Vittorio, 1963, *Religions of the Oppressed*. New York: Alfred A. Knopf.

Liebman, Charles S. and E. Don-Yehiva, 1983, *Civil Religion in Israel*. Berkeley and Los Angeles: University of California Press.

Lofland, John, 1977, *Doomsday Cult*. Enlarged edition. New York: Irvington Publishers.

Martin, David, 1981, 'Disorientations to Mainstream Religion.' Bryan Wilson (ed.), *The Social Impact of New Religious Movements*. New York: The Rose of Sharon Press.

Marty, Martin, 1974, 'Two Kinds of Civil Religion.' R. E. Richey and D. G. Jones (eds.), *American Civil Religion*. New York: Harper and Row.

McFarland, H. Neill, 1967, *The Rush-Hour of the Gods*. New York: Macmillan.

Mol, Hans, 1976, *Identity and the Sacred*. Oxford: Basil Blackwell.

——, 1982a, *The Fixed and the Fickle*. Waterloo, Ontario: Wilfrid Laurier University Press.

——, 1982b, *The Firm and the Formless*. Waterloo, Ontario: Wilfrid Laurier University Press.

Moodie, T. Dunbar, 1975, *The Rise of Afrikanerdom*. Berkeley and Los Angeles: University of California Press.

Needleman, Jacob and George Baker, eds., 1979, *Understanding the New Religions*. New York: Seabury Press.

Nordquist, Ted A., 1982, 'New Religious Movements in Sweden.' Eileen

Barker (ed.), *New Religious Movements*. New York: Edwin Mellen Press.

Richey, R. E. and D. G. Jones, eds., 1974, *American Civil Religion*. New York: Harper and Row.

Robbins, Thomas and Dick Anthony, eds., 1981, *In Gods We Trust*. New Brunswick, NJ: Transaction Books.

Robbins, T., W. Shepperd, and J. McBride, eds., 1985, *Cults, Culture, and the Law*. Decatur, GA: Scholars Press.

Roof, W. Clark, 1978, *Community and Commitment*. New York: Elsevier.

Shupe, Anson D., Jr. and D. G. Bromley, 1980, *The New Vigilantes*. Beverly Hills, CA: Sage Publications.

Smart, Ninian, 1982, 'Asian Cultures and the Impact of the West: India and China.' Eileen Barker (ed.), *New Religious Movements*. New York: Edwin Mellen Press.

Stark, Rodney, 1981, 'Must All Religions Be Supernatural?' Bryan Wilson (ed.), *The Social Impact of New Religious Movements*. New York: The Rose of Sharon Press.

Stark, Rodney and W. S. Bainbridge, 1985, *The Future of Religion*. Berkeley and Los Angeles: University of California Press.

Tipton, Steven, 1982, *Getting Saved From the Sixties*. Berkeley and Los Angeles: University of California Press.

Troeltsch, Ernst, 1931, *The Social Teaching of the Christian Churches*. Olive Wyon, trans. London: George Allen and Unwin, Ltd.

Wach, Joachim, 1944, *Sociology of Religion*. Chicago: University of Chicago Press.

Wallis, Roy, 1976, *The Road to Total Freedom*. London: Heinemann Educational Books.

——, 1984, *The Elementary Forms of the New Religious Life*. London: Routledge and Kegan Paul.

Wilson, Bryan R., 1973, *Magic and Millenium: Religious Movements of Protest Among Tribal and Third-World Peoples*. London: Heinemann Educational Books.

——, 1982, *Religion in Sociological Perspective*. Oxford: Oxford University Press.

Wilson, Bryan R., ed., 1981, *The Social Impact of New Religious Movements*. New York: The Rose of Sharon Press.

Wuthnow, Robert, 1980, 'World Order and Religious Movements.' Albert Bergesen (ed.), *Studies in the Modern World-System*. New York: Academic Press.

Zaretsky, I. I. and M. P. Leone, eds., 1974, *Religious Movements in Contemporary America*. Princeton, NJ: Princeton University Press.

5

THE HINDU TRADITION IN TODAY'S WORLD

Frank Whaling
(Edinburgh)

1. Introduction

'He majestically stands there on His throne graciously smiling down to his devotees: stands as a unique symbol of the great flexibility and dynamics of Hinduism, of its capacity to absorb, integrate and remodel.'[1] This comment, made about a famous Hindu deity, the Lord Jagannātha of Puri, could well be applied to the Hindu tradition itself during much of its history and indeed during much of our period. Continuity and change have been characteristics of the Hindu tradition in the past, and they remain so during the present.

In contemporary India, the sacred geography of Hinduism retains its symbolic significance. Pilgrims travel round the sacred places in the four corners of India: Badrinath in the north,

---

*As this is intended for non-experts as well as experts in the Hindu tradition the following conventions have been used in regard to diacritical marks. The correct diacritical marks have been retained, in Sanskrit rather than Hindi where there is a choice, with the following exceptions: town names that are still in use (e.g. Puri for Purī); modern persons and movements (e.g. Gandhi for Gāndhī, Sathya Sai Baba for Sathya Sāi Bābā, Hindu Mahasabha for Hindu Mahāsabhā); festivals (e.g. Holi for Holī); and a few common conventions (Shiva for Śiva, Vishnu for Viṣṇu, Krishna for Kṛṣṇa, Chaitanya for Caitanya, Upanishads for Upaniṣads, and darshana for darśana).

* [1] G. C. Tripathi, 'Jagannātha: The Ageless Deity of the Hindus', in *The Cult of Jagannath and the Regional Tradition of Orissa*, edited by A. Eschmann, H. Kulke and G. C. Tripathi, New Delhi: Manohar, 1978, p. 490.

Puri in the east, Ramesvaram in the south, and Dvaraka in the west. The Himalaya mountains and the Ganges river, together with a network of other geographical points, remain symbolically important for many Hindus. At the same time the context within which the Hindu tradition operates is changing at the present time. Within India, the coming of Independence to India and Pakistan on the basis of partition, and the setting up of the free secular state of India were clearly important factors implying political, social and religious consequences. The further spread of the Hindu *diaspora* outside India is also important for both the Hindu and other religious traditions, and a significant extension of this emigration of Hindus to other lands has happened since the Second World War. In addition to this, Hindu ideas and movements have become better known to people outside India, especially in the West, and there has been the development of an incipient world Hindu religious tradition. These two broad factors, the coming of Indian Independence in 1947 and the spread of Hindu peoples and ideas outside India, are two of the most important in the evolution of the Hindu tradition since 1945.

2. Complexity and Elusiveness of Hinduism

To summarise the Hindu tradition in the contemporary world is a difficult undertaking, such is its complexity and its elusiveness. We need guidelines for our task, but before we set them out, let us pause to reflect that the very interest in the question 'What is a Hindu?' is indicative of a process of thoughtful self-questioning on the part of contemporary Hindus.

There have been numerous views of the Hindu tradition on the part of outsiders as well as Hindus themselves, and discussion continues concerning the basic question 'What is a Hindu?' Insofar as the Hindu tradition, compared with some other religious traditions, had no founder, no central authority, no credal formulations, and a wide variety of sacred texts, it is clear that any generalisations about the Hindu tradition are fraught with difficulties. Wilfred Cantwell Smith has pointed out that the term 'Hinduism' is 'a particularly false conceptualisation, one that is conspicuously incompatible with any adequate understanding of the religious outlook of Hindus.'[2] He would prefer to concentrate upon the cumulative tradition of the Hindus that has been transmitted down the generations, and the faiths of Hindus that has produced that tradition and lies behind it. This is a helpful way of looking at the question but it has not prevented Hindus from giving more specific answers concerning the nature of their own tradition, and a brief review of some of their suggestions will indicate some of the different currents within the Hindu tradition today.

At one extreme Dandekar offers a wide suggestion that 'a Hindu is one who is born of Hindu parents and who has not *openly* abjured Hinduism.'[3] In fact this statement is not really wide enough, for it leaves out of account those who may convert to the Hindu tradition. Moreover it is negative rather than positive. Elsewhere Dandekar states that, in the last analysis, 'a study of Hinduism would invariably amount to a study of the various Hindu castes and sects.'[4] Pragmatically this suggestion has much to commend it, for the Hindu tradition historically has in the main emphasised the role of caste at the social level of relationships between people, and the role of sects (*sampradāyas*) at the vertical level of relationships between persons and the divine. However, in the contemporary period, as we shall see, there has been frequent discussion among

[2] W. Cantwell Smith, *The Meaning and End of Religion*, New York: New American Library (Mentor), 1964, p. 61.

[3] R. N. Dandekar, *Insights into Hinduism*, Delhi: Ajanta Publications, 1979, p. 4.

[4] *Op. cit.*, p. 7.

Hindus, especially those living in Indian cities and outside India, about the relevance and place of the caste system. Also the Hindu sects are many and varied, and to focus on them individually is to leave out of account what features hold them together and constitute them as being Hindu. Another view of the Hindu tradition is that it is such because it recognises the authority of the Veda. According to this viewpoint, the Veda was the touchstone whereby the Jains and Buddhists were seen to be outside the tradition, and it is also a criterion for determining who is in the tradition. Again there is cogency in this view, for most Hindus down the ages have appealed to the Veda and have seen themselves as being in some sort of continuity with the Vedic tradition. As J. L. Mehta puts it, the original Veda (the Ṛgveda) has remained the 'animating source' of the religiousness that has generated and sustained the Hindu tradition.[5] However, as we shall see, the contemporary period has witnessed discussion as to what was the Veda—was it the original Ṛgveda, was it a much wider body of ancient sacred texts including the Upanishads, should later texts such as the Bhagavad Gītā be included under its umbrella, and how should the whole be interpreted? This brings us to the realm of concepts, and another view of the Hindu tradition has suggested that it is characterised by certain implicit beliefs. These will normally be held to include the notion of Brahman as the ultimate reality, the notion of Ātman as the real self of human beings, and the notion of rebirth (saṃsāra) according to deeds (karma) as the human condition from which release (mokṣa) is required. However not all Hindus hold to these beliefs, though they are reasonably widespread, and even among those that do hold them a process of reinterpretation of the classical views is

[5] J. L. Mehta, 'The Hindu Tradition: The Vedic Root', in *The World's Religious Traditions: Current Perspectives in Religious Studies*, edited by F. Whaling, Edinburgh: T. & T. Clark 1984 & New York: Crossroad 1986, p. 33.

often part of the contemporary situation. Partial views as to what is a Hindu, for example the notion that Hindus venerate the cow and are vegetarian, are less important and universal. Nevertheless any total view of the Hindu tradition in the contemporary age can hardly ignore completely the fact that India has about a third of the world's cattle on three per cent of the world's land area, that her cattle represent the largest concentration of domesticated animals anywhere in the world, that her animal homes are 'essentially religious institutions', and that lying behind them are notions of cow veneration, avoidance of meat, and *ahiṃsā*, non-violence to living creatures.[6]

What we call the Hindu tradition can therefore be seen in a number of ways and from many angles by Hindus themselves as well as by external observers. These different viewpoints are not always consonant with each other. Yet, as Dandekar puts it, 'the true glory of Hinduism consists in presenting all these polarities and paradoxes as also the various levels of doctrine and practice as constituting a single well-coordinated religious system.'[7]

3. Indian Independence and the Hindu Tradition

What then are the distinctive trends in the contemporary development of the Hindu religious tradition? As space is limited we shall concentrate upon four: the significance for the Hindu tradition of the coming of Indian Independence, the impact of neo-Hinduism upon contemporary India, the spread of the Hindu tradition outside India, and some continuing aspects of traditional Hinduism.

[6] Deryck O. Lodrick, *Sacred Cows, Sacred Places*, Berkeley, Los Angeles and London: University of California Press, 1981, especially 'Animal Homes and the Sacred Cow of India' pp. 198–206.
[7] R. N. Dandekar, *op. cit.*, p. 8.

India became independent in 1947. She became, and has since remained, the world's largest democracy. Unlike Pakistan, which became a Muslim state, India opted to become a secular state. She did not inherit the whole land-mass of the Indian sub-continent because the territories in the north-west and north-east became West Pakistan and East Pakistan, and later the latter became Bangla Desh. However within the area of the new India, freedom of religion was proclaimed within a secular constitution. Therefore, although over eighty per cent of the new India were Hindus, equal privileges, respects, rights and freedoms were given to the other religious traditions namely the Muslims, Christians, Sikhs, Buddhists, Jains, Parsis, and Jews.

From the state's point of view, a significant reason for the setting-up of a secular state was the threat of communalism to the unity and integrity of the new India. The birth-pangs of the new nation included communal violence between Hindus and Muslims on a large scale as the time for partition approached. The Jammu-Kashmir area, although mainly Muslim, came under the sovereignty of India rather than Pakistan and remained a bone of political contention with religious under-tones. Sikh aspirations in the Punjab, and Tamil aspirations in Tamil Nadu, as well as Tamil concern for their fellow Tamils over the water in Sri Lanka (Ceylon) over against the Buddhist majority there remained legitimate causes for concern. The existence of a secular state was a focus of unity to counter-balance potential communal tension both between and within religious traditions.

3(a) Hindu Secularism

Hindus adapted to and participated in the secular state of India in four different ways. One group, typified by Nehru, adopted secularism. He wrote, 'We have to get rid of that narrowing religious outlook, that obsession with the supernatural and metaphysical speculations, that loosening of the mind's discipline in religious ceremonial and mystical emotionalism, which come in the way of our understanding ourselves and the world. We have to come to grips with the present, this life, this world, this nature . . .'[8] Although deeply influenced by the West, Nehru was Indian in his interpretation of the secular state. But the fountains whence he drew his inspiration for the new secular India were less obviously Hindu than was the case with the other groups we are considering.

3(b) Hindu Religious/Secular Gradualism

The second group saw clearly the rationale for a secular state but remained uneasy about it because it seemed to undervalue spiritual and moral ideals. There had been a certain ambivalence among some Hindus in the fight for Indian Independence. They had seen the need for co-operation with persons of other religious traditions but, like Gandhi in his aim that the new India should fulfil the ideal of Rāmarājya (the Kingdom of Rāma), they had wrestled with the question as to whether religious values could be incorporated more directly in the workings of a secular state. In 1957 P. S. Narayan stated, 'The justification of morality is to be sought in the sphere of religion and this holds good in the private sector of the individual and in the public sector of the state . . . Loud and frequent announcements of the "secular" nature of the State are likely to sap the springs of morality in religion.'[9] Pragmatically they acquiesced in the need for a secular state but not with alacrity like Nehru but with a twinge of regret. Interestingly Hindus who thought along these lines were also quizzical about the value of western-style

[8] Jawaharlal Nehru, *The Discovery of India*, Bombay: Asia Publishing House, 1961, pp. 552–555.

[9] See P. D. Devanandan and M. M. Thomas, *Human Person, Society and State*, Bangalore, Christian Institute for the Study of Society and Religion, 1957, pp. 72–74.

descriptive Comparative Religion because it seemed to avoid existential concern in the reality of religion.

3(c) Hindu Nationalism

The third group was opposed to the idea of India being a secular state on the grounds of what they called *Hindutva*, 'Hinduness'. Finding attractive the work of Dayananda Saraswati (1824–83) who had founded the Arya Samaj in 1875 to purify the Hindu tradition without recourse to the West, and the work of B. G. Tilak (1856–1920) who had interpreted the Bhagavad Gītā on militant Hindu lines, their recent impact has been through political bodies such as the Hindu Mahasabha, the Rashtriya Swayamsevak Sangh (founded in 1925), and the Bharatiya Jana Sangh (founded in 1951). Their aim is to heighten an awareness of the Hindu heritage throughout India, and to work for the eventual creation of a Hindu nation based upon *Hindutva*. They are therefore not in sympathy with the separation of the Indian state from the Hindu tradition as far as the constitution is concerned, nor do they agree with the state's policy in regard to the caste system which they regard as a central part of the Hindu tradition. According to Golwalkar, the very word 'Hindu' 'at once reflects the unity, the sublimity, and the speciality of our people.'[10] Part of the work of this group of Hindus has been to try to strengthen the role of the classical language Sanskrit and its modern spoken successor Hindi. This means that their influence has been greater in northern India than in the south where the Dravidian rather than Sanskrit-type languages hold sway. Another interesting feature of the Arya Samaj especially has been its work in *śuddhi*,[11] the reconversion back to the Hindu

[10] M. S. Golwalkar, *Bunch of Thoughts*, Bangalore: Rashtriya Swayamsevak Sangh, 1966, p. 98ff. See also P. H. Ashby, *Modern Trends in Hinduism*, New York and London: Columbia University Press, 1974, especially pp. 91–116.
[11] J. F. Seunarine, *Reconversion to Hinduism Through Śuddhi*, Madras: Christian Literature Society, 1977.

fold of Muslims, Christians, or others who had formerly been Hindus. This has sometimes been extended to the conversion of people into the Hindu community who have not been Hindus before. Clearly the Hindu communalism of this group is in marked contrast to the acceptance of the secular state on the part of the two groups mentioned above. Its members have also been ready to work for the implementation of the banning of cow-slaughter on the premise that veneration of the cow is an important feature of the Hindu tradition.

3(d) Neo-Hindu Reform

The fourth group, and an influential one, is that of the neo-Hindu reformers who have provided the theoretical undergirding for the religious pluralism lying behind the secular state of India. Paul Hacker has remarked that the neo-Hindu reformers have received more attention than they deserve because of their facility in the English language, because of their formation in western intellectual ideas, and because of the publicity resulting from their élite position. Traditional Hinduism, he claims, is much more alive than neo-Hinduism which 'sometimes looks stillborn'.[12] It may be admitted that there is some truth in this observation, but it raises a host of issues that, for reasons of space, must await discussion elsewhere: for example, What is traditional Hinduism? Is the religiousness of the Hindus to be found in the realm of ideas, in the realm of anthropological observation, or somewhere else? How can neo-Hinduism be characterised? Short of a series of the Indian equivalent of Gallup polls held throughout India and among Hindus throughout the world, it would be difficult to verify Hacker's remark. The fact remains that it is the neo-Hindu reformers that have set the agenda and set the pace for

[12] Paul Hacker, 'Aspects of Neo-Hinduism as Contrasted with Surviving Traditional Hinduism' pp. 580–608 in Paul Hacker, *Kleine Schriften*, Wiesbaden: Franz Steiner Verlag, 1978.

significant development within the contemporary Hindu tradition and for this reason their importance is out of proportion to their numbers. We will look briefly at the general issues raised by their work, and then we will look in more detail at some of the more important of these neo-Hindu figures.

4. Contemporary Neo-Hinduism

4(a) Historical Background

With the benefit of hindsight we can trace four stages in the development of the neo-Hindu tradition.[13] The first stage, symbolised in the work of Ram Mohun Roy (1772–1833), had seen an active turning towards the West in the spheres of education, social reform, respect for science, the use of the English language, and reform of the Hindu tradition. Through his work for social betterment such as the abolition of *sati* (widow-burning), through his support for education in the English language, and through his foundation of the Brahmo Samaj to reform the Hindu tradition on the lines of Upanishadic theism, the morning-star of the Hindu renaissance admitted the need for Hindus to take seriously the seemingly stronger western culture and religion. The second stage, symbolised in the work of Ramakrishna (1834–86), had seen a growth of internal self-confidence within the Hindu reform movement. The Hindu tradition was seen to have something to offer to the Christian West as well as something to receive from it. Ramakrishna's deep spiritual experience, incorporating aspects of Sufi Islam and Christ as well as devotional, Tantric and

---

[13] This analysis is my own. See also V. S. Naravane, *Modern Indian Thought: A Philosophical Survey*, Bombay: Asia Publishing House, 1964; D. S. Sarma, *Hinduism Through the Ages*, Bombay: Bharatiya Vidya Bhavan, 1973 (1st ed. 1956), especially pp. 60–278; Trevor Ling, *A History of Religion East and West*, London, Melbourne and Toronto: Macmillan, 1968, especially pp. 364–377.

Advaita Hinduism, was seen as a corrective to the materialism and spiritual shallowness of the West; moreover, his Hindu universalism, through its potentially all-embracing inclusivism, not only queried the need for conversion to other persuasions but also promised them hospitality alongside it within the total religious spectrum. The third stage, symbolised in the work of Swami Vivekananda (1863–1902) and Mahatma Gandhi (1869–1948), saw the neo-Hindus embrace the nationalist movement that was seeking to achieve ultimate independence for India. The attraction of the West remained at the same time as India sought political independence from it. The West was still a place to find training (as was the case with Gandhi and various other neo-Hindu leaders), a place to be influenced (following the pattern set by Vivekananda at the Chicago Parliament of Religions in 1893), and a source of borrowing (as in the case of democracy, science, educational ideas and the English language). The fourth stage, from independence to present day, forms the contemporary era of the neo-Hindu tradition. The influence of the West in India has declined, both physically and emotionally, but neo-Hindu ideas remain significant in contemporary India. We will glance at three elements within modern neo-Hinduism.

4(b) Contemporary Elements
(i) One such element is religious pluralism. Although pluralism, toleration, and inclusivism have not been absent in the Hindu past, despite episodes such as the medieval demise of the Buddhists in India, modern Hindu pluralism is essentially a creation of the neo-Hindus. Religious traditions are equal paths to the same goal; there is an essential unity of all the religions; different religions are branches of the same tree—the neo-Hindu phrases roll on. They are not talking in terms of a universal religion formed by choosing the best parts of all the world religions. Their aim is partly political—to obviate the threat of

communalism; but it is also religious—to make the point that the Hindu tradition is not so much a set of doctrines as a way of life characterised by tolerance and a wide vision. Thus persons of all religious backgrounds were welcomed in the Congress Party, and neo-Hindus such as Radhakrishnan were ready to welcome the re-emergence of a growing Buddhist tradition in India. However, the very generosity of some forms of Hindu inclusivism, such as the encompassing of the Sikh tradition within the Hindu worldview or the inclusion of Christ as an honorary *avatāra* of Vishnu, was not always accepted in the spirit in which it was offered. Neo-Hindu tolerance is not merely tolerance of other religious traditions. It is in continuity with a strand of Hindu openness which includes 'tolerance of the new, the unusual, and the different, a capacity to reshape itself in changing conditions, a quickness of comprehension, and a willingness to seek for new solutions to new problems.'[14]

(ii) A second element in neo-Hindu thought relates to its implicit support for governmental reforms of traditional Hindu practice. Since 1945, Indian governments have had no strong links with traditional Hindu religious leaders. Part of the reason for this is that there are few formal religious structures within the Hindu tradition to supply those links. Another part of the reason is that the government and the neo-Hindus have seen the need to reform Hindu cultic life and the supervision of Hindu temples which are felt to have become too conservative and rigid. Whereas British officials had rarely interfered in the affairs of Hindu priests and temples, in some states the rules changed after Independence. For example, Fuller's study of the great Mīnākṣī temple at Madurai in Tamil Nadu shows how the Mīnākṣī priests found themselves in conflict with their

---

[14] Norman Brown, 'Class and Cultural Tradition in India', in M. Singer (Ed.), *Traditional India: Structure and Change*, Philadelphia: America Folklore Society, 1959, p. 39.

government, with its religious endowments department, and with the government's allies, the neo-Hindu élite. As Fuller puts it, 'the Minaksi priests have ceded much of their status and authority to the Temple administration over the last fifty years or so, and they have also (like other temple priests) come under a lot of pressure from the government and the reformist movement.'[15] Thus the Indian government, aided by neo-Hindu principles, has been pressed into service as an agency of religious reform.

(iii) A third element in neo-Hindu thought relates to the caste system. In regard to caste, as in regard to most other matters, contemporary Hindus have gone in three main directions. The secularists, such as Nehru and K. M. Panikkar, have desired the dismantling of the caste system; the communalists, such as the Arya Samaj, the Hindu Mahasabha, and the Bharatiya Jana Sangh, have desired to maintain it with full force; the neo-Hindus and the ambivalent supporters of the secular state have sought to purify and reform rather than dismantle the caste system. The Hindu Marriage Act of 1955 allowed divorce and disallowed polygamy, and as far as the civil law was concerned caste was abolished as a necessary requirement for a valid marriage. Caste became irrelevant to marriage from the viewpoint of the courts. Later Acts, the Hindu Adoptions and Maintenance Act and the Hindu Succession Act, safeguarded the rights of girls to be adopted and to be heirs. Thus government legislation moved all Indians, including Hindus, in the direction of a uniform civil code of law.

Discussion of caste in contemporary India raises a number of issues: Is caste part of the Hindu religious tradition? How strong does it remain, whatever the civil law may say—in cities, in towns, in villages? How can we gain evidence concerning the

---

[15] C. J. Fuller, *Servants of the Goddess: The Priests of a South Indian Temple*, Cambridge: Cambridge University Press, 1984, p. 162.

present state of caste that is representative of the real situation, as opposed to evidence that is true for one part of India but not for another, and as opposed to evidence that tells us more about the group that offers it than the objective facts that group claims to put forward? How do we define caste anyway? These questions are partly intractable, but it would be churlish to ignore them altogether.

The three Hindu groups mentioned above go in predictable directions as far as the relationship between caste and Hindu tradition is concerned. The secularists, such as K. M. Panikkar, denied that there was any necessary connection between caste and religious Hinduism so that, from their point of view, one could be a Hindu while repudiating caste. The communalist Hindu parties and traditional Hindu orthodoxy consider that the caste system is an integral part of the Hindu religious tradition and for this reason they are opposed to the state's attempt to impose a social pattern in which caste is disregarded. The neo-Hindus and their supporters have taken a mid-way position. Gandhi, for example, affirmed the four *varṇas*, sought to reform the caste system, attacked untouchability as a blot on Hinduism, and aimed to purify the attitudes of higher-caste Hindus within the overall framework of the caste system. He saw it as part of the Hindu religious tradition that was in need of urgent renewal. Neo-Hindus more interested in influencing the West, such as Vivekananda and Radhakrishnan, have been inclined to lay greater stress upon the religious philosophy and spiritual experience centred in the Vedanta as expressing the soul of the Hindu tradition which was imperishable whereas the caste system belonged to a particular set of social arrangements which expressed the body of the Hindu tradition and was therefore more perishable. They thought that modern science, the process of industrialisation, and the advent of a technological society would erode the caste system slowly so that while it was presently part of the Hindu tradition, it was not an essential part of true Hinduism and its departure would not mean the demise of the Hindu tradition.

Hard evidence concerning the present strength of the caste system is not plentiful. Negative evidence about its strength comes from those who rebelled against it because they felt that it was an integral part of the Hindu worldview. The Dravidian movement in Madras, associated with the name of E. V. Ramaswamy Naicker, opposed the caste system as part of a total religious outlook based upon Brahmin domination. Later the Dravida Munnetra Kazagham (DMK) moderated the more extreme views of Naicker to condemn instead the caste mentality of 'Brahminism'. Nevertheless their stance was clear. Even clearer was the action of B. R. Ambedkar who in 1956 led his outcaste followers in a mass conversion to the Buddhist tradition. He saw caste as central to the Hindu religious tradition so that 'to ask people to give up caste is to ask them to go contrary to their fundamental religious notions.'[16] For him caste was a primary feature of Hinduism—that is why he wanted to escape from it.

Anthropological research has also shown the continuing strength of certain aspects of the caste system in Indian villages. Indeed Louis Dumont's book on the place of the caste system in Indian society, *Homo Hierarchicus*, has become a classic of its kind.[17] In another work he states plainly, 'the Hindu belief in gods is secondary and derived in relation to the fundamental religious values of caste.'[18] For anthropologists, then, whatever

[16] B. R. Ambedkar, *Annihilation of Caste*, Bombay: Bharat Bhushan Publishing Press, 1937, p. 39. On Naicker and the DMK, see Robert L. Hardgrave Jr., 'Religion, Politics and the DMK' in D. E. Smith (Ed.), *South Asian Politics and Religion*, Princeton: Princeton University Press, 1966, pp. 213–234.

[17] Louis Dumont, *Homo Hierarchicus*, Chicago: Chicago University Press, 1970.

[18] Louis Dumont, *Religion, Politics and History in India*, Paris, The Hague: Mouton, 1970, p. 16.

the civil law may say, caste is seen to be built into the religious scheme of things, and it still persists in various strengths. Moreover Paul Hacker, an Indologist, shows that the traditional view of *dharma* as relating to caste and the four stages of life (*varṇāśramadharma*) remains strong in traditional Hinduism.[19] Thus while the neo-Hindus may be winning the battle in the realm of ideas and among the élite it is by no means clear that they are winning the battle in the sphere of practice in rural India where eighty per cent of the people still live in villages.

Most reports claim that life in cities, study at universities, secularisation and industrialisation do have some effect upon caste practice, and common sense also commends this viewpoint, but it is not easy to back up this claim with the thoroughness of detail that is warranted. Some evidence is available: for example Ashby's study of Hindu students at Andhra University in South India, Gosling's study of the impact of scientific ideas upon the beliefs and practice of Hindu scientists in institutions in Delhi, Bangalore, Madurai, and Kottayam, A. M. A. Ayrookuzhiel's study of the 'Sacred' within the social structure of Chirakkal in North Malabar, and Judith M. Brown's study of religious observance among lecturers in Poona, and other places.[20] The evidence is ambivalent according to context and author, but it generally points to tradition and change standing side-by-side in different states of balance, with tradition generally more to the fore in the village setting and change more to the fore in the city and university setting. It is obvious that caste ties remain in most

[19] Paul Hacker, *op. cit.*, pp. 589–591.
[20] Philip H. Ashby, *Modern Trends in Hinduism*, New York and London: Columbia University Press, 1974, especially chapter 3 'Hinduism and Contemporary Indian Youth' pp. 49–70; A. M. A. Ayrookuzhiel, *The Sacred in Popular Hinduism*, Madras: Christian Literature Society, 1983; David L. Gosling, *Science and Religion in India*, Madras: Christian Literature Society, 1976; Judith M. Brown, *Men and Gods in a Changing World*, London: SCM Press, 1980.

parts of the Hindu community but that sanctions against those who offend against caste *dharma* are much less strong among the educated and in the cities.

5. Seminal Contemporary Figures

Before we leave the neo-Hindus, we will glance briefly at the work of three seminal figures during our period. They are Vinoba Bhave, Radhakrishnan, and Sri Aurobindo. They represent three contrasting but important pieces within the neo-Hindu jigsaw.

5(a) Vinoba Bhave—Hindu Socialism

Vinoba Bhave, born in 1895, was a follower of Gandhi, and he has developed especially the social side of Gandhi's teaching through the medium of the Sarvodaya movement. As he puts it, 'I want to root out the wrong ideas and erect the new society on the basis of religious ideas.'[21] In spite of his desire for a social revolution, he has not stressed politics *per se*, in either the communist or socialist mode, but he has worked for a change in the social order from below by means of religiously motivated ideals that would in turn change the state, the government and the very life-structure of India. In effect, because of his stress upon the moral element in social reform, and through his appeal to the principles of association and mutual help, he has represented a form of Hindu socialism.

Bhave has appealed to the altruism of Hindus. He has transmuted and universalised the Bhagavad Gītā's stress upon *karma-yoga* into a principle of serving others without thought of reward especially in the social and economic sphere. Thus the

[21] Vinoba Bhave, *The Principles and Philosophy of the Bhoodan Yagna,* Tanjore: Sarvodaya Prachuralaya, 1955, p. 3.

notion of *sevā*, service, which in classical Hindu thought had implied the service of the higher castes by the lower, becomes the service of all beings by all persons; the notion of *karma*, which in classical Hindu thought had been focussed upon ritual works, becomes focussed upon good works performed for others in the world; the notion of Brahman, which in classical Hindu thought had been a metaphysical principle signifying ultimate reality, becomes a principle of equality in that all people, including the poor, partake of Brahman and should be treated as such; the notion of *bhakti*, devotion, which in classical Hindu thought had meant devotion to God, becomes also devotion to human beings. For Bhave, the Hindu tradition achieves deep economic and social relevance because, for him, its basic religious ideas point in the direction of altruistic service of others in the world. He represents the'extreme working-out of the strand of social reform woven into the neo-Hindu tradition from the time of Ram Mohun Roy. The age of degeneration, *kali yuga*, has come to an end, he proclaims. The time has come for resolute action in the world to re-establish *satya yuga*, the age of truth.

In practice, Bhave has travelled round from village to village disseminating his ideas and calling upon people, especially landowners and rich people, to make sacrifices on behalf of others. He is best known for his request for gifts of land, *bhūdan*, to be given to the many landless people in India. 'We must make sacrifices for the poor',[22] he states. 'I am asking for land. It is just a symbol of that spirit of sacrifice.'[23] He has also called for other kinds of sacrifice: the gift of labour (*shramdan*), the gift of wealth (*sampattidān*), the gift of intelligence (*buddhidān*), the gift of love (*premdān*), and even the gift of life (*jīvandān*). He is a symbol of the neo-Hindu concern for ethics and social involvement applied in very practical ways in the economic sphere.

[22] S. Ramabhai, *Vinoba and his Mission*, Wardha: Sevagram, 1954, p. 59.
[23] *Op. cit.*, p. 59.

5(b) Sarvepalli Radhakrishnan—Hindu Ideas Reinterpreted

Sarvepalli Radhakrishnan, who was born in 1888, was a thinker rather than a doer. Although he did have political interests, culminating in his service as President of India from 1961–67, his main contribution was to the realm of neo-Hindu thought. If Bhave symbolises the *karma-yoga* of the Bhagavad Gītā, Radhakrishnan symbolises the *jñāna-yoga* of the Bhagavad Gītā, the yoga of knowledge. His many writings, written lucidly in beautiful prose, not only reinterpret the classical Hindu doctrines in the light of the modern situation, they are also a specifically Hindu contribution to the study of religion and to the academic enterprise in general.

Radhakrishnan, together with his neo-Hindu colleagues, wishes to accomodate the ongoing Hindu tradition to various modern and western notions such as history, the importance of this world, the role of the individual, the world process, religious experience, national development, and the march of science. This involves him in a process of reinterpretation, for the Veda and later Hindu texts do not appear to contain some of these ideas except by a complicated process of hermeneutics. And this is what Radhakrishnan engages in. He interprets *māyā*, illusion, to give it a creative rather than illusory nuance; he interprets the law of *karma* to make room within it for repentance and forgiveness; he interprets *saṃsāra*, the unending world process, to enable it: to include progress towards an ultimate destiny; he interprets the *sanātana dharma*, the eternal (Hindu) religion, so that it can be a foundation of tolerance, peace and vision that the planet needs.

Radhakrishnan also makes a valuable contribution to the wider study of religion from a Hindu perspective. His output includes not only classical works on Indian thought such as *Indian Philosophy*, and works of Hindu apologetic such as *The Hindu View of Life*, but also other works in which a creative

146

Hindu outlook is inserted into the bloodstream of religious scholarship. To put it in other words, the neo-Hindus have not only borrowed from the West they have also enriched the West. Thus Radhakrishnan stresses the role of philosophy in the study of religion but he has a Hindu insight into the way philosophy works. It is integrally intertwined with religion, it uses intuition as well as intellect, and it recognises mystery as well as reason. Moreover he is not afraid to emphasise the role of religious commitment in academic scholarship. He is unashamedly an idealist for whom 'Vedanta is not a religion, but religion itself in its most universal and deepest significance.'[24] Here indeed we have Hindu inclusivism and a 'counter-attack from the East' (to use Joad's phrase) with a vengeance, yet couched in academically appealing terms! Furthermore Radhakrishnan has a concern for dialogue with other religions, and a concern that the Hindu tradition and religious traditions in general should contribute to the building of a global culture that will provide a creative future for humankind. As he puts it, 'the different religions are to be used as building stones for the development of a human culture in which the adherents of the different religions may be fraternally united as children of one Supreme. . . . The world will give birth to a new faith which will be but the old faith in another form, the faith of the ages, the potential divinity of man which will work for the supreme purpose written in our hearts and souls, the unity of all mankind.'[25]

5(c) Sri Aurobindo—Hindu Spirituality Reformulated

This concern for human unity is carried even further by our

[24] S. Radhakrishnan, *The Hindu View of Life*, London: Allen & Unwin, 1954 (9th impr.), p. 23.

[25] L. Rouner (Ed.), *Philosophy, Religion and the Coming World Civilisation*, The Hague: Martinus Nijhoff, 1966, p. 296. See also F. Whaling, 'The Study of Religion in a Global Context' pp. 391–443 in F. Whaling (Ed.), *Contemporary Approaches to the Study of Religion: The Humanities*, Berlin, New York and Amsterdam: Mouton, 1984.

third neo-Hindu, Sri Aurobindo (1872–1950). Aurobindo's first twenty-one years had been steeped in the English language and western culture in India then in England, but when he came back to Baroda he immersed himself in Indian languages and the Hindu tradition as well as becoming involved as an early leader of the fledgling Indian Independence Movement. After being arrested, imprisoned, tried and acquitted in connection with his political activities, he renounced politics in his famous Uttarapara speech of 1909 and made his way eventually to Pondicherry, then in French India, where he was to spend the rest of his life in meditation, writing, and yoga within the bosom of his Pondicherry Ashram superintended by the Mother, a figure equally as charismatic as himself. Insofar as the Mother only died recently at an advanced age, and insofar as the city of Auroville is still being built as a material symbol to perpetuate and expand Aurobindo's vision, this most original of the neo-Hindus is relevant to our chapter—and he is so for four main reasons.

In the first place, he appropriated the theory of creative evolution in a peculiarly Hindu way, blissfully unaware that Teilhard de Chardin and Sir Muhammad Iqbal were pursuing similar paths within the Christian and Muslim traditions.[26] Brahman, he argued, has become involved in the world process right down as far as matter through creative involution. Now the process is going in the other direction: from matter, through plant life, through animal life, through human life, and through an advanced human consciousness back up into Brahman through a process of creative evolution. Thus Brahman is dynamically active in evolution, and the universe and human life are in a state of becoming, they have not yet reached their appointed goal, which is a spiritual goal. Creative evolution can

---

[26] See F. Whaling, 'Śrī Aurobindo: A Critique' in *The Journal of Religious Studies*, 7(2), 1979, pp. 66–103.

be seen as a growth of consciousness, and human beings are at the centre of, not separate from, this evolution. Thus Aurobindo sees a vibrant future for humanity—he is a prophet of hope—and as far as he is concerned we may anticipate the emergence of a new species of humanity with new goals and new triumphs. It is clear therefore that he takes the cosmos, humanity, matter, history, and the world process seriously. He also takes science seriously—this is a typically neo-Hindu perspective—but he puts it into a gradation that ranks it lower than true spirituality. Science and technology are to be granted the respect they deserve, but that respect is to be kept within proper limits.

Secondly, Aurobindo emphasised what he called integral yoga. That is to say, he not only engaged in the yoga of world involvement of his political days, he not only engaged in the yoga of knowledge of his student and writing days, above all he engaged in the yoga of spirituality. His own life and the life of his ashram were meant to be powerhouses of spirituality, the vibrant currents of which would percolate out to influence the contemporary issues of his day. The seeming paradox of this apostle of creative evolution spending his time in meditation and spiritual endeavour in the heart of an ashram is resolved when we realise that his ultimate vision was the divinisation of the whole life of humanity. Thus his integral yoga was the synthesis of all other yogas. He was concerned about the body, mind, soul and spirit of human beings; he was concerned about the material, mental, moral and spiritual parts of the personality; he was concerned about the natural, humane, moral and spiritual sciences; he was concerned about nature, the indivdual, the social group and transcendent reality; he was concerned about the ways of deeds (*karma*), knowledge (*jñāna*), and devotion (*bhakti*); he was concerned about bodily yoga, mental yoga, heart yoga, and spiritual yoga. He assimilated the essentials of all elements of yoga into an integral (*pūrṇa*) yoga that had as its aim, for himself and for others, the life divine. True spirituality did not abandon matter, the world, human beings, and the world process—it completed them. Thus Aurobindo's integral yoga in the Pondicherry ashram was helping to hasten on the process of creative evolution.

Thirdly, he used as his sources a wide variety of Hindu sacred texts. Like many of the other neo-Hindus he had a high regard for the Bhagavad Gītā which is not in fact part of the Veda. It is a singular fact that since 1945 numerous editions and translations of the Bhagavad Gītā have been produced so that it has become very popular even though it is not part of the original Hindu *śruti*, 'revelation'. Aurobindo also paid unique attention to the fountain-head of the Veda, namely the Ṛg-Veda itself. Apart from Dayananda Saraswati, the other Hindu reformers had ignored it in favour of the Upanishads. Aurobindo took it seriously. However he paid due attention to the Upanishads as well. In addition to using the Ṛg-Veda, the Upanishads, and the Bhagavad Gītā, Aurobindo also used the Tantras of his native Bengal with their references to the Goddess. Thus his Hindu sources were wide and varied. It is true that he reinterpreted them in the light of the contemporary situation—nevertheless Kees Bolle has shown how the insights of Aurobindo are in continuity with the long history of the Hindu tradition. In other words, Aurobindo and the neo-Hindus illustrate yet again the Hindu genius for assimilating new insights—in this case the insights of the modern West—into the ongoing Hindu tradition.

Fourthly, Aurobindo's vision is being given concrete expression in the growing town of Auroville which is being built near Pondicherry by over five hundred people from over twenty-four countries as a symbol of international co-operation in the fashioning of a new world. With the possible exception of Sri Chinmoy, a living Hindu who has exercised a positive spiritual influence within the United Nations organisation, it is

Aurobindo who has most persuasively articulated a Hindu vision of future human unity. As the Auroville Charter puts it: 1. Auroville belongs to nobody in particular. Auroville belongs to humanity as a whole. But to live in Auroville one must be a willing servitor of the Divine Consciousness. 2. Auroville will be the place of an unending education, of constant progress and a youth that never ages. 3. Auroville wants to be the bridge between the past and the future. Taking advantage of all discoveries from without and from within Auroville will boldly spring towards future realisations. 4. Auroville will be a site of material and spiritual researches for a living embodiment of an actual Human Unity.[27]

6. Hinduism as a World Tradition

6(a) Introduction

We may appropriately pass on from the neo-Hindus to consider our third main topic, the Hindu *diaspora* from India into other parts of the contemporary world. It is, of course, true to say that for 2,000 years the Hindu tradition has not been confined to India. In the first 500 years of the Common Era, when Christians were expanding throughout the Roman Empire, and when Buddhists were expanding throughout China, the Hindus were expanding throughout South East Asia. We have only to examine the widespread influence of the Rāmāyaṇa story throughout South East Asia to see the evidence for this.[28]

Hindus remain in parts of further Asia. Nepal is a specifically Hindu nation, the only one in the world. There are significant

---

[27] See The Mother, *Auroville: Cradle of a New World*, Pondicherry: Sri Aurobindo Ashram, 1972, pp. 1–6. See also R. McDermott (Ed.), *The Essential Aurobindo*, New York: Schocken Books, 1973.

[28] K. R. Srinivasa Iyengar, (Ed.) *Asian Variations in Ramayana*, New Delhi: Sahitya Akademi, 1983.

numbers of Hindus in Bangla Desh, Pakistan, Sri Lanka, and Mauritius. Further afield the Hindu populations of Bali, and Fiji are reminders of continuing Hindu influence in outer Asia. South America harbours Hindu communities in Guyana and Suriname; Hindus are present in Trinidad in the West Indies; and Hindus form an important part of the Indian constituency in South Africa. Thus Hindus are present, albeit often in small numbers, in every part of the world. All Indians are not Hindus, neither are all Hindus Indians.

6(b) Hindu Movements Outside India

In the contemporary world the main movement has been towards Africa and above all towards the West. We will look especially at the Hindu *diaspora* into the West, and we will concentrate upon the role played by particular Hindu sects and gurus in taking the Hindu message into the West. Among the extremely varied Hindu groups which have come to the West, we select five that give a reasonable cross-section of types of Hinduism in that part of the world: the Swaminarayan community's work among Gujaratis in East Africa, Britain and the United States, the work of the Hare Krishna Movement, the influence of Sathya Sai Baba, the spread of Raja-Yoga, and the appeal of Transcendental Meditation. Not only do these movements form bridges between the Hindu tradition in India and elsewhere, they also form bridges between medieval and modern forms of Hinduism.

6(b)(i) Swaminarayan Movement

The Swaminarayan tradition dates back 200 years to Sahajanand Swami who was born in 1781 and is now worshipped as Swaminarayan.[29] He taught in Gujarat. This area has remained central to the Swaminarayan tradition, and insofar as a

[29] R. B. Williams, *A New Face of Hinduism: The Swaminarayan Religion*, Cambridge: Cambridge University Press, 1984.

preponderant number of Gujaratis have emigrated to East Africa, Britain and the United States the Swaminarayans have played an important role in *diaspora* Hinduism. Intelligent estimates would place the number of Gujaratis affiliated to the Swaminarayans at over five million, and in view of the strength of the Swaminarayan tradition abroad this may well be a conservative estimate.

The Swaminarayan community had established a foothold in East Africa since the influx of Gujarati construction workers to build railways in 1895, but its first temple was built at Nairobi in 1945. By 1968 the two main Swaminarayan branches had reached their zenith in East Africa. They had grown in tandem with the rapid growth of the Gujarati community, representing as they did an important vehicle for the deepening of Gujarati cultural religion among the immigrant community. With the coming to independence of Kenya, Tanzania, and Uganda between 1962 and 1964, their scope became more limited. The sequence of events from the Kenya Immigration Act of December 1968 to Amin's forced exodus of the Indians from Uganda in 1973–73 further reduced their numbers and activities, although active temples and communities remain in a number of cities of Kenya and Tanzania.

Subsequent emigrations of Indians from East Africa to Britain have led to the formation of a large Swaminarayan community in the UK, and the relaxing of the United States immigrant laws in 1965 resulted in many Gujaratis entering that land as part of the 'new ethnics', with Swaminarayan groups and temples important among them. Thus it will be seen that the role of the Swaminarayans was not to act as an evangelising agency among East Africans, Britons, or Americans, but rather to service the Gujarati communities which emigrated to those lands. They are essentially a Hindu service agency for Hindus, and especially Gujarati Hindus, with their religious base remaining in Gujarat.

The Swaminarayans are a modern devotional Hindu *sampradāya* (sect) centred upon devotion to Swaminarayan who is viewed as the fullest manifestation of the eternal Nārāyaṇa (Vishnu). Sahajanand Swami himself followed in a succession of North Indian devotional saints dating back to Rāmānanda and Kabīr, but he has also been described as 'the first of the neo-Hindu reformers'.[30] In fact, he is unique. He has been 'deified' more than the medieval saints or the neo-Hindu reformers, yet paradoxically his movement has retained a Gujarati image while at the same time making a deep mark among Hindus in East Africa, Britain and the United States.

6(b)(ii) Hare Krishna Movement

Our second modern movement, the Hare Krishna movement, incorporated in 1966 as the International Society for Krishna Consciousness (ISKCON), has developed into a service movement for Hindus abroad.[31] However its beginnings were different. It dates back to the work of Swami Prabhupada who was born in 1896. Prabhupada was initiated by his guru in 1933 into a succession that dated itself back to the great Krishna devotee Chaitanya. Although his guru died in 1936, Prabhupada had already heard the call to preach Krishna Consciousness to the English-speaking peoples, but it was not until 1965 that he set sail for the United States at the age of 70. Thus it was that the familiar Hare Krishna mantra became known in the streets and parks òf western cities: 'Hare Krishna, Hare Krishna, Krishna Krishna, Hare Hare; Hare Rama, Hare Rama, Rama Rama, Hare Hare.' The initial aim was to promote Krishna Consciousness among westerners, and especially young westerners, alienated by the materialism of western society. By 1975 this aim had been successfully

[30] *Op. cit.*, p. 24.
[31] See Phillip Hammond's chapter in this book on 'Cults and Civil Religion'.

achieved, and over 100 temples had been set up at places as far apart as the United States, Canada, Mexico, South America, Britain, Holland, France, Germany, Spain, Switzerland, Australia, East Africa, Hong Kong, Indonesia, Iran, Japan, New Zealand, and South Africa. In these temples, Rādhā Krishna deities were honoured, classes on the Bhagavad Gītā and the Bhāgavata Purāṇa were held, the Hare Krishna mantra was chanted in congregational fellowship (sankīrtan), and many visitors were welcomed.

During the last decade, the Hare Krishna movement has turned its attention far more to serving Hindus who have come to live in the West. Its potential scope is wider than that of the Swaminarayan movement because it is not culturally confined to Gujarat, and it has a more universal appeal to different kinds of Hindus. The activities promoted by the Hare Krishna movement are many and varied. For example, on October 20 1985 the largest Hindu temple outside India was opened in Durban, South Africa, by the Hare Krishna movement.[32] The movement is also an important motivating factor in ECHO, the European Council of Hindu Organisations, which has some of the following aims: to promote the concerns of over three million Hindus living in Europe, to educate Europeans concerning the Hindu way of life, to influence European schools to take the Hindu tradition seriously, to promote literature about the Hindu tradition, to enable Hindu festivals such as Diwali, Dusshera, Janamashtami, Holi and Durga Puja to be celebrated and Hindu sacraments to be performed in Europe, to construct Hindu temples and community centres where needed, to have access for Hindu viewing time on radio and television, to allow Hindus to take court oaths on the Bhagavad Gītā, to encourage the appointment of a European Ombudsman for

[32] ECHO News: Newsletter of the European Council of Hindu Organisations, Amsterdam. Winter 1985, 86, p. 1.

Hindus, and to promote multi-cultural concerns in Europe. Vidya Sagar Anand, chairman of ECHO, at a conference of the Vishwa Hindu Parishad held in Copenhagen in July 1985 gave words to these new aspirations, 'No longer can we see Hinduism as confined to the Indian subcontinent only, or to the people of Indian extraction. Rather it has become a religion of universal appeal. It draws adherents from all corners of the earth. It is now at last beginning to fulfil the prophecy of Chaitanya Mahaprabhu . . . the light of Hinduism is shining . . . and in every society in which we find ourselves we must participate more fully.'[33] From encouraging a Hindu Festival of Chariots in Trafalgar Square to helping to repair a temple in Slough, UK, damaged by hooligans, the Hare Krishna movement is active in pursuing the interests of Hindus outside India in a variety of different ways. By the same token, much more attention is being given now to Hindus of Indian extraction living outside India by comparison with the situation in 1965 when the main aim was to attract westerners into the orbit of Krishna Consciousness.

6(b)(iii) Sathya Sai Baba Movement

Our third example of a modern Hindu movement that has had some influence in the West centres on the work of Sathya Sai Baba. He was born in 1926, and he did not aim consciously to influence the West, but he has done so through his spiritual vitality. To this extent, he belongs to a group of gurus including Ramana Maharshi, Anandamayee Ma, Neelakantha Tathaji, Sri Dattabal, Muktananda Paramahamsa, and Sri Aurobindo whose spirituality has influenced the West from India rather than by prolonged sojourns in the West (as would be true of Swami Prabhupada, Guru Maharaj Ji of the Divine Light

[33] *Op. cit.*, p. 3, Didya Sagar Anand, 'Hindus Gather in Copenhagen for World Conference'.

Mission, and Maharishi Mahesh Yogi of TM who have visited and consciously targeted the West).[34]

Like other contemporary Hindu gurus, Sathya Sai Baba is not perhaps as 'new' as he seems to be. He stands in a succession (implicit if not explicit) that includes Upasani Baba and Mata Godavari, and lying behind them is Sai Baba (1856–1918) of whom Sathya Sai Baba is taken to be a rebirth. Lying behind Sai Baba is the influence of Kabīr, the Nāthpanthi yogis, and the medieval Sants.[35] Unlike his predecessors, Sathya Sai Baba has the advantage of being portrayed in the modern media, including television, of being within easy access of visitors from abroad, and of appealing to a worldwide rather than a purely Indian following. Central to his appeal to Indian and foreigner alike is the age-old attraction of the Indian realised saint: charismatic spirituality mediated mainly through presence, gesture, relationship and spiritual power as well as through well-turned phrases either written or spoken. For this reason, there is not much academic writing on gurus such as him, either past or present, but their contemporary influence is real.

Although Sathya Sai Baba's influence in India extends to millions of people, for the purposes of this chapter I intend to refer to his contribution to the Hindu *diaspora* and the Hindu influence upon non-Hindus. In Britain, for example, there are over fifty Sathya Sai Baba groups devoted to study and service ranging alphabetically from Birmingham to Woking, and geographically from West Cornwall to mid-Scotland.[36] They include Indians but their main clientele is non-Indians, and there

[34] See P. Brent, *Godmen of India*, London: Penguin Press, 1972; Khushwant Singh, *Gurus, Godmen and Good People*, Bombay: Orient Longman, 1975.

[35] See Charles S. J. White, 'The Sāi Bābā Movement: Approaches to the Study of Indian Saints' in the *Journal of Asian Studies*, Vol. xxxi, 1971–72. pp. 863–878.

[36] See *A Quarterly Magazine Dedicated to Sathya Sai Baba*, Tunbridge Wells Kent, Summer 1985, No. 8, pp. 31–33.

is a continual stream of visitors between Britain and the guru's ashram at Puttaparthi outside Bangalore.

To his devotees, Sathya Sai Baba is an omnipresent divine force as well as a physical swami. As Peggy Mason puts it, 'When Swami stands so close to you and says, "I am in your heart", or "I am always with you", one is only fully aware of this when away from the physical form.'[37] Personal gifts and desires are offered up to Sathya Sai Baba by his followers in Britain, America and other parts of the world: for example tithing of money is fairly common, disciplined eating habits are practised, time is dedicated in a relaxed but structured way, and energy is surrendered in order to be accepted back and used in helping others.

The five pillars of Sathya Sai Baba's teaching have been brought together in a Programme of Education in Human Values.[38] To use the programme's own terminology those five pillars are: truth (*sathya*), right action (*dharma*), peace (*shānti*), love (*prema*), and non-violence (*ahimsā*). These have been further elaborated into a theory and method of education which is attracting attention among some theorists and a few practitioners of education at the global level and also at some specific local levels in India and elsewhere.

Recently there has been increasing stress within the movement upon service (*sevā*). Service to fellow humans is seen as service to the divine; work done for Sathya Sai Baba is seen to be as important as devotion to him; hands that help are seen to be as consecrated as hands that pray. Thus in Britain since 1983 over thirty service projects have been taken up ranging from meals on wheels to helping the handicapped, from Age Concern to Oxfam, and from prison visiting to animal welfare; in addition the Sri Sathya Sai World Foundation UK, established

[37] *Op. cit.*, p. 6.
[38] *Op. cit.*, pp. 6–9.

in 1979, has as its aims 'the advancement of education; the relief of poverty and sickness and the support of any existing charitable organisation or organisations the trustees may select.'[39] Thus it will be seen that education and service have been combined with meditation as the main avenues of devotion to Sathya Sai Baba. In this respect he is similar to a number of other Hindu gurus who have been influential in the West: the initial devotion and meditation they inspire is supplemented by educational and social service projects.

6(b)(iv) Raja-Yoga Movement

Our fourth Hindu-type group active in the West is similar in some ways to the Sathya Sai Baba movement but it is also different in others. It is the Raja-Yoga movement.[40] It too has educational aspirations (its headquarters is in fact a university, the Brahma Kumaris World Spiritual University at Mount Abu in Rajasthan, India); it too aims to serve the world (since 1980 it has been affiliated to the United Nations as a movement recognised to be working for harmonious relationships personally and globally); however its basic stress is upon meditation. Unlike the Sathya Sai Baba movement, it downplays the role of gurus. Unlike other similar groups, it does not use mantras, nor does it engage in vigorous proselytisation. It is essentially centred upon exemplary spirituality rather than charismatic spirituality.

The Raja-Yoga movement began in the 1930s through the

---

[39] See last page of *United Kingdom 60th Birthday Souvenir* published by the Sathya Sai Baba Council of the United Kingdom, 1985, on the 'Sri Sathya Sai World Foundation—UK' See also N. Kasturi (Ed.), *Sathya Sai Speaks: Discourses*, Vols 1–10, 1970–80, Sri Sathya Sai Books and Publication Foundation India.

[40] B. K. Jagdish Chander, *The Way and the Goal of Raja-Yoga*, Mount Abu: Prajapita Brahma Kumaris Ishwariya Vishwa-Vidyalaya, 1977; B. K. Jagdish Chander, *Adi Dev*, Mount Abu: Prajapita Brahma Kumaris Vishwa-Vidyalaya, 1981.

experience of a member of the prominent Sindhi Lekh Raj family who became known as Prajapita Brahma. Although he was deeply respected as an instrument, leadership of the movement eventually passed into the hands of female leaders, and after the partition of India the headquarters finally became centred at Mount Abu in India rather than at Karachi in Sindh in Pakistan. From 1971 onwards Raja-Yoga has spread from India into over fifty countries and it has over fifteen hundred service centres around the world. It is unique in that all these centres are strictly speaking branches of the Spiritual University so that the movement is a worldwide university of spirituality.

Raja-Yoga recommends a total life-style including vegetarian diet, abstinence from alcohol, smoking and drug-taking, celibacy, and the systematic improvement of life-quality; however its central stress is upon meditation and the realisation of the true nature of the self. Compared with the eight limbs of Patañjali's system of classical yoga, which involve a long and complex discipline, this movement teaches theoretically and experientially an 'easy Raja Yoga which is based on Soul-consciousness and God-consciousness.'[41] Daily study and meditation lie at the heart of its practise, at both an individual and group level, and rapid growth in consciousness becomes possible.

This growth of consciousness, and the practical service that flows from it, is based theoretically upon a cluster of Hindu-type ideas: we are in an age of confluence at the end of the present kali yuga; this may end in a nuclear holocaust; there will soon be a new golden age; human beings are essentially souls rather than bodies; the soul is conceived as having the form of a point of light and it can radiate outwards to form loving connections with the rest of existence; natural peace and happiness lie in this soul-consciousness; it is obtained through

[41] B. K. Jagdish Chander, *The Way and the Goal of Raja-Yoga*, p. 204.

mental union with God the Supreme Soul; this is a vibrant age for the spread of this sense of union which can be acquired through Raja Yoga. This cluster of ideas, in the form of daily *murlis* or messages, is delivered in Hindi at Mount Abu and is sent to all the centres around the world—the London centre being used as a place of translation and transmission for other nations—so that the movement is held together in a common spirituality.

Prajapita Brahma was ahead of his time in authorising women to become leaders of the Raja-Yoga movement. He was unwittingly echoing some of the ideas of his contemporary Carl Jung, and anticipating work on the importance of the right and left hemispheres of the brain in regard to intuitive as well as cognitive modes of leadership, not to mention some of the insights of women's and ecological movements. Although regarded with suspicion for this and other reasons, in some Hindu quarters, Raja-Yoga is symbolic of a spread of Hindu-type spirituality into the wider world.

6(b)(v) Transcendental Meditation Movement

Our fifth movement can be dealt with briefly. It is the Transcendental Meditation movement arising out of the work of Maharishi Mahesh Yogi.[42] Although this movement has a Hindu guru, uses Hindu mantras, and has created organisations to help forward its work (notably the Students International Meditation Society, the Spiritual Regeneration Movement, the International Meditation Society, the American Foundation for the Science of Creative Intelligence, and the Maharishi International University), it has for most of its adepts become cut off from its Hindu roots, and functions as a means to better physical and mental health, to increased efficiency of living, and to a more rewarding life-style. As such it may be seen as part of a general wider Hindu influence upon the planet earth.

[42] Jack Forem, *Transcendental Meditation*, London: Allen & Unwin, 1974.

6(b)(vi) General Hindu Influence Outside India

Part of the nature of religion in today's world lies in the interpenetration of religious ideas, and before we leave our present topic we will indicate briefly other ways in which the Hindu tradition has influenced the wider world. If the Hindu tradition has been affected by other religious traditions, especially Christianity, as M. M. Thomas points out in *The Acknowledged Christ of the Indian Renaissance*,[43] other traditions have also been affected by Hindus as Raimundo Panikkar points out in *The Unknown Christ of Hinduism*[44] and his other works. Through the inter-religious dialogue movement, Hindu spirituality has influenced wider spirituality, Gandhi's creative non-violence has influenced Martin Luther King in the USA and Sarvodaya movements in various Asian lands, Coomaraswamy's thought has influenced the *philosophia perennis* movement which is a factor in the search for global religiousness, and Hindu religious pluralism has fed into the search of Wilfred Cantwell Smith and John Hick for a global theology.[45] If Vivekananda was an exotic star at the Chicago Parliament of Religions in 1893, it is fairly certain that Hindu ideas and figures will be at the centre of the centenary Parliament of Religions to be held in 1993.

6(b)(vii) Hindu Global Ecumenism

An offshoot of the Hindu input into global ecumenism, and of

---

[43] M. M. Thomas, *The Achnowledged Christ of the Indian Renaissance*, London: SCM Press, 1969.

[44] Raimundo Panikkar, *The Unknown Christ of Hinduism*, London: Darton Longman and Todd, 1964.

[45] See the chapters by John Hick on 'Religious Pluralism', S. H. Nasr on 'The Philosophia Perennis and the Study of Religion', R. Panikkar on 'The Dialogical Dialogue', J. Carman on 'Bangalore Revisited', and F. Whaling 'Introductory Essay' in F. Whaling (Ed.), *The World's Religious Traditions: Current Perspectives in Religious Studies: Essays in Honour of Wilfred Cantwell Smith*, Edinburgh: T. & T. Clark, 1984 and New York: Crossroad, 1986.

the Hindu *diaspora*, is an increased interest in Hindu ecumenism. What is it that holds Hindus together in a global world? There is no answer to this query, as was made clear at the beginning of this chapter, but one of the increasing number of feed-backs from *diaspora* Hinduism into general Hinduism is a concern for this question. One attempt to grapple with this search for a Hindu ecumenism was given by Dr Karan Singh, President of the Virat Hindu Samaj, at the tenth World Hindu Conference held in New York in 1984. The context for his search was global, the human crisis in the nuclear age, and for him the Hindu response lies in 'a restatement of five fundamental concepts that are embedded in the Hindu tradition, the external principles of Vedanta and they flow logically from each other.'[46] They are: the fact that this entire universe is pervaded by the same divine power; this divine power is also found in the heart of every human being; all humans are therefore members of a single human family; there is an essential unity of the world's religious traditions; and it is necessary to seek for the welfare and happiness of the entire human family. The fact that there are world Hindu organisations such as the Virat Hindu Samaj, and the Vishwa Hindu Parishad led by Maharana Bhagwat Singh, is indicative of an attempt to service the Hindu tradition on a worldwide basis and to conceptualise Hindu ecumenical teachings in order to spread them to a wider public. There will be increasing interplay between Hindu ecumenism and local Hindu movements in different parts of the world.

7. *Traditional Hinduism Today*

7(a) Introduction
Finally let us return from our vista of global Hinduism to

[46] Karan Singh, *Keynote Address* at the Tenth World Hindu Conference New York 1984, New Delhi: Ramayana Vidyapeeth, 1984, p. 5.

traditional Hinduism at grassroots in Indian towns and villages. This bedrock remains the core within which contemporary Hindu movements have emerged and within which they have diverged. It would be wrong to suggest that there is an unchanging traditional Hinduism in opposition to which modern Hindu movements have 'rebelled'. The situation is far more subtle than this. Since 1945 the total Hindu tradition, with its congeries of groups, movements, families and individuals, has been in flux. The flux has been greater for some people and areas than others, it has not been absent for any element within the Hindu tradition as it has changed and modernised. However, as we said at the beginning, the sacred geography of Hinduism retains its symbolic significance, and we will glance briefly at the basic elements of that sacred geography, at the different levels within traditional Hinduism within recent history, and at the ways in which Hindu traditionalism has modernised during our period. In attempting this analysis, we remain at the mercy of the vastness of the Hindu tradition and the paucity of research evidence, nevertheless it is important to try to fit in these last pieces of the jigsaw of the Hindu tradition in today's world.

7(b) Hindu Sacred Geography and Traditional Background in Today's World

For many Hindus, India itself is a sacred land, with symbolic holy places at the four corners of the subcontinent, sacred natural features such as the Ganges and the Himalayas, and key holy cities such as Banaras. As the Kāshī Khaṇḍa puts it concerning Banaras (Kāshī):

> Are there not many holy places on this earth?
> Yet which of them would equal in the balance one speck of Kāshī's dust?
> Are there not many rivers running to the sea?

Yet which of them is like the River of Heaven in Kāshī?
Are there not many fields of liberation on earth?
Yet not one equals the smallest part of the city never forsaken by
Shiva.[47]

Itinerant holy men (*sādhus*) travel round the sacred land,
resident *sādhus* run some of the monasteries in the holy places,
householders when occasion allows go for festival or pilgrimage
or sacred rite to Banaras. Yet, having stated this, the opening
sentence quoted above is significant, 'Are there not many holy
places on this earth?' The Ganges and the Himalayas may be
sacred, so are many local rivers and hills; Banaras may be holy,
so are many local towns and villages; Shiva may be a great
divinity, so is Vishnu as Lord of the universe or in the form of an
avatāra such as Rāma or Krishna, so is the Goddess in her various
forms from the darkly numinous Kālī to the more benign
Pārvatī, so are the legion of local gods including the *grāma
devatās* of the smallest villages. Hindus talk about 'going for
darshan', about 'going to see' the image of a god, but they do not
need to treck to Banaras for *darshan* of Shiva or to holy
Badrinath in the Himalayas for *darshan* of Vishnu or to sacred
Puri in the East for *darshan* of Krishna.[48] They can go for *darshan*
to a local pilgrimage place, or a local temple, or a nearby Shiva
lingam, or to their own chosen deity in their own prayer room;
they can go for *darshan* to a local *sādhu*, or a passing itinerant
holy man, or a realised saint (such as Sathya Sai Baba if
accessible); they can see the divine through the sacramental
ritual life of their own family, for fourteen of the traditional
sixteen *saṃskāras* centre upon the family, and the main ones now
focus on birth, initiation, marriage and death; they can go for

[47] *Kāsī Khaṇḍa* Gurumandala Granthamālāyā No. XX, Vol. IV, Calcutta,
1961, 35. 7–10. See Diana L. Eck, *Banaras City of Light*, London: Routledge &
Kegan Paul, 1983.
[48] Diana L. Eck, *Darśan: Seeing the Divine Image in India*, Chambersburg,
Penn: Anima Publications, 1981.

darshan at times of local festival through the medium of the enacted story of Rāma at Ram Lila, through the beauty of lights at Diwali, through the riotous joy of Holi, through demonstrations of the power of the Goddess at Durga Puja, through celebrating the birthday of a Lord such as Krishna at Janamashtami, through the remembrance of Shiva at Shivaratri, through the brightness and colour of a simple fair to a local god. Hindus can 'see the divine' in a myriad of ways through various aspects of nature, through family life and worship, through the devotional sect they may belong to. Traditionally the Hindu ability to see the divine and the Hindu way of seeing the divine has been structured by their stage of life (as a student, as a householder, as a retired person); by their place within the caste system; by the sacred texts revered in their home or locality; by the concerns of their particular sect if they have one; and by their sense of whether they are due to continue in the round of rebirths or whether final release from the round of rebirths is nigh. In the latter case, more attention may be paid to 'seeing the divine' within as invisible, without qualities (*nirguṇa*), in addition to or instead of 'seeing the divine' in the external world, with qualities (*saguna*).

Thus today's world inherited a Hindu tradition that was already a kaleidoscope of local traditions seeking to become part of the Great Tradition (to use Redfield's phrase),[49] seeking to adapt or reform the part of the wider tradition they knew, or seeking to remain the same yet being changed willy-nilly by circumstances beyond their ken or control. It inherited a series of movements and sects (*sampradāyas*), realised gurus, itinerant *sādhus*, monasteries and family traditions; it inherited a series of rituals centred on family sacraments or worship, centred on temple worship, centred upon festivals and pilgrimages; it

[49] See Robert Redfield, *The Primitive World and its Transformations*, Ithaca: Cornell University Press, 1953.

inherited a system of situational ethics (*dharma*) that outlined for Hindus their place in the wider universe, their place in the social structure, and the duty that lay before them; it inherited a system of strong social involvement through the ramifications of the caste system but weak political involvement in the wider nation; it inherited a plethora of sacred texts focused in theory on the Veda yet incorporating in practice a bewildering variety of other 'scriptures'; it inherited a pattern of concepts that did not have the force of beliefs (for Brahman is beyond beliefs) but which, insofar as the philosophical systems that referred to them were termed '*darshanas*', could themselves be ways of seeing the divine; it inherited a plethora of aesthetic images: ornate temples, classical dances, musical *rāgas*, intricate sculptures, stylised paintings, popular literature—a veritable visual theology; it inherited a diverse spirituality adapted to varied psychological and temperamental modes such as ritual and social action (*karma*), metaphysical knowledge (*jñāna*), devotional feeling (*bhakti*—whereby the divine could be worshipped as Lord, Master, Friend, Child, or Lover), and above all inward realisation.[50]

7(c) **Hindu Secularisation and Modernisation**

We have analysed in this chapter some of the more striking developments within the Hindu tradition since 1945 whereby the traditional pattern, already changing, further modernised itself or perhaps we should say further 'traditionalised' itself.[51] For it is important to state that the Hindu tradition does not easily fit into two of the more familiar anthropological models of modernisation: the notion of westernisation according to

[50] In this brief analysis I have used my own model of a Religious Tradition as containing the eight elements of religious community, ritual, ethics, social involvement, scripture/myth, concepts, aesthetics, and spirituality.

[51] Milton Singer, *When a Great Tradition Modernises*, London: Pall Mall Press, 1972.

which there is an inherent conflict between Hindu traditionalism and western secularisation whereby victory must go to one of these forces (by implication westernisation), and the notion of social evolution according to which the Hindu tradition, by means of internal changes, will attain the 'modern rung' of a universally similar ladder of social evolution. If the Hindu tradition is affected by secularisation, secularisation is also affected by the Hindu tradition so that it becomes Hindu secularisation rather than westernisation; if internal changes within the Hindu tradition are moving it along a ladder of social evolution, it is a Hindu rather that a universal ladder of social evolution. In short, the Hindu adaptation to change and innovation since 1945 is a continuation, in slightly more dramatic terms, of the Hindu adaptation to change and innovation over the last two thousand five hundred years.

In 1961 K. M. Panikkar said:

> The basic fact in respect of Indian History is the continuity of the Hindu people since the time of their first integration. The continuity is one of the marvels of history. Excepting China and to some extent Persia, in no country has a people had so unbroken an existence, an existence which gives to their history in social, religious, political and artistic spheres a unity which is truly remarkable. In each of these spheres Hindu life remains today a development and continuation of what it was when the Hindus were first integrated into a people.[52]

Allowing for a certain poetic exaggeration of the unity of the Hindu tradition which must be balanced by a stress upon the diversity which Hindus themselves have admired within their history, this statement is even more true today in the light of the disruption caused to China and Iran by the Cultural Revolution and the Khomeini Revolution. The ability of the Hindu

[52] K. M. Panikkar, *The Determining Periods of Indian History*, Bombay: Bharatiya Vidya Bhavan, 1962, p. 3.

tradition creatively to adapt since 1945 to changing circumstances has been assisted by her own long history of assimilation whereby her own Great (and mainly Sanskrit) Tradition has grown and spread and transmuted by internal adjustment, and by the willingness of some Hindus (mainly but not only the neo-Hindus) to 'pass-over' into key facets of the western experience introduced willy-nilly by the British Raj and to return again with the fruits of their experience to renew the Hindu tradition by enabling it to assimilate the 'foreign' elements into the ongoing story.[53] We will close by analysing one of two more examples of the creative adjustment and assimilation which constitutes the Hindu tradition in her new situation in independent India.

7(c)(i) Incorporation of Tribal Elements

In the first place, the tribal element within Indian life is receiving more attention recently, partly for political and partly for cultural reasons. Surajit Sinha claims that tribal cultures are a 'relatively untransformed section of the original primitive culture, arrested in its development mainly as a result of ecological factors of isolation and also perhaps because of some unknown series of historical accidents.'[54] Whether this is historically accurate or not, it is the case that in some areas there are attempts to bring tribal cultures and religions into the obit of the Hindu tradition at the present time. Tribal cultures are in flux throughout the world and it is natural that they should safeguard and develop their riches by assimilation into a Great Tradition whether it be an African Independent Church or the

[53] The classical study of 'passing-over' is John S. Dunne, *The Way of all the Earth*, Notre Dame: University of Notre Dame Press, 1978.

[54] Surajit Sinha, 'Tribal Cultures of Peninsular India as a Dimension of the Little Tradition: A Preliminary Statement' in M. Singer (Ed.), *Traditional India: Structure and Change*, Philadelphia: American Folklore Society, 1958, p. 300.

Hindu tradition. It is likely that this assimilation of Indian tribal religion into Hinduism will increase.

7(c)(ii) Influence of Mass Media

In the second place, there is the interesting question concerning the effect of the mass media on popular Hinduism. Radio, television, film and popular literature are becoming increasingly ubiquitous in towns and villages around India. On the one hand they educate about the Great Tradition in far-flung areas—it is the same mass-produced pictures of the well-known gods and goddesses that are present on walls throughout the land. On the other hand they can also promote spontaneous innovation within the Hindu tradition as is evidenced by the growing popularity around North India of the cult of a new goddess, Santoshi Ma, attractive especially to women, which derived originally from a film.

7(c)(iii) Sociological Variations

In the third place, there is evidence to show that although there is interaction between the Hindu tradition in villages and urban areas there are also differences between them. In both villages and cities there are inter-linking networks deriving from trade, local government, marriage, pilgrimage, festivals, and the work of priests, monks or travelling *sādhus*. Through these networks the more universal forms of the Hindu tradition are transmitted to local groups, and local religious elements are assimilated into the wider tradition. However in larger towns and cities the networks are more complex, the speed of adjustment is faster, and the impact of western elements is more pronounced. To this extent, village Hinduism is more conservative and urban Hinduism more innovatory although the difference is in degree rather than in kind.[55]

[55] See also D. E. Smith, *Religion, Politics and Social Change in the Third World*, New York: The Free Press, 1971; D. B. Forrester, *Caste and*

7(c)(iv) Modernising Progressions

In the fourth place, the more obvious innovations namely those from abroad tend to come through individuals and families of upper-caste status within the cities, as well as through reforming religious leaders. They have a secure status, they are more likely to go abroad or be in touch with new ideas, as an upper-caste élite they can both innovate and conserve at the same time. Milton Singer has described a common series of progressions whereby new elements move from the status of being rank innovations to being accepted as part of the tradition.[56] In this way contemporary ideas, artefacts, life-styles, religious views derived from abroad are traditionalised and creatively incorporated into ongoing Hinduism.

7(c)(v) Some Problems with Modernisation

In the fifth place, although the positive note sounded in this chapter has substantial foundation, there are hesitations of confidence in some strata of the contemporary Hindu tradition. For example, the number of Hindu leaders adept in the oral traditions is declining rapidly relative to the rapid growth in population, the morale of priests such as those in the Mīnākṣī temple at Madurai is not high, the Sanskrit language is less revered in the modern setting, some of the sacraments (saṃskāras) are less observed than of yore, and the civil law questioning of the caste system causes uneasiness in some

Christianity, London: Curzon Press, 1979; S. D. Pillai, (Ed.), Aspects of Changing Indian, Bombay: Popular Prakashan, 1976; Bardwell L. Smith (Ed.), Hinduism: New Essays in the History of Religions, Leiden: E. J. Brill, 1976; Y. Singh, Modernisation of Indian Tradition, New Delhi: Oriental Press, 1973; M. N. Srinivas, S. Seshaiah, V. S. Parthasarathy (Eds), Dimensions of Social Change in India, Bombay: Allied Publishers, 1977; T. S. Epstein, South India Yesterday Today and Tomorrow, London: Macmillan, 1973.

[56] M. Singer, When a Great Tradition Modernises, London: Pall Mall Press, 1972, Part Four 'Modernisation and Traditionalisation' and Part Five 'Beyond Tradition and Modernity' pp. 245–412.

quarters. At the intellectual level, contemporary genetic concepts, sub-atomic theories, astronomical discoveries and evolutionary models pose probing questions to elements within the Hindu world-view such as rebirth, traditional cosmology and cyclical views of history.[57] The problems are not necessarily insuperable, and elsewhere neo-Hindu thinkers and others have suggested ways forward in relation to these problems, but if their potential solutions are not available to the individuals and groups in need at the right time the mental unease is not dispelled.

7(c)(vi) Creative Tensions

Finally, as we have seen throughout this chapter, there are creative tensions within the contemporary Hindu tradition. The coming of independence, the advent of a secular state, the creation of the world's largest democracy, the setting up of an atomic reactor, the rapid growth in population, the proportionate growth of the Hindu segment within India with the siphoning off of Muslims into Pakistan, the appearance of a technologically-minded Prime Minister, the emergence of a global world would have taxed any religious tradition. Hindu secularists, Hindu communalists, the lukewarm Hindu advocates of a secular state, and the neo-Hindus have offered varying insights into how to deal with religious pluralism, how to reform archaic Hindu practice, how to handle the caste system, how to modernise the Hindu tradition, how to live in a global world. The neo-Hindus have innovated in different directions ranging from Bhave's Hindu socialism through Radhakrishnan's intellectual modernism to Aurobindo's integral yoga. Hindus have left India and found that ecumenical

---

[57] D. L. Gosling, *Science and Religion in India*, Madras: Christian Literature Society, 1976 analyses some of this discussion albeit the issues have shifted somewhat in the last ten years.

Hinduism and world Hinduism in Europe, America, Africa and further Asia have to cope with different environments and face different questions from those posed to Hindus in India. The many Hindu movements working outside as well as inside India, of which we looked at the Swaminarayans, the Hare Krishnas, the Sathya Sai Babas, the Raja-Yogas and Transcendental Meditation, have had to take cognisance of the wider perspective, as have Hindu ecumenical movements which have tried to unite Hindus on a global basis. Such is the variety, adaptability and assimilative power of the Hindu tradition that the Lord Jagannātha of Puri still 'majestically stands there on His throne graciously smiling down to his devotees: stands as a unique symbol of the great flexibility and dynamics of Hinduism, of its capacity to absorb, integrate and remodel.'[58]

[58] See n. 1.

6

THE JAPANESE RELIGIOUS TRADITIONS IN TODAY'S WORLD

Brian Bocking

(Stirling)

1. Introduction

Any assessment of the religious situation in postwar Japan has to take into account the radical changes in Japanese religious life wrought by the military defeat in 1945 and the subsequent occupation of Japan by the Allied powers until 1951.

Just as the political and economic complexion of Japan today would have been inconceivable to the Japanese of the 1940s, so the present religious situation in Japan bears little apparent relationship to that prior to 1945. Until almost the moment of surrender, the Japanese had expected to win the armed conflict and take up their destined role as 'elder brother' of the South-East Asian nations, usurping the tyranny of the European colonial powers. Japan had never been defeated, much less successfully invaded, in all her long history, and she never would be. The proud traditions of Japan and the unique Japanese 'spirit', it was widely believed, could overcome overwhelming obstacles and enemies. Defeat in 1945 shattered these cherished assumptions. The Imperial line, presumed unbroken since its inception in the age of the gods may have remained intact (though the emperor was obliged to discount his own divinity), but the rest of the Shinto-based ideological edifice which had sustained the belief of the Japanese people in their own unique imperial destiny since the late nineteenth century, under the system of *saisei ichi* (unity of religion and state) was shown to be, if not an illusion, at least based on a deception. Military defeat was thus compounded by psychological and spiritual disorientation, soon to be followed by political and social changes unprecedented in Japan.

Under the sweeping legislative and constitutional reforms of the Allied occupation, the thoroughgoing suppression of religious dissent and religious innovation that had characterised pre-war Japanese religious life gave way overnight to freedom of religion. By a stroke of legislation, compulsory adherence to centralised, state-controlled Shinto was replaced by genuine religious pluralism. Moreover, a written constitutional guarantee of the separation of religion and state gave equal rights to all *bona fide* religious bodies. One result was that a large number of so-called 'New Religions' appeared as if from nowhere. Some faded away almost as suddenly as they had arisen. Others grew spectacularly over the next twenty or thirty years, and now form some of the largest and most active religious groups to be found anywhere in the world. Not only did new religions arise, but older lay religious groups such as Tenrikyō and Konkōkyō, which had been 'New Religions' when Japan was still closed to the world in the mid-nineteenth century, simultaneously distanced themselves from their wartime role as quasi-Shinto sects and took on a new independent religious identity. Today, forty years after the end of the war and in marked contrast to their patriotic and militaristic stance in the 1930s and 40s, Japanese religions overwhelmingly proclaim world peace and human co-operation as their goal, and strive to attain a global rather than a narrowly national perspective on human affairs. The transformation of Japanese religion since 1945 seems, in fact, to be complete.

Looked at another way, however, Japanese religion seems hardly to have changed at all. Many of the New Religions were actually founded before the war. The teachings and practices they propound today date from the 1920s or 30s, and only the exigencies of the prewar political situation prevented them from flourishing then as they do now. Shinto, which has had a long history and a variety of forms in Japan, was disestablished after the war and separated from the state, but Shinto had only recently *been* established—in the wake of the Meiji restoration in 1868. Its transformation into centralised, articulate and patriotic 'State Shinto' lasted less than sixty years of its two thousand year history. Mainstream Buddhism, the traditional sectarian temple-based form which had earned the soubriquet of 'funeral Buddhism' because it survived mainly by providing funeral and memorial services, had been disestablished to make way for State Shinto, and was hardly touched by the national disaster of 1945; it was still recovering from its own displacement by Shinto at the time of the Meiji restoration. Folk religion was widespread in Japan before the war, and is still today, in various forms. And as far as Christianity is concerned, there were proportionately more Christians in Japan in the sixteenth century than there were in the prewar period, or are today. How then can it be said that religion has been transformed in Japan?

There is a Zen saying: 'things are not what they seem, nor are they otherwise'. It is quite obvious that Japanese society and Japanese religion today are very different from what they were forty years ago, but the nature and depth of the changes which have taken place are often called into question. In the postwar period the Japanese have been deeply interested in the degree of continuity and change in their own society, and have instituted numerous surveys of national characteristics and values, in order to determine the direction of change. After a period of drifting away from tradition, in recent years (1973 seems to have been the turning point) the trend seems to have turned back towards 'traditional' values, including a reawakening of interest in religious observances such as ancestor worship. Yet at the same time Japan seems on the surface to be daily becoming more and more 'Westernised'. Is the apparent reversion to tradition merely a rearguard action as some assert, a last attempt to defend the 'Japanese way' in face of the inexorable advance of Western values? Or are we witnessing today a renascence of deeply-rooted beliefs and values, values which were simply suppressed by the occupation's *force majeure*? To analyse the religious situation in Japan today is not a straightforward matter, for Japan has in the postwar period provided many surprises for those who expected to see a traditional society change, in predictable ways, into a likeness of a modern Western nation. Where Japan is concerned, good Western theories often founder. This is not because Japan is somehow special or unique, except in the sense that all nations and cultures are unique, but because Japan is a modern and a successful major international power whose modernity and success has different roots, and draws upon different traditions, including religious traditions, from those with which we are familiar in the West.

2. *Japanese religion before 1945*

From 1931 to 1945 Japan was continuously at war, first with China and subsequently with the Allied powers. Both before and during this period, religion in Japan was dominated by what has now come to be called 'State Shinto' (*kokka shintō*). The process which gave rise to State Shinto began in the nineteenth century, for when the Shogunate fell and Imperial rule was restored in 1868, Shinto and Buddhism were declared officially separate, and from a position of relative insignificance in the Tokugawa or Edo period (1600–1868) Shinto was systematically developed and centralised under government sponsorship to become, in the prewar decades, an effective vehicle for nationalistic and militaristic government propaganda, channelling devotion to the native *kami* into zealous patriotic support for the mystically-conceived 'body of the state' (*kokutai*), at whose head stood the emperor, blood-descendant of the sun-goddess Amaterasu.

Official Shinto doctrine, taught in the classroom and summarised in brief ethical edicts such as the 'Imperial prescript on Education' and the longer treatise 'Cardinal Principles of the National Entity' stressed as sacred values loyalty and patriotism, vigorous and selfless service to the state, and obedience to authority. Religious ideas critical of State Shinto (particularly Christian ideas and some of the outspoken teachings of those New Religions which emerged before the war) were effectively suppressed, and virtually all religious groups in the pre-war period adopted either a neutral ethical stance or, in order to survive and even prosper, took on a State Shinto hue, emphasising devotion to the emperor and the virtues of loyalty and patriotism. Ironically, 'religious freedom' had been theoretically assured in Japan from the Meiji period onwards, but Shinto, alone among the Japanese traditions, was officially designated 'non-religious'. Paying reverence at a Shinto Shrine and adhering to State Shinto ideology, it was officially taught, was no more than the civic and patriotic responsibility of every Japanese citizen, but as such it took absolute precedence over personal preferences such as belief in particular religions. Any religion, such as Buddhism or Christianity, could be followed—so long as it did not interfere with the civic duty of adherence to State Shinto.

Such opposition as there was to this official ideology was diluted not only by the traditionally submissive attitude to authority engendered by Confucian training (which emphasises adapting and cultivating oneself to fulfil a predetermined role) but by two other rational considerations as well. Firstly, Japan was pursuing a policy of rapid modernisation and industrialisation in a bid first to catch up with and then to overtake the Western powers, and her policymakers believed (as they still do in most cases) that this could only succeed if the populace was united in a sense of national purpose. Secondly, Japanese culture and Japanese values were, in truth, under considerable threat from the West, and State Shinto was, at least initially, a deliberate response to this threat. After two and a half centuries of being a 'closed country' (*sakoku*), Japan had swung wildly towards the adoption of Western technology, political institutions and cultural ideals—including religious and social ideals—which for a time in the late nineteenth century threatened to submerge whatever was distinctive of the Japanese heritage. The deliberate cultivation of a national ethos under the aegis of a specifically 'Japanese' religious tradition—Shinto— was born of Japan's intent to take its place in the modern world on its own terms, not merely as a pale imitation of a Western state.

As part of the government's policy of thought control, it was determined that all religions, regardless of their sectarian differences, should come under the control of broad 'umbrella' groups (for example, Protestant Christian or Nichiren Buddhist). A few religious leaders took a stand against either the general direction of government policy or the specific restrictions on religion in the prewar period. The leaders of the nascent and exclusivist Soka Gakkai, a lay movement attached to a small Nichirenite Buddhist sect for example objected on essentially theological grounds to the government's lumping-together of different sects. In the outspoken tradition of Nichiren himself they declared that only true Buddhism (which to them meant the Nichiren Shōshū sect, not the other Nichirenite groups) could protect the Japanese empire, but they were arrested and the founder of Soka Gakkai died in prison during the war.

Other religious figures were prosecuted for crimes such as not paying due respect to the emperor, and many followers left the younger religious movements to avoid trouble with the authorities. Most religions however went along with the prevailing mood of patriotic nationalism. Among the Christian churches for example, the Protestant denominations, which had strong individual links with disparate mother churches abroad, sent many of their long-resident foreign missionaries home to avoid difficulties, and the various churches were then forced into a Protestant coalition, which survives in the new postwar age of Christian ecumenism with strongly ambivalent feelings about its unwilling origins, as the Nihon Kirisutokyō Kyōdan, the United Church of Christ in Japan.

Prior to 1945, therefore, religious freedom existed in name only in Japan. Despite the ever-existing potential for growth of new or diverse religious movements in Japan, religious life was in practice extremely restricted. Many Japanese people may have resented this restriction of religious expression, but traditional patterns of thought inhibited protest, encouraging those who chafed under restrictions on freedom of religion to reform their own thinking rather than attempting to reform the system to suit their own 'selfish' desires. In conformity with much traditional Japanese religious thought derived from Confucianism, State Shinto provided no support for the idea of individual conscience as distinct from social duty. Indeed 'individualism' was (and to a remarkable extent is still today) regarded as the very antithesis of religious virtue in Japan. To canvass one's individual views regardless of majority or senior opinion is generally thought to be evidence of weakness and selfishness. But State Shinto did not merely take away religious choice and religious freedom. It provided in their place a powerful and appealing alternative avenue for religious self-sublimation which emphasised traditional religious ideas, such as the need for repayment of infinite obligation to ancestors, superiors and, by extension, the emperor. State Shinto redirected religious action away from the gods and towards the state, via the figure of the divine emperor. Rather than attempting to alter the fundamental structure of religion, or to introduce totally new religious attitudes, State Shinto merely organised, centralised and most importantly shifted the focus of, religious devotion in Japan.

3. Japanese religion since 1945

3.1 Freedom of Religion

Japan's defeat in 1945 was followed by radical changes in the religious sphere. In the aftermath of the surrender the emperor was obliged, to all intents and purposes, to renounce his divinity. State Shinto was disestablished, and the Allied occupation of Japan which lasted from 1945 to 1951 ushered in a period of genuine individual religious freedom which has survived until the present day.

With the proclamation of religious freedom, numerous religious cults sprang up almost overnight, and at the same time older minority religions and pre-war 'new' religions whose activities had been curtailed by restrictions under State Shinto experienced a dramatic renascence, shedding their adopted Shintoist character and attracting thousands of new followers with promises of healing, prosperity and happiness.

The reforms of the occupation administration (Supreme Command Allied Powers—SCAP) provided for a written constitutional separation of religion and state, based on the United States (as opposed to, for example, the English) model. The intention of SCAP was clearly to avoid a recurrence of Shinto-inspired militarism and imperialism. The new constitution, which also relinquished Japan's right to use military force, reflected a widespread Allied distrust of official Japanese religion, which was perceived as incapable of adopting an ethical or ideological stance independent of dominant political currents. This distrust was understandable not only on account of the prewar experience but also in view of the close association, even identification of interests between institutional religion, whether Buddhism, Confucianism or most recently Shinto, and the Japanese state throughout Japan's history.

However, the imposition of the American-style constitutional pattern on a traditional society such as Japan's, in which religious and political values were traditionally undifferentiated, inevitably created tensions, increasingly apparent at the present time. Those who deplore 'Americanisation' which is often identified with materialism in Japan, and who advocate a return to traditional values, can and do point to other models of church-state relations in modern industrial powers. Meanwhile, influential Western scholars such as Robert Bellah have called for a revaluation of traditional religion as a remedy for the rootlessness of contemporary urban societies. The issue of the relation between church and state in Japan cannot therefore be considered as solved by the provisions of the SCAP constitution. For a number of reasons, chief among them Japan's territorial economic growth, the absence of any real threat to Japanese territorial security over the last forty years and the phenomenon of a remarkably stable society, the constitution has only been implemented, and not tested under stress, since 1945. While things go well for Japan, religious freedom is assured. Nobody however knows what the future will bring.

3.2 The Role of Religion in Modern Japan

Compared with most industrially developed modern urban societies, Japanese society today appears remarkably stable and homogeneous. The reality of Japanese life is somewhat different from the image of a smooth-functioning, consensual society, striving always for *wa* or harmony, that is often presented for outside consumption, but nevertheless postwar Japan is unusual for its ability to preserve many of the forms of traditional Japanese society on the one hand, and yet be flexible and ready to adapt to changing circumstances on the other.

That the Japanese can and do view themselves as a single and homogeneous people is perhaps testimony to the enduring power of the *kokutai* or 'body of the state' concept promulgated from the Meiji period up to 1945. In the postwar period, advanced communications and national radio and television networks, while no doubt presenting powerful alternatives to the Japanese way of life through a diet of foreign media offerings, have at the same time helped to underline the strong sense of belonging to a single unified social grouping—'we Japanese'—which characterises modern Japanese national consciousness. Japan has a single language, a high degree of social cohesion and shared cultural values and a low crime rate, which is not just a low reported crime rate, but actually reflects a sense of personal safety even in the densely populated inner cities which is probably unique in the world. Japan has also enjoyed political stability since the war and a marked uniformity of life-style. Japanese society, though thoroughly and minutely hierarchical, perceives itself to be essentially classless. There are minority and marginal groups in Japanese society; the traditional 'outcaste' groups found in most large Japanese cities are hardly assimilated and experience discrimination in jobs, educational opportunity and housing, and the Korean minority composed largely of descendants of Korean forced labourers brought to Japan in the prewar period are still insultingly treated as temporary foreign residents, forming as they do the bulk of the annual statistics on 'foreigners in Japan', but for the vast majority of Japanese these are problems neither encountered nor discussed in daily life. They are certainly not the problems addressed by either the traditional mainstream or new religions, which are overwhelmingly concerned with the day-to-day problems of the typical Japanese family. These problems may be loosely categorised as family problems, and problems of self-identity.

Life in Japan may be safe, but it is never easy. There is

183

tremendous pressure to conform, to be 'reliable', to succeed in one's assigned role in life and to fulfil obligations to others. In the postwar period the rapid growth of the industrial economy has produced many new problems. The sense of one's 'place' so important in traditional Japanese society is lost when traditional rural extended families are dislocated and fragmented by urbanisation, as so many have been since the war. The education system, reformed after 1945, has now become so competitive that schoolchildren regularly commit suicide, and classroom bullying of those who are in any way different, or who are thought to be holding the rest of the class back, has become a major social problem. Japanese men are under intense pressure from an early age first to succeed in the education race and then to make and maintain close personal and professional contacts in order to get a good secure job—any good secure job—whence flow the blessings of an economically sound future in Japan's highly competitive society. Many jobs in Japan are jobs for life in paternalistic companies, so that a lifetime of suppressing one's own preferences in order to get on with people one does not necessarily like in a job one does not enjoy is an inevitable discipline, with its own psychic costs and also benefits. Married women increasingly have a dual responsibility as mother and second breadwinner, and divorce is on the increase. The costs of health and education, retirement and the expenses of marrying off children are all heavy burdens carried by the family rather than the state. All in all, it is a major achievement if one is able to live a 'normal' life in Japan, with a happy family, a secure job, good prospects and reasonable health. The problems of what to do with one's life or how to deal with existential *ennui*, are not major concerns. Japanese religion reflects the reality of Japanese life. Religious practices are almost always pragmatic in orientation, and religions offer immediate benefits whether in terms of an improved mental attitude or an even more tangible blessing such as the cure of illness. A religion which, however 'true', does not offer such worldly benefits, it is said, is worse than no religion at all.

3.3 Secularisation in Japan

The concept of secularisation, arising as it did in the context of Western thought about religion and modernisation, runs into difficulties in Japan. The indices of secularisation include quantifiable churchgoing (not applicable to Japan, where temple visits are sporadic and often indistinguishable from sightseeing), religious beliefs (articulation of beliefs is a relatively insignificant aspect of religion in Japan) and the role which religion plays in political and social affairs (measurable only where religion is readily identifiable, whereas in Japan religion is often of the implicit kind recently discovered in the West). According to a recent Japanese survey of various indices of religious vitality (including possession of a *butsudan* (Buddhist ancestral home altar) and the consumption of Christmas cakes) it seems that religion, after declining somewhat is the 1960s, has been gradually increasing in Japan since 1973. This suggests that 'modernisation', does not entail secularisation in Japan. This perception has had the effect of making scholars rethink the secularisation theory in relation to the West as well.

Whether or not we can speak of secularisation in Japan, the question arises of religion's present role or position in Japanese society. At first glance Japan appears—as many outside observers believe it to be—a highly religious society. However, the ubiquity of temples and shrines is evidence only of a strong belief in the need for periodic ritual observances—in the case of Buddhist temples, for the periodic observance of ancestor worship. Religious beliefs and religious teachings are unlikely in Japan to exert a direct and measurable influence on all areas of an individual's life. More often, compartmentalisation of religious beliefs is the rule, such that when religiously-inspired belief and behaviour is appropriate it is performed, but when secular behaviour (or perhaps even behaviour required by another religion) is appropriate, the first religion plays no role. This compartmentalisation is itself however evidence of the contemporary influence in Japan of a religious tradition, that of Confucianism, with its emphasis on different standards of moral behaviour in different social contexts.

The Japanese ability to compartmentalise secular and religious beliefs finds parallels of course in other societies than Japan and in other religious contexts and is itself central to the idea of secularisation and the marginalising of religion. However in Japan compartmentalisation seems always to have been the rule rather than the exception, due to the influence of an overarching Confucian value-system that requires of the individual the moral virtue of being infinitely flexible in the execution of a variety of roles and behaviours in relation to other social actors. As a result, Japanese religiosity appears often to outsiders to be merely 'acted' religiosity, a religiosity picked up and discarded along with other roles and requirements as occasion demands. But on closer analysis it becomes clear that Japanese society is constructed in such a way that a person who is consistently guided by fixed religious ideas relating to specific behaviour patterns (never drinking, or never lying, for example) will incur the charge of selfishness and excessive individualism. The 'honest judge' who starved in postwar Tokyo rather than break the law by buying food on the black market is regarded as a curiosity rather than a moral exemplar in Japan. In a Confucian society it is not merely necessary but actively virtuous to play the game and adapt to the immediate situation.

3.4 Religion and economic growth

One of the most noticeable developments in postwar Japan has been the phenomenal growth of the Japanese economy. The existence of a Japanese work-ethic derived from the samurai ethic was analysed by Robert Bellah in *Tokugawa Religion* and the question may be posed, whether religion in Japan has anything to do with the postwar 'economic miracle'. Although a great deal of money is spent on religion in Japan today, religion and the economy are not obviously related, though as noted below many companies large and small have corporate affiliation to a Shinto shrine and regard a particular Shinto deity as their protective *kami*. There may also be some significance in the fact that Japanese companies regularly send their new employees for a short period of Zen training, to teach them single-mindedness. One aspect of the Japanese economy which is at least quasi-religious and seems to have contributed considerably to Japanese economic success over the last forty years however has been the role of the situational, Confucian-derived morality referred to above. Japanese ethical standards being essentially interpersonal and contextual rather than abstract and universal, Japanese behaviour often appears inconsistent and 'unprincipled' by the standards of universalist religious ethics found in the West, but Japanese morality is founded on sound Confucian principles of reciprocity and filial piety (often taking the form of loyalty to a superior). In the case of Japanese firms, the structure is frequently that of a (relatively) benevolent paternalism, and worker-management relations involve correspondingly less confrontation. Japanese ethics even today are informed by aspects of the strict Samurai ethic developed in the Tokugawa period (1600–1868) and generalised via state Shinto through the Japanese education system after the Meiji restoration. Though Confucian ethics are no longer taught in schools, important elements such as respect for elders and loyalty to one's social group are transmitted within the family (anyone over thirty in Japan either grew up in or was brought up by parents who grew up in, the 'old' education system) and in schools, through an emphasis on uniformity and group activities. An aspect of the Japanese world-view which 'mainstream' tradition(s) of Buddhism and Shinto, and the ethico-religious inheritance of Confucianism, the spectrum of Japanese religions during the last century includes also Christianity in various different forms, and a large number of so-called 'New Religions' (some in fact very old, some genuinely new, many of them ecumenical, a few fiercely exclusivist, some indigenous, others imported from overseas). Also influential in Japan are a range of Western secular ideologies such as Marxism and scientific materialism, and a rich diversity of traditional and neo-traditional folk-religious beliefs and practices. Many Japanese participate in several of these traditions either simultaneously (for example at a wedding, which may well contain Shinto and Christian elements) or by 'compartmentalising' different religious activities (for example belonging in a personal or family capacity to a Buddhist-derived New Religion but participating in corporate Shinto rites in one's role as a company employee). This kind of compartmentalisation is necessary in many areas of Japanese life since appropriate behaviour in Japan is generally understood to depend on the requirements of the particular social context, rather than on the consistent exercise of individual conscience or choice. The Japanese are trained from an early age to act wholeheartedly according to the demands of a particular context, and there is no evidence to suggest that this kind of compartmentalisation when applied to religious life causes undue psychic conflict, although certain combinations of religious ideas or practices are impossible, or extremely difficult, to combine in one person. An example would be ancestral rites and belief in Christianity. Belonging to the exclusivist Buddhist movement Soka Gakkai also precludes certain other religious observances, particularly taking part in Shinto and non-Soka Gakkai Buddhist rites. However, such incompatibilities, though significant, are recognised to be the exception rather than the rule to the inherent eclecticism of Japanese religion.

In the first two decades of the twentieth century the crystallising of State Shinto ideology had been accompanied by a government-inspired programme of centralising and merging local village or community shrines into larger shrines located in main centres. Villagers were henceforth expected to go to worship at the main or 'merged' shrine and to refrain from local rites. The purpose of merging the shrines was to inculcate in the predominantly rural populace the idea of Shinto shrines as points of entry into the quasi-mystical religio-political system centring on the figure of the emperor as the source of all legitimate power, the parent-ruler of the whole country.

A number of shrines which were officially 'merged' in the early 1900s have gradually reverted to their original locations in the postwar period, a move which underlines the importance of local and regional loyalties in relation to community shrines. The geographical distribution of shrines now is perhaps more like that of 1905 (before shrine mergers) than of 1945. This reversion to the pre-shrine merger situation is seen by some as evidence that Shinto is not essentially political or nationalistic but was only temporarily made so. On the other hand critics point to the fact that Shinto lacks any intellectual or spiritual resources with which it can resist politicisation, and also to its perennial association with the most conservative and patriotic currents of Japanese thought.

Predictably in the aftermath of the war newly-disestablished Shinto faced a crisis, both materially (since state support was summarily withdrawn) and theologically (since the religio-political claims of State Shinto were discredited by military defeat). Its response was virtually to abandon prewar doctrine and concentrate on traditional local shrine rituals and ceremonies, virtually devoid of theological implications. (One of the reasons for finding the term 'Shinto' difficult to define in the postwar period is that Shinto is different from what it was before the war, when its doctrinal standpoint was perfectly clear, and different again from what it was in the Tokugawa period (1600–1868) and earlier, when its doctrines were largely those of Confucianism or even Buddhism dressed up in the garb and vocabulary of Shinto).

Shrines in Japan traditionally drew their support from the local people, whom the enshrined *kami* is (or are) believed to protect. A Shinto shrine (*jinja* or *jingu*), which is usually the property of the priest's family, is a focus for individual acts of piety or petitionary prayer directed towards the *kami* and the venue also for seasonal festivals (*matsuri*). Shinto festivals are extremely diverse in character; they range from events which have the atmosphere of something like a school sports day, to highly theatrical masked dances and processions, and numinous ceremonies carried out at dead of night and attended only by a purified few. Quite commonly however a local festival contains a mixture of different elements, representing the ritual summoning, entertainment and sending-off to the spirit world of the *kami*, with perhaps a contest of strength included which may take the form of rival teams fighting for possession of a talisman or jostling with *mikoshi*, portable floats enshrining the *kami*. Shrines also sell a variety of amulets and religious memorabilia, and Shinto priests officiate at weddings, and perform rites of purification, for example at the beginning of construction of almost every new building in Japan, including government buildings.

Any real or apparent official sponsorship of Shinto is potentially controversial in Japan, and successful law suits brought by pressure-groups opposed to nationalistic Shinto have in recent years forced local government officials who attend such ground-breaking ceremonies to pay back an amount from their salary corresponding to the time taken up by the rites, to make the point that such ceremonies are not in any way official. It is unlikely however that most Japanese people approve of this legalistic approach. A recent test-case of attitudes to Shinto concerned a member of the Self-Defence Forces (the *Jietai*, the Japanese army) who was killed in an accident while on duty. The *Jietai* wanted to enshrine his remains in a Shinto shrine, but his widow objected on personal religious grounds. The public and legal debate that ensued demonstrated that while the constitution and the law may guarantee religious freedom on the basis of the individual's right to choose religious faith, Japanese 'common sense' still sees Shinto as essentially a matter for the community or indeed the nation (in this case represented by the armed forces), rather than the individual.

In the postwar period the upkeep of the many beautiful and ornate Shinto shrine buildings throughout Japan is accomplished with the help of collections in the neighbourhood, offerings made at the shrine, especially at festival times, and donations from businesses. Many Japanese companies ranging from large household-name international corporations to small family firms support local or tutelary Shinto deities, and modern office blocks and company premises frequently feature a miniature Shinto shrine representing a link with a larger local shrine. In the case of shrines of special architectural or historical significance, there is government support for the preservation of important buildings. The Ise Grand Shrine (where the imperial ancestral goddess Amaterasu 'Heaven-Shining' is enshrined) is a primitive-style Shinto shrine building which has to be reconstructed in exactly the same form using the same kind of materials once in each cycle of twenty years. The reconstruction process is expensive and before the war was the responsibility of the State. In the postwar period rebuilding of the shrine has been achieved by public donations but there is constant pressure from Shinto supporters to restore some measure of state support for what is, after all, an important symbolic cultural institution. As in the case of other historically important shrine buildings in Japan, the line between government support received for cultural, architectural or historical reasons and support received for religious reasons is sometimes so finely drawn as to be invisible, especially to opponents of Shinto, who see a renewed *rapprochement* between religion and state in Japan as an ever-present and threatening possibility.

Overall, the activities of Shinto shrines today are controlled by the Association of Shinto Shrines (*Jinja Honcho*) set up after the war which operates training programmes for Shinto priests and is closely associated with the two Shinto universities, in Tokyo and in Ise. About 94 per cent of shrines belong to the *Jinja Honcho*, which speaks collectively for the shrines from a 'Shinto' point of view. Recently the Shinto viewpoint has crystallised around a number of issues, in particular the issues of the relation between religion and the state, and the nature of moral education. The *Jinja Honcho* argues that the disestablishment of Shinto runs contrary to the natural identification of religious and political values in Japan, and can point to the many examples of established churches (and religious education) in other countries. Opponents of this Shinto view range from those who object on principle to any relationship between religion and the state, to those who approve of the idea of a national religion, but do not wish the religion in question to be Shinto. As Japan's international standing has increased, so Shinto has come to be more and more identified as a symbol of right-wing political opinion in Japan. The Shinto shrine to the war-dead in Tokyo—Yasukuni Jinja—constitutes a particularly sensitive barometer of official and public feeling in this regard. The Prime Minister of Japan regularly visits Yasukuni, in which are enshrined spirits of the dead including some convicted of war crimes. Up to 1984 successive premiers either stressed that they visited to pay their respects in the capacity of a private citizen (as many Japanese do), or they remained non-committal about the status of their visit. For the first time in 1985, Prime Minister Yasuhiro Nakasone described his visit to Yasukuni as official. This provocative step has undoubtedly greatly encouraged supporters of Shinto, but it is too early to say whether Nakasone's gesture will have any profound effect. Such official moves, which seem both to legitimise Japan's wartime role and to resurrect state Shinto ideas, provoke angry reactions from the Chinese and from other East Asian countries with memories of the Japanese empire, but they may be no more than tests of the political atmosphere both domestically and in Japan's relations with its East Asian neighbours. It remains to be seen also whether the 'Shinto' view will have any effect on the educational reforms proposed by the present government, which are aimed at reducing the worst pressures of the highly competitive education system and instilling into Japan's youth a sense of civic and perhaps patriotic responsibility.

4.2 Buddhism

While Shinto gradually recovers from its post-war disestablishment, Buddhism has seemed, during the postwar period, to be still wrestling with the problems posed for its future in the immediate aftermath of the Meiji restoration in 1868. As Buddhism fell from favour together with its long-term allies, the Shogunate and the samurai class, many Buddhist priests switched to Shinto overnight in order to survive. As the momentum of the nativist Shinto movement grew in the late nineteenth century to culminate in the Japanese government's adoption of Shinto as the national faith, and simultaneously Western ideas and ideologies crowded into newly-industrialising Japan, Buddhism was assailed from both within and without. After the banishment of Christians in the seventeenth century (one of the main purposes of *sakoku* or 'closure of the country' was to complete the eradication of Christianity), Buddhism was established as the state religion. By the nineteenth century Buddhism had grown introverted and complacent.

It was hardly a match for the vigorous advocacy of Western thought, whether Christian or humanist, which dominated Japanese intellectual and religious debate from the Meiji period onwards. Buddhism could not, despite its best efforts and the efforts of some outstanding individual Buddhist thinkers and reformers, achieve the status of a 'modern' faith, and it entered the postwar period of religious freedom in a demoralised and weakened state, not least because all the Buddhist leaders had backed the wartime government. This at least partly explains why the vigorous Buddhist movements have been the new lay organisations like Soka Gakkai and Rissho Kosei-kai, somewhat distanced from the ecclesiastical hierarchies. Traditional temple-based Buddhism continues and indeed prospers today however, as some of the wealth generated in Japan's economic advancement over the last forty years flows into traditional Buddhist observances, particularly funeral rites and memorial rites for the ancestors.

One feature of traditional Japanese temple Buddhism which shows no signs of change, so intrinsic is it to the continuing prosperity of the religion in Japan, is the close association between what might be called the 'pure' Buddhism of teaching, sermons, meditation, prayer and devotional rituals on the one hand, and the multitude of folk-religious or superstitious practices associated with Buddhist temples on the other. While the major source of income of Buddhist temples comes from funeral and memorial services, a good deal of income also derives from the range of protective amulets (*o-mamori*), fortune-telling devices (*o-mikuji*), souvenirs and religious paraphernalia on sale at every temple, and offerings made to bodhisattvas for such mundane benefits as easy childbirth, a good marriage, or magical healing. Some Buddhist priests do make the effort to introduce more profound Buddhist teachings to those attracted to temples by a desire for magical benefits, by providing Buddhist counselling or public talks on Buddhist doctrine. Many however, do not. Those priests who are aware of the disparity between the official teachings of their sect's founder (the majority of temples belong to sects founded by the medieval monks Kukai, Saicho, Honen, Shinran, Dogen, Eisai or Nichiren) and what actually goes on at their temple may approve (as most seem to do) or disapprove of the encouragement to superstition their temples provide, but whatever their attitude the priests realise that folk-beliefs only distantly related to the central concerns of 'pure' Buddhism are what keep the temples alive. Closely related to this phenomenon of temples actively encouraging folk-beliefs in Japan is the fact that Buddhist temples are businesses as well as religious institutions. The entrepreneurial spirit so conspicuous in the secular business world in Japan extends also to the temples, where priests have been quick to cash in on the various religious 'booms', such as the cult of *mizuko kuyo*, the recently-popularised practice of performing rites and setting up an extensive *jizo* bodhisattva statue in the temple grounds in order to avert the wrath and pacify the soul of an aborted infant. Such rites clearly create as well as satisfy religious needs, and there is an almost infinite market among people fearful of jeopardising their own luck for new variations on the Buddhist tenet that 'every cause' (e.g. buying a stone statue) 'has an effect' (pacifying the soul of a dead infant). Japanese Buddhism in general, with its largely married clergy and strongly sectarian divisions, appears sometimes to be almost non-Buddhist, when viewed by Buddhists from other countries including Buddhists from the West.

Some more immediately recognisable forms of Buddhism are flourishing in Japan of course, and the Zen sects in particular have been much encouraged by the degree of interest shown by the postwar West in the practice of *zazen* (meditation) and the application of Zen in the various traditional arts and ways of Japan, though most Zen temples in Japan remain indistinguishable from other centres of 'funeral Buddhism'. But of the two most popular forms of Buddhism in Japan today— Jodo Shinshu (True Pure Land, based on the teachings of Shinran) and Lotus (based on the teachings of Nichiren)—Jodo Shinshu involves no meditational practice at all, and Nichiren Buddhists (chief among them the around five million lay followers of Soka Gakkai) regard Nichiren, a pugnacious and outspoken Tendai critic of the Kamakura military government, to be in effect a Japanese Buddha, with the consequence that all previous Buddhas and their teachings are discarded. The central identifiably Buddhist practice of Soka Gakkai is the repetition of the mantra 'Namu Myōhō Renge Kyō' (an invocation of the title of the Lotus Sutra) but the interpretation of what Buddhism means is very much grounded in the day-to-day concerns of Japanese society, with an emphasis on positive mental attitudes and development of a group spirit to overcome life's difficulties. If Soka Gakkai had taught anything else, of course, it would not have been so successful.

It is Buddhism in Japan which has been in the modern era most actively involved in inter-religious dialogue, mostly with Christianity. Many interesting encounters take place between representatives of differet religions in Japan, but the particularly high level of activity in Buddhist–Christian dialogue reflects the position of Buddhist studies within the tertiary sector of Japanese education, where it occupies a place analogous to that of Theology in the Western world. It is estimated that 90 per cent of publications in the international field of Buddhist Studies are written in Japanese, and many Western scholars are attracted to Japanese Buddhist thought, which is highly sophisticated and subtle in the Japanese way, but with a rational core which is much easier to plumb than, for example, Shinto thought, since Buddhist thought is basically Indian (and hence Indo-European) rather than Japanese. Many able exponents of Japanese Buddhist teachings are able to engage with representatives of other religions at a high intellectual level, while at the same time accepting that, in another compartment of life, Japanese Buddhism in its present state is not by any means an international or universal religion, but is fully enmeshed in the particularistic concerns of Japanese society, concerns such as ancestor worship, marriage, health, children, and prosperity.

4.3 The New Religions

The phenomenon of the New Religions of Japan has been widely analysed both by scholars of Japanese religion and from a comparative perspective by those concerned with new religious movements throughout the world. There is general agreement that the term 'New Religions' is somewhat misleading in the case of Japan. The oldest examples of the New Religions (Tenrikyō and Konkōkyō) appeared before Japan opened up to the West, in the early to mid-nineteenth century. Moreover, many of the larger so-called 'postwar' New Religions such as Soka Gakkai and Rissho Kosei Kai were in fact founded in the pre-war period, but could not flourish then because of government restrictions on religious freedom and the vicissitudes of state Shinto. Apart from the question of date of origin of the New Religions, there is also the question of whether the New Religions are really new in terms of their doctrines and practices. Are they 'new' because they are novel, truly original, or just modern? It seems that all three types of 'new'ness may be present and perhaps need to be present for a New Religion to succeed in attracting and maintaining a substantial following.

Looking back over forty years it is possible to see that the New Religions are not the unified phenomenon that they might at first sight appear, and moreover that they have changed even in this brief period, passing through at least three distinct stages of development.

Most of the New Religions which existed in the prewar period entered a weak or dormant state during the war, their survival and size of following depending largely on their degree of conformity to State Shinto during the pre-occupation period. Reiyukai (Spirit Friends' Association) for example began in the 1920s as a lay movement emphasising ancestral rites and a return to 'traditional' values. It adopted State Shinto type teachings and flourished during the prewar and wartime period. On the other hand Rissho Kosei Kai (a group which grew out of Reiyukai) and Soka Gakkai, both fledgling movements in the late 1930s, lost the majority of their followers after running foul of the law. The leaders of Soka Gakkai (which is attached to the 'True' Nichiren sect, Nichiren Shōshū), were imprisoned for resisting amalgamation with the other Nichirenite sects, which they regarded as heretical, and incapable of protecting the nation. Other groups simply disbanded during the darkest days of the war. Bunce gives the following example:

> To illustrate the difficulties encountered by small religious organisations in their struggle for existence, the Hito no Michi (Way of Man) group first appeared as part of Mitake-kyo, later transferred to Fuso-kyo, was suppressed altogether during the war, and in 1947 was revived as the PL Kyodan.

Thus the first stage in the postwar period may be identified as the stage of 'new beginnings' for most of the New Religions. This stage was characterised by rapid growth, often within a fairly limited geographical area, with close personal contact among pioneer members, highly motivated and enjoying freedom to spread their religion unhindered for the first time. In the period of reconstruction of war-torn Japan the New Religions emphasised this-worldly benefits such as prosperity, overcoming of diseases such as tuberculosis, and happiness in family life. The first postwar leader of Soka Gakkai, Josei Toda in this period described the *qohonzon*, the mandala worshipped by members of Soka Gakkai as 'a machine for producing happiness'. Most of the successful New Religions put proselytising high on the agenda of religious activities, to the extent that a member's status in the movement depended largely upon the number of converts acquired. Indeed the main purpose of the religion could often seem to be the spread of the religion itself by enthusiastic new converts. The emphasis on evangelism in the New Religions was partly explained by the desire to bring other people happiness through sharing one's religion, and partly by the Japanese tendency to equate truth with consensus. Religious certainty may quite legitimately in Japan be derived from others' opinions, so that superiority in number of followers is evidence for the superiority in truth of a religious teaching.

The second stage in the development of the New Religions took place in the late 1950s and '60s and may be called the stage of religious mass-movements, when the New Religions were for the first time seen as really significant forces in Japanese society. Soka Gakkai had pushed itself to the fore at this time with a forceful and abrasive conversion campaign, highly successful to the extent that its membership was numbered in millions, but also threatening to other sectors of society, and perhaps also embarrassing to some of the other New Religions with more modest aims. Soka Gakkai sought, and achieved, political power through the centrist political party which it created called Kōmeito, but the combination of mass movement, exclusivist religious ideology and political influence raised the spectre of fascism, the new constitution was invoked, and Soka Gakkai was obliged to break at least its official ties with Kōmeito. Other of the New Religions at this time such as Seichō no Ie (House of Growth) adopted a more conservative political stance, though none so overtly as Soka Gakkai. Some other New Religions have remained neutral, restricting their political lobbying to directly relevant issues such as religious freedom. The stage of mass movements showed up fundamental problems in the structure of some of the larger New Religions. Personal contacts between members of the New Religions—in particular the primary religious bond between a believer and the converts she or he had made (a relationship of 'guiding parent' to 'spiritual children') tended to diminish as, in Japan's increasingly urbanised and mobile society, people moved away from each other and lost touch. The New Religions which retained their members and continued to flourish were primarily those which responded to the new social conditions by reforming their organisational structure, emphasising neighbourhood groups rather than individual ties and training people from each local area to exercise spiritual and administrative guidance derived from a strong central authority.

Such re-structuring led to the third and present stage, that of institutionalisation of the New Religions, in which many members are second or even third generation descendants of the original 'pioneers', and where membership has reached a plateau, or is perhaps falling. From the point of view of religious content, the claims of healing and instant prosperity made by these institutionalised New Religions are far less dramatic now than they were in the postwar period (though Tenrikyō, for example, still guarantees easy childbirth on request, even for non-believers). This is partly because the Japanese are far more prosperous and careful of their health than they were in the prewar depression and in the immediate aftermath of the war, and partly because the New Religions have adjusted their teachings in the light of long experience and now emphasise more intangible though none the less real benefits such as self-improvement and the development of character. Examples of the kind of spiritual virtues advocated by a number of New

Religions include endurance to overcome any difficulty, preserving an attitude of faith despite all, and becoming a less selfish and a brighter person (in the spiritual rather than intellectual sense of the word). Such aims are not dissimilar to the goals of many traditional religious sects and movements in Japan.

4.4 The 'New New Religions'

At the present time most of the postwar New Religions, having reached the stage of institutionalisation, are not regarded as particularly 'new' any more. The mantle of novelty has instead passed to the so-called 'new New Religions' such as Mahikari or Agonshū, which have grown up within the last decade and are related to the 'occult boom' which has been sweeping Japan as it did the West. Sukyō Mahikari (True-Light Supra-Religious Organisation) which is actively and successfully evangelising in Japanese cities today, has been described as 'an exorcistic sect . . . whose teachings attribute illness and misfortune to evil spirits. By casting out these spirits, members are able to cure diseases, repair broken television sets, change the weather, and even bring dead goldfish back to life.' This description may raise a smile, but the influence of Mahikari is strong and growing in modern urban Japan, and the beliefs which it encourages, particularly the belief that evil spirits—sometimes of other, living people—are maliciously responsible for misfortune and bad relationships between members of a family or colleagues at work, have a long pedigree in Japanese religion.

5. *The future of Japanese religion*

5.1 The Japanese way

The future course of Japanese religion depends on a number of factors including the direction of Japan's political and economic development. The present elder generation were educated into a quasi-religious vision of Japan as the land of the gods. Postwar educational reforms replaced this vision with the concept of a secular democracy, a free and modern society. But the Western vision of freedom and individuality is tarnished in the 80s by visible social and economic decline, while Japan's star has continued to rise not because Japan has uncritically accepted Western values and institutions but because, whether intentionally or not, Japanese society today represents a marriage of Western democratic and constitutional freedoms with Japanese values, not least those of paternalism in the home and workplace. Paternalism, which rests on a belief in the moral authority of elders and superiors, is in Japan akin to and shades off into ancestor reverence, which is of course one of the major preoccupations of the New Religions.

At the present time the Japanese, fully aware of their success in the international economic field, are entering a phase of new-found confidence in the 'Japanese' way (a confidence reflected particularly strongly in the younger generation of Japanese). It seems likely that this developing self-confidence will lead, in the religious sphere, to a period of more active evangelisation outside Japan, especially on the part of the New Religions, which have now consolidated their position within Japanese society and in many cases feel that they have something to offer the rest of the world in the face of mounting social problems. Pre-eminently this 'something' amounts to guidance on how to reform relationships with other human beings, usually by cultivating a new awareness of the important role played by human agents, particularly ancestors and parents but also others upon whom one depends in the course of daily life. Japanese religious teachings have been often described as 'this-worldly', but their orientation to the present—to the particularity of ordinary, quotidian family life for example—might be seen as an attractive and powerful corrective to the extreme individualism and existentialism of much Western popular ideology, both religious and secular. The notion of reciprocal dependence among human beings is *a priori* in Japanese religion, just as the notion of human aloneness before God is *a priori* in Western religion.

5.2 Westernisation

Japanese values, in 1985, almost as much as in 1945, are oriented 'backwards' (by Western reckoning) to the debt owed to those family members, parents and teachers who have gone before, as much as 'forwards' to a vision of a new and freer future created by present and future generations. There are few Japanese in Japan even today who have any real concept of what personal choice and the exercise of individual conscience in the Western manner really mean, so deeply ingrained is the Japanese habit, and so positively valued is the practice, of depending on others for guidance and reassurance in any course of action. The 'parent/child' (*oyabun-kobun*) type of relationship, characterised by the old Confucian virtue of filial piety (the parent sustains and guides while the child depends and obeys) extends to every area of Japanese society wherever personal relationships exist, be it organised crime, scientific research, art, politics or religion. While many Japanese people, exposed to a diet of modern Western myths on television, undoubtedly feel in some ways restricted by the closely-enmeshed character of interpersonal relationships in Japanese society (the average Japanese housewife exchanges about twenty presents of carefully calculated value each month), the Western ideal of individualism and personal freedom is too intangible and alien to Japanese traditions to be considered seriously as a solution to the problems faced by Japanese people in their everyday life. However irresistible the march of Westernisation may seem to Westerners looking at Japan, it would be a mistake to assume that Japanese society will become more 'Western' with time. In fact the reverse may be the case.

Westernisation, while perhaps only skin-deep in many cases, has nevertheless affected some aspects of Japanese religion. Pure Land (Shin) Buddhism long ago made a deliberate effort to 'Protestantise' to the extent that a Pure Land service may resemble in major respects a Christian service, even down to the hymn tunes. This is in clear recognition of the similarities between Shin Buddhism and Protestant Christianity, both of which emphasise grace, helplessness of the believer and the importance of giving oneself over to a greater Power.

However Shin Buddhism in Japan, like other sects of traditional Buddhism, has not achieved the transformation into a religion of the individual which some of its reform-minded leaders had hoped for. Adherence to Buddhism still remains essentially a family or household matter, with individual religious commitment as it were an optional extra.

Some of the most important elements in modern Western religion, for instance the emphasis on religiously-inspired philanthropy or charity, find no parallel in Shin or other Japanese Buddhist teachings, nor in Japanese culture or religion in general. The biblical parable of the Good Samaritan, which legitimises and encourages uncalculating giving to unknown recipients, has never had appeal in Japan, where a gift bestowed implies a debt incurred on the part of the recipient, and the bigger or more undeserved the gift, the greater and more onerous the corresponding burden of debt. Giving, whether of time, money or simply one's attention, can never be done lightly in Japan. As a matter of fact, despite its Western appearance, Pure Land Buddhist worship is conceived of as essentially an attempt to *repay* by active thankfulness the debt owed to Amida for his freely-bestowed grace.

Quite recently the concept of charity in the modern Western form of humanitarian relief work has been adopted by some of the New Religions. An example is one of the largest of the 'New' and more ecumenical Buddhist lay movements, Rissho

Kosei Kai, which combines faith in the Lotus Sutra with group counselling on basic Buddhist teachings. Rissho Kosei Kai regards itself as a partner rather than an opponent of Christianity in Japan, and under the guidance of its still-living founder has been developing since the late 1970s peace, religious freedom and international aid programmes. Rissho Kosei Kai has a membership of some two million families and its overseas aid budget in 1985 was approximately four million US dollars, much of it disbursed through United Nations relief agencies. Currently Rissho Kosei Kai is engaged in a drive to persuade its own members and others in Japan to skip a few meals every month and give the money saved to relief work, especially among refugees. Rissho Kosei Kai's charitable work is carried out without any obvious attempt to proselytise outside Japan, and its approach is ecumenical and non-sectarian, although the movement clearly expects to gain a certain amount of kudos in international circles for its generosity, and is keen that others should appreciate exactly how much it gives. Rissho Kosei Kai seems to be one of the New Religions most directly influenced by the Western ideal of charitable giving as a form of religious action. Rissho Kosei Kai is not the only group moving towards a position of giving without thought of reward, but many other religious groups in Japan target their members' giving more selectively, the concept of charity in these cases being identified primarily with service to the religion itself.

5.3 Developments in Shinto

At the moment the future course of Shinto is uncertain. Shinto shrines support the same variety of folk-religious beliefs and practices (concerned with healing, magic and wishes) as do Buddhist temples, and for the majority of the population Shinto means little more than the shrine itself and the seasonal or occasional festivals which people participate in or just go along to watch. With little or no teaching about Japanese religions in schools (Christianity by contrast is quite widely studied as a key to understanding the mentality of the West), public knowledge about Shinto and its teachings is extremely limited, and this situation is not helped by uncertainty on the part of Shinto writers and theologians themselves about what Shinto really stands for. A reluctance to reduce the 'way of the Kami' to mere words is no doubt part of Shinto tradition, but in a culture like modern Japan's which relies so heavily on the written and broadcast word, it may be felt that Shinto scholars should at least be able to agree on *what* it is that cannot be fully put into words. It seems that, as the influence of the prewar generation lessens, Shinto is more and more closely identified with conservative and right-wing values, whether these are applied to politics or home life. Plans for educational reform are currently under discussion at governmental level in Japan, and the Shinto establishment hopes to influence educational policy in the direction of reawakening a sense of national pride in the coming generations of schoolchildren. However, the teachers are the most radical group of professinals in Japan, and any suggestion that ethics teaching in Japanese schools should echo the prewar diet of civil religion will undoubtedly be hotly resisted.

5.4 The Future of the New Religions

The New Religions made their biggest impact in the '50s and '60s, when they started to acquire political influence, most noticeably in the case of Soka Gakkai which sponsored its own political party Kōmeito. There was tremendous public opposition to the idea of a religiously-based political party, especially one based in a religion which made no secret of the fact that it desired total political power and was out to convert everyone from the Japanese emperor downwards to belief in Nichiren Buddhism. The new constitution quite clearly excluded any possibility of such a religio-political monolith, and in the end Soka Gakkai and Komeito were offically separated, though their interests remain closely allied. In any case Soka Gakkai soon modified its aim of total world domination as, like other New Religions which had grown rapidly in the postwar years, its membership reached a plateau. Perhaps as the price of success, many of the New Religions in the postwar decades seem to have gone through fundamental crises involving basic questions of leadership, authority and direction. Rissho Kosei Kai's came in the late 1950s when a fundamental split in the movement was narrowly avoided by the death of Myoko Naganuma, one of Rissho Kosei Kai's two founders, who was the leader revered by a potential breakaway faction (the other founder is the present highly successful leader, Mr Nikkyo Niwano). Soka Gakkai's leadership went through very troubled times in the late 1970s after Daisaku Ikeda, the charismatic and powerful lay leader of Soka Gakkai, fell out with the ecclesiastical hierarchy of the Nichiren Buddhist sect to which Soka Gakkai is affiliated. The dispute was over religious and personal authority within the movement but also involved two different conceptions of modern Buddhism, one espoused by the priests and emphasising ecclesiastical authority and the mystical transmission of the *dharma*, the other represented by Ikeda which stresses the independent role of lay people guided by the teachings of Nichiren as interpreted by Soka Gakkai. Ikeda's teachings owe a good deal to the original educational impulse of the prewar Soka Gakkai under the leadership of its founder, the educationalist Tsunesaburo Makiguchi. It is tempting to predict that the 'soft' version of Buddhism advocated by Ikeda which stresses education and the pursuit of world peace will prevail, but the Nichiren strand of Buddhism based on the Lotus Sutra has always been uncompromising, so that the long term direction of Soka Gakkai is far from clear. Though doctrines are not the main thing in Japanese religion, they do play a part, and Soka Gakkai's present 'peace and

neighbours and friends, and in 1986 Mahikari or Agonshu leaflets and advertisements were appearing in the newspapers or through the letter box more or less every day. These religions appeal to millions in Japan, and they require—or perhaps it is truer to say contact with them engenders—a belief in miraculous processes and mystical powers which leaves the adherent little room for critical reflection.

In conclusion, then, Japanese religion seems set to develop in a number of different directions. Freedom of religion seems assured for the foreseeable future, though a very un-Western attitude of deep respectfulness amounting almost to credulity towards acknowledged authority, whether religious or secular, seems an inescapable and indeed positively-valued fact of Japanese life. Where there is deep respect for authority in religious life, much depends on the quality of religious leadership. Japanese religious leaders are no longer perhaps regarded as 'living *kami*', gods in human form, but a dividing line between elders, superiors, ancestors and deities has never been clearly drawn in Japan and figures like Nikkyo Niwano, Daisaku Ikeda, recently-emerged figures like the renowned high priest and founder of Agonshu, and the living founders of the smaller New Religions or their anointed descendants are men (usually) whose every word is taken and recorded as freshly-minted gospel by their devotees. A great deal of the wisdom of the group therefore depends upon the wisdom of the leader. Japanese religion is, in general, rather unpredictable, because the authoritative gospel of next year may not yet have been uttered.

Bibliography

Books

Bunce W. K., *Religions in Japan* (pub. 1948), Tokyo: Tuttle, 1976.

Caldarola C., *Christianity, the Japanese Way*, Leiden: Brill, 1979.

Davis, W., *Dojo: magic and exorcism in modern Japan*, Stanford: Stanford UP, 1980.

Earhart, H. B., *Japanese Religion: Unity and Diversity*, Encino: Dickenson, 1974.

———, *Religion in the Japanese Experience: sources and interpretations*, Encino: Dickenson, 1974.

———, *Religions of Japan: many traditions within one sacred way*, San Francisco: Harper & Row, 1984.

Hardacre, H., *Lay Buddhism in Contemporary Japan: Reiyukai Kyodan*, Princeton: Princeton UP, 1984.

Hori, I. (Ed.), *Japanese Religion: A Survey by the Agency for Cultural Affairs*, Tokyo: Kodansha, 1972.

Morioka, K., *Religion in Changing Japanese Society*, Tokyo: Univ. of Tokyo Press, 1975.

Murakami, S., *Japanese Religion in the Modern Century*, Tokyo: Univ. of Tokyo Press, 1980.

Journals

Japanese Journal of Religious Studies, (formerly *Contemporary Religions in Japan*).

Japanese Religions.

The Eastern Buddhist.

7

THE JEWISH TRADITION IN TODAY'S WORLD

Louis Jacobs

(London)

The two events which transformed Jewish thought and life in the period from 1947 to the present day were the destruction of six million Jews—a third of the world population of Jewry—in the Nazi Holocaust and the establishment of the State of Israel in 1948. Both events—the one utterly catastrophic, the other providing a measure of release from unbearable despair—compelled Jews to engage in searching, not to say ruthless, re-thinking of Jewish identity and the significance of Judaism in a world in which the old values had appeared to be shattered. On the theological level serious thought was given to such questions as why did God not prevent the horrors of the death camps; what meaning could now be given to the idea that God works through human history, that the Jewish people is 'chosen' in some way? Whatever the answers—and they were varied—given to these questions there was a resolve, strengthened by the new challenge presented by the State of Israel, not to allow Hitler, in the words of Emil Fackenheim, to have the last word. Naturally, the tensions in Judaism between universalism and particularism tended to become weighted, during this period, towards the latter, though in a faith like Judaism the belief that God is concerned with all His creatures could never be abandoned. Practically all the changes in Jewish life during our period can be traced either to the impact of the State of Israel or the Holocaust or both.

Accurate statistics are not available but the Jewish population of the world at the present is estimated to be around fourteen million. The largest section of Jewry is in the Americas (around six million). In Europe there are around three million, over two million of these in the Soviet Union (and, because of their isolated situation, with far less contact with other Jews). There are around three and a half million Jews in the State of Israel. These demographic conditions have resulted in a repetition of the situation in the first centuries of the present era, where there were two great (and rival) centres of Jewish life, one in Palestine, the other in Babylon. The two contemporary centres are those in Israel and in the USA. There is much debate on whether Israel is, or should be, the centre of Jewish life; some denying its centrality, others affirming it to the extent that Jewish life outside Israel is only legitimised as second-best with an ever-constant obligation for Diaspora Jews to emigrate to Israel as soon as possible. It can be surmised that the majority of Jews do look upon Israel as occupying a central role but with Diaspora Jewry entitled to work out its destiny and work for its future in the conviction that for as long as there can be permanence in human affairs the Diaspora communities will be permanent features of Jewish life.

The old division of Jews still obtains into the Ashkenazim, Jews of German descent, and Sephardim, Jews of Spanish or Oriental descent. The vast majority of Jews today follow the Ashkenazi traditions but it has to be appreciated that the differences between the two communities are only in matters of local custom, melodies for the prayers, preferences in diet and the like. There are no doctrinal differences between the two groups. The difference between Reform and Orthodox Judaism, on the other hand, does have doctrinal implications, though it is incorrect to understand the difference between Reform and Orthodoxy as resembling that between Protestantism and Roman Catholicism in the Christian Church. Both the Orthodox and the Reform regard themselves as belonging to the Jewish faith and people and there is no suggestion that the doctrinal differences are sufficient to make of the two groupings two different sub-religions. Especially in the USA, there is a third grouping known as Conservative Judaism (in Israel this is known as the M'sorati Movement), a middle-of-the-way position. Orthodoxy accepts the doctrine 'the Torah is from Heaven' in its traditional sense, that the Pentateuch and its traditional explanation as found now in the Talmudic literature were given in a direct manner by God to Moses at Sinai. It follows from this position that all Pentateuchal criticism, whether higher or lower, is forbidden and that there must be strict adherence to all the laws of the Torah, such as the dietary laws, in all their details. Not all Jews, of course, who belong to Orthodox synagogues are totally observant but they subscribe in theory at least to the Orthodox position.

Reform Judaism, accepting the findings of Biblical and historical criticism, relegates the ritual observances to a secondary place, preferring to see the essence of Judaism in the belief in ethical monotheism or, as it has often been called, prophetic Judaism. Conservative Judaism adopts a middle-of-the-road position between Orthodoxy and Reform in that it accepts belief in the doctrine 'the Torah is from Heaven' but understands this in the light of modern knowledge as God revealing Himself *through* the Jewish people not only *to* the Jewish people. For the reasons mentioned at the beginning of this chapter, a determined swing to the right can be observed in all three groups. Reform Judaism, for instance, has abandoned the view of many of its leaders at the beginning of the century that Zionism, with its stress on Jewish peoplehood in nationalistic terms, is a betrayal of the Jewish universalistic ideal. With hardly any exception, Reform Jews are committed to the State of Israel. Similarly, many Reform Jews are moving towards a greater appreciation of traditional observances. As a rough generalisation it has been said that while all three groups believe in God, the Torah and Jewish peoplehood, Reform places the emphasis on God, Orthodoxy on the Torah and Conservative Judaism on Jewish peoplehood. It must be noted that the actual term Orthodoxy is taken from Christian theology and, in fact, was originally used by the Reformers as a term of reproach, much as to say, you are hidebound and unduly conservative. This is why some Orthodox Jews today prefer some other term like 'Torah-true' to describe their position.

One of the most astonishing features of Jewish religious life today is the growth of Orthodoxy and its increasing attraction for Jews disillusioned by pre-War liberalism in thought and practice. Orthodox Jews today have been sub-categorised in the groups known as 'The Yeshivah World'; the Hasidim; and the 'Modern Orthodox'.

In pre-War Europe the intellectual élite obtained their education in the Torah in Yeshivot ('Colleges', 'Higher Institutions of Learning'). There were numerous Yeshivot in Hungary but the Yeshivah institution reached its most powerful form in Lithuania. The two main subjects taught in the Lithuanian Yeshivot were Talmud (which included the Codes of the Halakhah, the legal side of Judaism) and Musar ('Instruction'; 'Rebuke'; 'Ethical and religious pietism'). The students of the Yeshivot devoted themselves, under the guidance of skilled masters of the Law, to the intricate discussion of subtle Halakhic analysis. Musar was not so much studied as assimilated in the form of pietistic exercises; the singing of texts from the Jewish moralistic literature in a melancholy voice until they became part of one's nature, as it were. The language of instruction was Yiddish, except for the very few Sephardi Yeshivot where instruction was in Hebrew.

Although the Yeshivot were destroyed in the Holocaust, the few Yeshivah masters who managed to escape gradually succeeded in transplanting the Yeshivot in the USA and in

Israel, as well as in some other countries. On the face of it the Yeshivot, in their new environment, were continued, in our period, as if nothing had changed. Both Talmud and Musar continued to be the chief subjects, often to the exclusion of all others, even that of the Bible; and in the major Yeshivot the language of instruction is still Yiddish, though modern Hebrew in Israel, and English in the USA, are increasingly used as a supplement to Yiddish. As in the Lithuanian centres, all secular studies are banned from the Yeshivah proper. At the most, general studies are permitted by the Yeshivah heads for students who do not wish to become Rabbis. These are sometimes permitted to study, outside the Yeshivah, courses such as accountancy, physics or mathematics, which can lead to a career. But the main aim of the Yeshivot is to produce learned men (it is a male occupation), whether they will become Rabbis or not, who are capable of devoting most of their leisure time throughout their lives to the study of the Torah. Since the Yeshivot pursue a common aim, and their alumni adopt a common pattern of life, the teachers, students and graduates of the Yeshivot and those sympathetic to their aims are now said to belong to the Yeshivah World.

Hasidism, the mystical movement founded by Israel Baal Shem Tov (1700–1760) had such popular appeal that, despite the strong opposition of the Rabbinic authorities, it managed to capture at least half of the communities of Eastern Europe by the turn of the nineteenth century. Hasidism eventually produced dynasties of Masters. The function of the Guru-type leader, the Zaddik (or Rebbe, to distinguish him from the traditional Rabbi) was to guide his followers in the spiritual way, to lead them to God and to pray on their behalf. Although, again, the main centres of Hasidic life were destroyed in the Holocaust and many of the Rebbes perished together with their followers, some of the dynasties were re-established in Israel and in the USA. Hasidism was even more resistant to change than the

Yeshivah World. Hasidim still wear the traditional Hasidic garb, long black coats and hats, ringlets at the corners of the head, and, among most of the Hasidim, sable hats on the Sabbaths and Festivals. There is often fierce rivalry among the adherents of different Rebbes, each Hasid considering his Master as the sole authentic guide, at least for the group he leads. It is difficult to obtain any correct estimate but the Rebbes of Sotmar and Lubavitch (both in the United States) probably have around 100,000 followers each, residing in practically all the Jewish communities of the world. (It is indicative of the conservative nature of Hasidism that the Rebbes are known by the names of the towns in Eastern Europe in which the dynasties were established).

Hasidim have their own places of worship in which the particular customs of the group are followed. Common to all the Hasidic groups is the cultivation of spiritual joy in the service of God, total loyalty to the Rebbe and his family, song and dance as religious exercises, and the pursuit of holiness in daily living. There are frequent ritual immersions in the belief that this leads to purity of soul. It is also considered of high religious significance for the Hasidim to tell tales illustrating the miracle-working powers of the holy Masters.

Despite the many things they have in common, each Hasidic group follows its own particular way. Of the two major groups, Lubavitch is anxious to win adherents and encourages non-observant Jews to keep the rituals, whereas Sotmar is more inward-looking and less interested in those outside the group. Lubavitch has its own publishing house in New York, from which there is a constant stream of publications in Hebrew, English and other languages, and Lubavitch vans often parade through Jewish neighbourhoods with ritual appurtenances urging Jews to carry out a *mitzvah*, a religious act. In connection with Hasidism, it might be mentioned that a large number of non-Hasidic Jews are attracted to the Hasidic way as sympathisers. As in the non-Jewish world, there is a renewed interest, to which Hasidism caters, in the mystical side of religion. Together with their own special emphasis, Hasidim are strictly observant of the Jewish laws. Artificial methods of contraception, for example, are virtually unknown among the Hasidim and they have large families, which has led some students of the Jewish scene to conclude that, numerically at least, the Hasidim will become a major grouping in the Jewish world.

The Modern Orthodox subscribe to the doctrine 'The Torah is from Heaven' in its traditional sense but do not regard Orthodoxy as demanding that the Jew isolates himself from Western society. The Modern Orthodox Jew does not engage in secular studies merely in order to become equipped to earn a living but he tends to see value in its own right in Western culture. He will tend to dress in the modern style, he will usually be well-educated, having attended college or university, he will still be observant but in a less severe way than would be the case among the Hasidim and the Yeshivah World. As a result of the general swing to the right, the Modern Orthodox are increasingly on the defensive, having to justify what those who consider themselves to be 'really' Orthodox hold to be a radical departure from the tradition. In some instances, at Yeshivah University in New York and at Bar Ilan University in Israel (the two major strongholds of Modern Orthodoxy) historical investigation into the classical Jewish sources is not only tolerated but held to be praiseworthy and even a moderate Biblical criticism is engaged in but this latter is never allowed to be applied to the Pentateuch, which, on the Orthodox premiss, is the very Word of God and hence completely sacrosanct.

In the State of Israel Orthodoxy has a monopoly in certain areas. There is, for instance, no civil marriage in Israel and all marriage and divorce laws and other laws of personal status are administered solely by Orthodox Rabbis. There are a number of Orthodox members of the Israeli Knesset and it is under their influence that no public transport runs, in most Israel towns, on the Sabbath. The two largest of these parties, Mizrahi and Aggudat Israel, have members who do not live in Israel affiliated to them. Aggudat Israel was, in the pre-War period, opposed to Zionism on the grounds that the Zionist leaders were not observant Jews and, more especially, because, in their view, the establishment of a Jewish State had to await the coming of the Messiah sent by God. With the actual establishment of the Jewish State Aggudat Israel has softened its opposition considerably, though it is reluctant to read too much religious significance into the State. Nevertheless, only a handful of Orthodox Jews still maintain the old objections to a Jewish State. Mizrahi from its inception has held the settlement of the land of Israel to be a high religious duty and has welcomed enthusiastically the new State as a religious advance of the highest order. It is very widespread in Mizrahi and similar circles to see the State of Israel as 'the beginning of the redemption', that is, as the forerunner of the advent of the Messiah. The State of Israel is not seen in terms of actually realised eschatology but it does have numinous overtones. The redeemed world has not yet come into being and the Messiah has not yet come but is on the way in a more intense form than has been the case for well-nigh two thousand years.

In our period the term 'ingathering of the exiles' was used not only for the ability of homeless Jews to find a home in Israel but also for the determined attempt to bring system and order to the religious classics of Judaism. This has taken the form of huge collections of material in the form of Encyclopedias, Anthologies, Digests and Dictionaries. In the State of Israel were published the Biblical Encyclopedia: *Encyklopedia Mikrait*; a general Encyclopedia in Hebrew: *Encyklopedia Ivrit*, containing, in addition to general articles, summaries in impeccable scholarship of the present state of the question on very many specifically Jewish topics; the great digest of Talmudic and Halakhic law: *Encyklopedia Talmudit*; the comprehensive digest of opinions on Jewish marriage law: *Otzar ha-Posekim*; and the English *Encyclopedia Judaica*. New scholarly editions of mediaeval texts have been published in Israel and in the USA together with numerous photo-copies of religious works of the past of every description. Translation of the classical works of Judaism from the original Hebrew and Aramaic into English has also proceeded apace, some of it extremely competent, some of it less than adequate. The Responsa tradition, in which famous Rabbis reply to questions addressed to them regarding Jewish law in new situations, has continued in profusion. Among the questions discussed in our period are: the Jewish doctrine of the just war; the right to strike for better wages in Jewish law; whether it is right to give up territory in the holy land in exchange for peace; the introduction of new rituals to mark the establishment of the State of Israel; the ways in which a modern Jewish State can function without an infringement of the laws against sabbath desecration; in-vitro fertilisation, the use of organ transplants and the whole new area of bio-ethics. There has been little theological work among the Orthodox beyond re-affirming the tradition in all its details. In Reform and Conservative circles there has been a good deal of theological probing, much of which has found its way into print. Jewish theologians have explored the meaning of revelation; the language used of God; the nature of God; and the problem of dogma and authority in Judaism.

Two new trends have emerged in our period, represented by the Jewish feminine movement and the *baal teshuvah* movement.

In the traditional Jewish scheme, women are exempt from the performance of those rituals which take place only at given times. They do not wear phylacteries or a prayer-shawl during the prayers; they are not called to the reading of the Torah in the synagogue; they do not sit together with the men in the synagogue; and they cannot serve as prayer leaders (Cantors). Women, moreover, have no obligation to study the Torah, though women learned in the Torah are certainly not unknown in the tradition. There is no legal objection to women functioning as Rabbis, if they have competence in the Torah, especially since the Rabbi is not a priest but, traditionally, simply one who renders decisions in Jewish law. Since, however, women were not usually at all learned in the law they did not function as Rabbis in the past.

The Jewish feminist movement began effectively to challenge all this, even among the Orthodox, though its clamour for greater participation in religious life has up to date, largely gone unheard. There have been no women Rabbis among the Orthodox, even though the modern Rabbi has functions— pastoral, preaching, social welfare—that are, in any event, untraditional. For some time, despite initial resistance, Reform has ordained women Rabbis. The issue divided the Conservative movement in the USA for some years but the main Conservative Seminary, the Jewish Theological Seminary in New York, eventually decided to accept women as students in the Rabbinic class leading to ordination.

In both the Reform and Conservative movements girls have a Bat Mitzvah ('daughter of the commandments'—for boys the ceremony is, of course, Bar Mitzvah) ceremony when they come of age; in most of these congregations, too, the Bat Mitzvah girl as well as other females are called to the reading of the Torah. Many Jewish women, including the Orthodox, believing that Jewish law is male-orientated and unfair to women in certain areas such as divorce, have campaigned for greater equality between the sexes. Some of the more extreme Jewish feminists, especially in the USA, have been critical of the exclusively male vocabulary of the traditional liturgy and have added the words: 'God of Sarah, Rebecca, Rachel and Leah' to the traditional: 'God of Abraham, Isaac and Jacob'. Some have gone much further to speak of God as She as well as He, of 'Our Mother' as well as of 'Our Father'. It is hard to detect whether these innovations will be accepted and become respectable but at the moment the whole feminine movement in Judaism is in its infancy and some have forecast its speedy demise.

The term *baal teshuvah* ('one who repents') refers in the Jewish tradition to a penitent sinner who expresses remorse for his sins and resolves to lead a better life. But, in our period, there has been a remarkable return on the part of young people brought up in non-Orthodox or non-observant homes to the leading of a full Jewish life. These have taken the name *baaley teshuvah*. Orthodoxy has established in Israel and in the USA special Yeshivot to cater for the needs of the *baaley teshuvah*. In the USA the *baaley teshuvah* have formed themselves into a kind of special class, even using the initial BT (for *baal teshuvah*) as a status symbol, distinguishing them from the FFB ('*frum* from birth', 'pious from the beginning'). In many of the *baaley teshuvah* Yeshivot there has been an awareness on the part of the teachers that only a gradual introduction into the niceties of observance will succeed in winning over the hitherto non-observant, with the result that a degree of picking and choosing among the observances has been tolerated. Some Orthodox leaders have been apprehensive that this approach might sow the seeds of compromise to affect Orthodoxy and, for this and other reasons, have been somewhat lukewarm to the whole *baal teshuvah* movement.

The problem of Jews marrying out of the faith has been acute ever since the Emancipation of the Jews at the beginning of the nineteenth century. The majority of Jewish teachers, recognising how widespread marriage with non-Jewish partners has become, have, in our period, tended to relax to some extent the rigorous demands made of converts to Judaism in order to encourage the non-Jewish partner to convert to

Judaism. Where the non-Jewish partner is unwilling to embrace Judaism, the majority of Rabbis refuse to participate in any kind of religious ceremony for the couple. Some Reform Rabbis in the USA have permitted themselves, however, to participate in a form of religious ceremony in these instances, even, at times, together with a Christian priest. In the tradition, the Jewish status of a child born of a mixed marriage is determined by the status of the mother, not the father. The child of a Gentile father and a Jewish mother is Jewish; the child of a Jewish father and a Gentile mother is not Jewish. In Reform circles, especially in the USA, there have been moves to treat the child as Jewish if either of the parents is Jewish provided it is the sincere intention of the parents for the child to be brought up as a Jew. The Orthodox and the Conservative Rabbis continue to insist on matrilineal descent as determining the Jewish status of a child.

There has been an advance in ecumenism in this period both within and outside the Jewish ranks. There have been very few meetings of Jews and Muslims because of the tensions in the Middle East and even less between Jews and Buddhists and Hindus. Christian-Jewish dialogue, on the other hand, has flourished despite opposition to it in some Orthodox circles. There has also been considerable debate on whether the idea of a Judaeo-Christian tradition has any significance; whether the two faiths have sufficient in common for them to be considered, for all their doctrinal differences, as friendly rivals of the same religious stock. The opponents of such a position stress the differences as so acute and categorical that only confusion is caused by any suggestion that they belong together however tenuously. On the whole, it is this latter view that has prevailed. In some Reform circles it has been argued, without much success, that it is time for Judaism to become, as evidently it once was, a missionary religion; seeking to win converts, if not among Christians, at least among the polytheistic faiths. Against this there has militated the natural reluctance for Judaism to give up its particularity or to compromise this in any way and the view that in an age of religious tolerance it is offensive for Jews to wish to convert others. The traditional view is still maintained that in the Messianic Age all mankind will come to acknowledge the One true God but before that age each faith should develop its own institutions, especially since, according to official Jewish teaching, 'the righteous of all peoples have a share in the World to Come', so that there is no need for a Gentile to embrace Judaism in order to find 'salvation'. The result has been that, with few exceptions, conversions to Judaism in our period have been for matrimonial reasons.

Within Jewish ranks it cannot be denied that there has developed greater polarisation. Increasingly, the Orthodox have tended to regard Reform and Conservative Jews as heretics and sinners, though still Jews and with little or no blame attached to them for being what they are, with whom, in the interests of preserving an undiluted faith, it is better not to associate if this can be avoided. Nevertheless, there are areas—philanthropy, work for Soviet Jewry and for the State of Israel—where there is and has been close cooperation between all the branches of religious Jews.

In classical Reform synagogues (generally called 'Temples') the vernacular was used for many of the prayers. This was, in fact, one of the issues between Reform and Orthodoxy from the days of the establishment of the Hamburg Temple in 1813. After the establishment of the State of Israel and the widespread use of Hebrew as a living language, there has been a definite shift back to Hebrew even in Reform circles, though some prayers are still recited in the vernacular. Conversely, Orthodoxy, now more secure, has often introduced some vernacular prayers into the service.

Another issue between the Reformers and the Orthodox at the beginning of the nineteenth century was whether the traditional prayers for a return to Zion and the rebuilding of the

Temple could honestly be recited since, in the Reform view, the Messianic hope was understood as being realised in Germany, France and England and wherever the new liberal ideas were being advocated. Reform still maintains its belief in a Messianic Age rather than a personal Messiah but the older Reform objection to prayers for a return to Zion has been made obsolete by the establishment of the State of Israel. Orthodoxy still hopes for the personal Messiah, sent by God to redeem His people and ultimately the whole of mankind, who will rebuild the Temple in which the old sacrificial system will be restored. Reform Jews do not pray for the restoration of sacrifices and continue to omit these traditional prayers from their prayer books. Conservative Jews do not believe in the restoration of the sacrificial system but, because the traditional prayers have been hallowed, use the words of the prayers but with a slight alteration so that the reference now is to the glories of the past rather than to a hope for the future i.e. instead of: 'and there (in Zion in the Messianic Age) we will offer the sacrifices Thou hast commanded' they say: 'and there our ancestors offered the sacrifices Thou hast commanded'. Another Reform position, reflected in the liturgy, is the substitution of the doctrine of the immortality of the soul for the traditional doctrine of the resurrection of the dead.

Judaism is organised, today as in the past, around the community, with the synagogue only one of the communal institutions and, to a marked degree, entirely independent of communal control of any kind. Synagogues are formed by a group of Jews wishing to worship together, though, naturally, the synagogue will usually have loose affiliations to one of the larger synagogual bodies in a particular community, Reform, Orthodox or Conservative. Some synagogues are even independent of these. Every community has its own burial plot, though Reform does not frown on cremation where it is requested by the family. Marriages are generally performed in

the Conservatives; and the Conference of Reform Rabbis. The Hasidim recognise the right of Rabbis to decide on matters of Jewish law and will, as observant Jews, accept Rabbinic decisions. But the only real authority for the Hasidim is the particular Rebbe to whom they owe allegiance. The Orthodox Aggudat Israel, however, is organised as a world movement with a hierarchy of famous Rabbis and Hasidic Rebbes. Although this, too, is largely a matter of policy, not of doctrine, nevertheless the opinions of the 'Council of Sages' of the Aggudah will lay down opinions not only on matters of Jewish law but even on political matters such as voting in the State of Israel and the correct attitude to be adopted to the non-Jewish government authorities in other lands. The Aggudah has grown in strength and its Council of Sages has acquired increasing authority. Moreover, there has emerged in other circles as well the idea that certain very pious and learned Rabbis have acquired a kind of built-in Torah response to every situation with the result that in some Orthodox circles charismatic personalities have come to be accepted as world authorities on Judaism and on how Jewish life should be lived. These have never been elected and owe the respect in which they are held to their charisma and, more especially, to their popular acceptance as holy men by a large proportion of the Jewish population. For all that, Judaism maintains its traditions of independence from any spiritual hierarchy. The ultimate authority is the Torah, not any person no matter how saintly or learned. There is a Sephardi World Organisation but its authority sits very loosely on Sephardi Jews. The Sephardi Rabbi is generally known not as 'Rabbi' but by the older name of Hakham ('Sage') though his functions, according to tradition, are the same as those of his Ashkenazi colleague. Here and there among Sephardi and Oriental Jews there have been charismatic personalities who have been revered as saints and miracle workers such as Baba Salah of Morocco and Modercai Sharabi of the Yemen both of whom lived in Israel and died in 1983. Indicative of the reverence in which these men were held was the publication, full of miracle tales, of biographies of each within a year of their death. The Sephardim in Israel have continued the Kabbalistic tradition, establishing schools for the study of the ancient lore. Originally the study and practice of the Kabbalah was an élitist affair open only to initiates. It has now become, thanks to the interest in mysticism, a much more popular pursuit. Among the Ashkenazim, too, especially among the Hasidim, and in some measure even in non-Orthodox circles, the Kabbalah is studied and works on the Kabbalah published. Professor Gershom Scholem and his school have created, at the Hebrew University in Jerusalem, what amounts to a new discipline in Jewish studies, the study of Jewish mysticism. Pursued purely as an academic discipline this study has nevertheless had a great influence on the popularity of the mystical approach among practising religious Jews.

The major theological Jewish journals are in English in our period. These are: *Tradition* for Orthodoxy; *Conservative Judaism* for the Conservatives; *The Central Conference of American Rabbis Journal* for Reform, all published in the USA. Also published in the USA is the Quarterly *Judaism*, a journal the pages of which are open to every variety of religious expression, as is the much smaller *Sh'ma*. In these, theological debates and discussions are presented with a high level of sophistication.

Judaism as practised in our period is especially concerned with religion in the here-and-now: in social justice; striving for peace on earth and better international relations; the alleviation of poverty; human rights, tolerance and freedom. Yet there can also be discerned a renewed interest in the other-worldly aspects of the faith: in the fate of the individual soul in the Hereafter; in this world as a 'vale of soul-making'; in the individual's spiritual quest and his relationship to God in an intensely personal way.

Perhaps more than at any time since the emergence of the Jew into Western society at the end of the eighteenth century, Judaism, in our period, is interpreted as being both this-worldly and other-worldly. As one of the Talmudic Rabbis put in in the second century: 'Better is one hour of repentance and good deeds in this world than the whole life of the world to come but better is one hour of bliss in the world to come than the whole life of this world.'

Bibliography

Bulka, Reuven P., ed., *Dimensions of Orthodox Judaism*. New York: KTAV, 1983.

Cohen, Samuel S., *Jewish Theology*, Assen: Van Gorcum, 1971.

de Lange, Nicholas, *Atlas of the Jewish World*, Oxford: Phaidon, 1984.

Frankel, William, ed., *Survey of Jewish Affairs 1982*, London/Toronto: Fairleigh Dickinson, 1984.

——, *Survey of Jewish Affairs 1983*, London/Toronto: Fairleigh Dickinson, 1985.

Freehof, Solomon B., *Reform Responsa* and *Recent Reform Responsa*, two volumes in one, New York: KTAV, 1973.

Goldin, Judah, ed., *The Jewish Expression*, New Haven, Conn.: Yale University Press, 1976.

Gordis, Robert, *Understanding Conservative Judaism*, New York: KTAV, 1978.

——, Waxman, Ruth, ed., *Faith and Reason: Essays in Judaism*, New York: KTAV, 1973.

Heilman, Samuel C., *Synagogue Life*, Chicago: Chicago University Press, 1978.

——, *The People of the Book*, Chicago: Chicago University, 1980.

Helmreich, William B., *The World of the Yeshiva*, New York: Free Press, 1982.

Jacobs, Louis, *A Jewish Theology*, New York: Behrman, 1973.

Kellner, M. M., ed., *Contemporary Jewish Ethics*, New York: Sanhedrin Press, 1978.

Lamm, Norman, Wurzburger, W. S., ed., *A Treasury of Tradition*, New York: Hebrew Publishing, 1967.

Litvin, Baruch, Hoenig, Sidney B., ed., *Jewish Identity*, New York: Feldheim, 1965.

Rabinowicz, Harry, *Hasidism and the State of Israel*, London: Oxford University Press, 1982.

Roth, Cecil, editor in chief, *Encyclopedia Judaica*, 16 vols, Jerusalem, 1972; Yearbook 1973–82, Jerusalem: Keter Publishing House, 1982.

Roth, Leon, *Judaism A Portrait*, London: Faber & Faber, 1960.

Siegel, Seymour ed., *Conservative Judaism and Jewish Law*, New York: KTAV, 1977.

8

HE MUSLIM TRADITION IN TODAY'S WORLD

W. Montgomery Watt
(Edinburgh)

In order to understand what has been happening religiously in the world of Islam since 1945 it is necessary to have some idea of how Muslims had been responding to the West during the previous two centuries or so. In a sense Islam first felt the impact of Europe in India and south-east Asia after Vasco de Gama discovered the route to the Indies round the Cape of Good Hope in 1498. For the lands round the eastern Mediterranean, however, the effective impact of Europe began with the invasion of Egypt by Napoleon in 1798. Since the fiteenth century, of course, the Ottoman Empire had been established in south-east Europe and had been engaged in wars with various European powers; but it was only when Ottoman defeats led to the humiliating treaty of Karlowitz in 1699 that there may be said to have been an impact of Europe on the Ottomans.

The impact of Europe took many forms. At first it was mainly economic, political and military. The discovery of the route to the East Indies led to trade with that whole region, but trade which was on the whole more to the advantage of the Europeans. Trade led to political agreements, then to military intervention leading to the establishment of colonies and other forms of political control. The nineteenth century saw the impingement on Islamic lands of various aspects of the European intellectual outlook, while the twentieth century, with greater ease of travel and so greater intermingling of peoples, has seen the Muslims exposed to every aspect of Western culture.

Much of what is happening in the Islamic world is a response to this impact. It has to be emphasized, however, that it is not a purely passive reaction, but an active, willed response. When things have happened it has been because some Muslims wanted them. They wanted the comforts and luxuries produced by European technology; they wanted to be respected by the Europeans and not regarded as inferior; and the few who realized the importance of European intellectual achievements wanted Muslims to share in these.

It so happens that precisely in 1945 Sir Hamilton Gibb (as he later became) delivered the Haskell Lectures in Chicago under the title of 'Modern Trends in Islam'.[1] The title is a little misleading since Gibb did not try to describe all the contemporary trends but only those which were modernistic or modernizing on the intellectual level, as seen in men like Muḥammad 'Abduh and Muḥammad Iqbal. He naturally mentions incidentally the secularizing trend, especially evident among statesmen, and the reaction of the ulema to this by accusing the secularizers of 'apostasy'. These points may be developed further.

Islam has never, strictly speaking, had a clerical class, since it has had no priests, pastors or other clergymen; but it has had an important class of religious intellectuals who are known by various names such as ulema and mullahs, and who are primarily jurists. By the nineteenth century the ulema of the Ottoman empire had become a powerful body, hierarchically organized under the Shaykh al-Islam, whose position in the empire was inferior only to that of the sultan and the grand vizier. The body of ulema controlled all higher education, all the administration of justice, and the formulation of law. In

---

[1] Published Chicago: University of Chicago Press, 1947.

233

Islam even the ruler of a great empire like the Ottoman sultan had no power of legislation. The law of an Islamic state was the Sharī'a or divine law, defined by the Qur'ān and Ḥadīth (the records of the inspired example of Muḥammad); if the principles implicit in Qur'ān and Ḥadīth had to be applied to novel circumstances, only the ulema were qualified to do this. By the eighteenth century, however, the ulema had become very inflexible in their outlook, and rulers and statesmen were aware of this.

After the withdrawal of the French from Egypt, for example, an Ottoman general Muḥammad 'Alī made himself effective master of the country by 1805 and was acknowledged as governor by the Ottoman sultan. He had become well aware of the superiority of European armies, and wanted to form one in Egypt on European lines. He realized, too, that for this purpose it was necessary to have an officer class with some of the attainments of European officers; and he also saw that the ulema would never agree to the introduction of the necessary new subjects into the curriculum of Islamic education. He therefore imported teachers from Europe for the training of his officers. This was the beginning of the introduction into the Islamic world of a vast system of European-type education. By the early twentieth century there were two systems of education throughout the Islamic world: the traditional Islamic system, whose curriculum had not changed for centuries, and a system of the Western type. At some points this type of education had been provided by Christian missionaries, but more and more it was Muslims themselves who developed it because they wanted it for their children. By 1945 in most Muslim countries there were Western-type primary schools, secondary schools and universities; and the majority of well-educated persons were the products of this system. Such persons received little formal religious education in school, since the religious experts with a traditional training could not follow Western methods of teaching. There was, of course, informal education within the family and through private reading.

The statesmen began to disregard the ulema in matters also of law. By the middle of the nineteenth century the Ottoman empire had a considerable volume of foreign trade, largely with European countries, but the Sharīʿa as traditionally understood created what to many seemed unnecessary obstacles. Consequently in 1850 the Ottoman sultan promulgated a Commercial Code. Ostensibly this contained not new laws but only regulations to show how existing laws based on the Sharīʿa were to be applied, and this was something the sultan was entitled to do; but the regulations were in fact new laws based on a French code. When there was little protest from the ulema in general over this code, others followed: a Penal Code in 1858, a Code of Commercial Procedure in 1861, a Code of Maritime Commerce in 1863, and so on. New courts were then established to apply these codes. Finally in 1927 the Turkish republic got rid of the Sharīʿa altogether and adopted a Civil Code based on the Swiss. In the quarter of a century before 1945 most of the newly independent Islamic states were applying the Sharīʿa only in matters of personal status—marriage, divorce, inheritance—and not always even there.

All these changes meant a severe loss of power and status for the traditionally trained jurists, the ulema. They still controlled some education, but most education at all levels was outwith their control. They still controlled the Sharīʿa courts, but much judicial business was done elsewhere in courts in which they were not qualified to practise. And since the Sharīʿa was being neglected at many points, their right of interpreting the Sharīʿa had lost much of its value. It is thus not surprising that a prominent factor in Islamic life both before 1945 and increasingly since then has been the desire of the ulema to recover something of their lost power and prestige.

Another important factor, not yet apparent to observers like

Gibb in 1945, nor even to Bishop Kenneth Cragg in his *Counsels in Contemporary Islam*[2] in 1965, was the widespread feeling among ordinary Muslims that they were in danger of becoming completely Westernized and losing their Muslim identity. It is significant that Anwar el-Sadat, who became President of Egypt in succession to Gamal Abd-en-Nasser in 1970, entitled his autobiography *In Search of Identity*[3] and in it emphasized that he was seeking not just his own identity but that of Egypt. A similar point is made in the publisher's announcement of a series of seven volumes containing revised versions in English of papers read at the First World Conference on Muslim Education held at Mecca in spring 1977.[4] Some of the announcement is worth quoting, since it shows that the conservative ulema who dominated the conference accept much of the analysis given above.

'Muslims in the twentieth century are passing through a period of self-examination and self-awareness. The Muslim majority countries that extend from Morocco to Indonesia have adopted the Western system of education in order to acquire modern knowledge so that they may become intellectually and materially advanced. This system of education has long ago been separated from the sphere of the Divine and is at present secular in approach, since basic assumptions behind Natural, Applied and Social Sciences and Humanities are not drawn from religion. Along with these concepts, a modern way of life which contradicts the traditional way of life governed by the Sharia is becoming established in Muslim society and is being encouraged by radio, television and other mass media programmes. A cultural duality has therefore appeared everywhere in the Muslim world. The traditional Islamic education that still persists is supporting the traditional Islamic group, whereas modern secular education is creating secularists who know or

[2] Edinburgh: Edinburgh University Press, 1965.
[3] London: Collins, 1978 (paperback).
[4] Islamic Education Series, Jeddah 1979.

care little about their traditions and values or pay only lip-service to them.

As the secular education system is dominant in Muslim countries, Muslim thinkers have become worried that gradually the Muslim world will lose its identity by losing its Islamic character and will thus suffer from the same moral disintegration and confusion as the West. It can preserve that identity and save the Ummah from the confusion and erosion of values and from the conflict between religious and secular groups only if Muslims receive a truly Islamic education.'

The fear of a loss of identity is probably the main factor which has led to a resurgence or revival of Islam during the last two decades. It appears to be a widespread popular movement with a genuine religious component. The twenty-year-old son of a leading Egyptian gynaecologist not merely tells his father to stop drinking whisky but gets up early in the morning to go to the mosque. The popular feeling, however, has certainly been encouraged and in part directed by the ulema as part of their struggle to regain power.

The first significant event after 1945 for Islam as a religion was the creation of the independent state of Pakistan in 1947, a state consisting of those regions of the Indian subcontinent where there was a Muslim majority. This state came into existence because, in the years when independence was being negotiated, some of the leading Muslim statesmen abandoned the idea of an All-India Federation in favour of a separate state for Muslims. The underlying consideration was that Muslims were unlikely to be fairly treated in a state where there were at least twice as many Hindus. Superficially, then, it would seem that Pakistan was a state whose basis was Islam; and this fits in with the common belief that Islam can only truly be itself when it is embodied in a state. The realities here, however, were somewhat different. Those who worked for the establishment of Pakistan were largely Westernized statesmen, while the religious leaders opposed the project for a separate state. During the constitutional debates the ulema strove to ensure that the state would be truly Islamic by having the principle accepted that all legislation should be examined by qualified jurists to see that it was in accordance with the Sharī'a; but the statesmen, apprehensive of the reactionary outlook of most ulema, were not prepared to agree to this. In the end Pakistan, though apparently created for specifically Islamic reasons, differs little from states like Egypt and Indonesia. Since about 1980 the government, urgently requiring the support of the conservative ulema, has had to yield to some of their demands, such as making the amputation of a hand the punishment for theft in certain cases.

The partition of the subcontinent also had a profound effect on the forty million Muslims remaining in the new, officially secular and predominantly Hindu, India. There were Muslim leaders who had opposed partition, and these were ready to participate fully in the new state. Dr. Zakir Husain, a Muslim, was President of India for a term. Another prominent upholder of full participation in the new India, and one of the outstanding Muslims of his generation, was Mawlana Abul-Kalam Azad, a deeply religious man and something of a theologian. He wrote a long commentary on the Qur'ān in Urdu, which has been translated into English under the title *The Tarjumān al-Qur'ān*.[5] Living in a multi-religious society he takes the view that all spiritual religion is in essence one. Even the essence of Islam, he thinks, has been obscured by the work of the early scholars, such as their acceptance of Greek philosophical categories. In attempting to recover this essential Islam it is necessary to allow the Qur'ān to interpret itself; and this is what he attempts to do in his commentary. He also includes discussions, in terms of current Western thought, of some basic Qur'ānic concepts. His

[5] London: Asia Publications, vol. 1, 1962; vol. 2, 1967.

views were found attractive by many of the more Westernized Muslims, and are well suited to life in a secular state, where religion is a private and communal matter and does not affect law and government.

Apart from the millions of non-Westernized Muslims in India there were traditionally-trained ulema, and these had responsibility for administration of the Islamic law of personal status. The result of partition was to make such people even more rigid and inflexible, unwilling to make the slightest adjustment to the formulation of the law which might alleviate some obvious problem, because they feared that, if they did so, they would then have pressure put upon them to make further changes.

In the 1920s under Mustafa Kemal Atatürk the Turkish Republic became a wholly secular state, and Islam was discouraged. Islam nevertheless persisted, and, since the death of Atatürk in 1938, has recoverd some of the ground it had lost, at least in respect of religious practice, though not in the sphere of legislation. In 1949 a theological faculty was established in the University of Ankara, and this has been followed by similar faculties in other universities. These faculties, however, have not been organized on the lines of a traditional Islamic college (*madrasa*), but make use of Western methods, and many of the professors are moderately Westernizing in attitude. Other professors are more conservative, but not fanatically so. The faculties are mainly concerned with the training of teachers to give religious instruction in schools. Apart from the inclusion of Islam in the school curriculum the practice of Islam in Turkey has become a matter for the individual, and there is a degree of freedom to write and think about religious matters.

Muslim intellectuals in Muslim-minority countries have the fullest freedom to rethink their religious position. Many books and articles now appear in French, English and other European languages, and pursue many different lines of thought. Two

239

names may be mentioned to give a sample of the avenues being explored, though they cannot convey the variety of approaches. Mohammed Arkoun is an Algerian who is now professor at the Sorbonne in Paris. He is conversant with all the latest thinking among French intellectuals, especially in the field of linguistics, and has written a large number of articles showing how this thinking may be applied to Islam in ways which lead to the deepening of the faith of Muslims—in contrast to the purely secular attitude of many Western Islamologists.[6] Mahmoud Ayoub spent some years in a Christian school in the Lebanon, and has a much better understanding of Christianity than most Muslims. Because he realizes the central place in Christian faith of the belief that Jesus died on the cross, he has reinterpreted the Qur'ānic passage (4.157–9) which is commonly taken as denying that death, and he has tried to show that the passage can be taken in a way that does not deny the death. He has also a book on *Redemptive Suffering in Islam*[7] which combines careful scholarship with deep religious experience, and shows that at some points the difference between Christianity and Islam is not so great as is often supposed.

Western observers of Islam in the early part of this century were greatly impressed by the modernizing and Westernizing tendencies, and concentrated their studies mainly on these. Perhaps they thought these would create the Islam of the future, and hoped it would be closer to Christianity. The resurgence of the last two decades or so, however, is clearly the outcome of forces which must have been developing quietly under the

[6] Most relevant are three volumes of reprinted articles and essays: *Essais sur la pensée islamique*; *Lectures du Coran* (sc. ways of reading it); *Pour une critique de la raison islamique*—Paris 1973, 1982, 1984. See also W. M. Watt, 'A Contemporary Muslim Thinker', *Scottish Journal of Religious Studies*, vi (1985), 5–10.

[7] *Redemptive Suffering in Islam: a Study of the Devotional Aspects of 'Āshūrā' in Twelver Shī'ism*, The Hague 1978: 'Towards an Islamic Christology, II: The Death of Jesus, Reality or Delusion', *Muslim World*, lxx (1980), 91–121.

surface during the previous half-century. Sir Hamilton Gibb
was aware of such forces. He applied the term 'revolutionary
Mahdism' to movements which hoped by 'a violent assertion of
the supremacy of the sacred law' to establish an alternative to
secularized government; and he went on to note that 'Mahdism
has linked up with extreme nationalism to produce the swelling
tides of popular discontent and revolutionary ardor which are
familiar to all observers of the Muslim world today.'[8] Let us
now look more closely at two of these movements.

The Muslim Brotherhood (Al-Ikhwān al-Muslimūn) had
become sufficiently important by 1945 to be mentioned by Sir
Hamilton Gibb in a footnote. Founded by Ḥasan al-Bannā' in
1928, it has passed through many ups and downs. It is difficult to
describe it in a few words because it has many aspects. Some
were attracted to it because it was a kind of sufi order (ṭarīqa).
For others it was a club for cultural, athletic and other activities.
More and more, however, it tended to attract political activists,
looking for reforms along Islamic lines, and not always averse to
violence. In its origins it was under the influence of Muḥammad
'Abduh, but its basic attitude came to be anti-Western. It had no
clear intellectual principles, however, on which to found its
policies, and tended to be interested in whatever reforms were
in the public eye at a given moment. In recent years, not
surprisingly, it has been moving closer to the fundamentalist
ulema.

In India in 1941 Mawlānā Abū-l-A'lā al-Mawdūdī (often
Maududi in English), a journalist by training, founded the
Jamā'at-i-Islāmī, an association not unlike the Muslim
Brotherhood, but with more of a theological basis. Though
originally opposed to partition Maududi decided to accept it
and to live in Pakistan. He believed that the Sharī'a contained
the final idea for all humanity, and that Muslims had nothing to

[8] *Modern Trends*, 117, 120.

learn from non-Islamic sources; and thus he was among those who worked—in the end unsuccessfully—to make Pakistan a truly Islamic state in accordance with the Sharī'a. He believed in theory that the regulations based on the Sharī'a could be adapted to new situations, but in practice did little about this and on most points agreed with conservative ulema. He was particularly insistent that women should observe strict purdah, and he also thought that usury should be avoided. He was fond of criticizing the immorality of the West, but thought Muslims were justified in taking over what they found useful of Western science and technology. His views gave expression to the outlook of the traditionalist middle class in India who felt their identity and sometimes their livelihood threatened by the West.[9] This is the first clear statement of the attitudes underlying the present resurgence of Islam.

Since 1979 Iran may be said to have become the spearhead of this resurgence. Even in 1965 Kenneth Cragg made no mention of any 'contemporary counsels' in Iran. Yet under the surface the social pressures were increasing which led to the revolution. They were similar to those in other parts of the Islamic world— above all the feeling that the Westernization of the country was endangering its Muslim identity. With swelling oil revenues Shah Muhammad Reza accelerated the process of Westernization, and this not only increased apprehension about Islamic identity, but also had an adverse effect economically on various groups. Again in Iran, as in other parts of the Islamic world, the ulema (usually known as mujtahids) were trying to regain some of their lost powers. In Iran, however, they were in a stronger position than elsewhere. The medieval Sunnite caliphs could claim to be in a sense the successors of the Prophet politically, and so to have authority over the ulema; and something of this attitude may have persisted towards

[9] Malise Ruthven, *Islam in the World*, Harmondsworth 1984, 326–329.

contemporary Muslim rulers. In Iran, however, since the official religion was the Imāmite or Twelver form of Shīʿism, the ulema could claim to know more about the mind of the 'hidden imam' than the actual ruler, who was only a kind of caretaker. This was theory, but in practice since the later nineteenth century the ulema had at various points shown themselves the defenders of ordinary people against oppressive rulers. They had also, over a long period, wherever a shah was weak and needed their support, wrested concessions from him; and in particular they now had control of the revenues from which their salaries came, and so could not have economic pressure brought to bear on them to conform to the policies of the government.

When discontent with the shah and his policies spread to many different groups of people, one of the ulema, Ayatollah Khomeini, was able to get all these groups to act together to overthrow the shah. The general programme on which they were agreed was a return to an Islamic way of life; but in some of his writings Khomeini had gone beyond the usual aim of ulema of having a committee to ensure that legislation and other government acts were Islamic; he had asserted that the ulema themselves should be the rulers. This is more or less what happened in Iran. The ulema, of course, lacked the necessary administrative skills to run a modern country, but they were able to retain sufficient civil servants, politicians and army officers to keep the machine of state in running order. There have naturally been tensions between all these and the ulema, and indeed between different groups among the ulema, but so far under this system Iran has continued to function as a state.

After this review of some of the salient features of the religion of Islam during the past forty years, the remainder of the chapter will try to outline its present position and future prospects.

The first point to be made is that there has been little decline in the practice of their religion by vast numbers of Muslims, probably the majority, as is evidenced by attendance at the mosque on Fridays and at other times, and by observance of the fast of Ramaḍān. There has been some falling off in religious practice among those with a Western education, but they are a minority, and numbers of them have remained devout and practising Muslims. Some sufi orders continue to flourish among ordinary people, urban and rural, but the position varies from country to country. A number of persons with a mainly Western education also practise certain forms of sufism.

The most significant feature of Islam today, however, is the continuing power of the ulema. Though they have lost most of their former functions in respect of education and the administration of justice, they still have considerable influence over the minds of the masses of ordinary Muslims. It remains to be seen whether this will be affected by the spread of television in Islamic lands. A man of moderate Westernizing outlook might be able to get a greater following through television than the ulema, who would not necessarily be able to make such effective use of the medium. At the present moment, however, the ulema seem to be able to sway the masses against any reforming movement of which they disapprove.

An outstanding characteristic of the ulema is their inflexibility. Muslims in general have taken over the nomadic-Arab ideal of unchangingness. The word for 'heresy' is simply 'innovation' (bid'a). The ulema are constantly striving to keep Islam as it originally was and always has been; and for them this means keeping it in accord with the 'picture' or 'image' of the earliest Islam which was developed by ulema later in the middle ages. This picture or image contains all aspects of Islam—law and social morality, the interpretation of the Qur'ān, theology and even history. It has been handed on for centuries by traditional Islamic education, while all possible alternatives have been denied expression. It is thus virtually impossible for Muslims to think about their religion and religious community except in terms of this image—apart, that is, from those exposed to strong doses of Western education. Though the image was originally the work of scholars, it may be said to be held by the masses in a popular version. For example, medieval scholars were well aware that there were officially seven *qirā'āt* (sets of readings) of the Qur'ān, as well as many unofficial variants; but the modern popular belief is that there is one single text of the Qur'ān to which there are no variants. This is a matter on which Islam is thought to be superior to Christianity, and slightly sophisticated young Muslims today will maintain that the official *qirā'āt* are altogether different from the Christian textual variants.

Sir Hamilton Gibb in 1945 saw one of the chief weaknesses of Islam as 'romanticism' or the exaltation of imagination over reason and the failure to use reason to check imagination. One example of this is the fact that historical criticism was developed by the historians up to a point but then was gradually abandoned; and what followed was a 'subordination of historical method and thought to the demands of religious emotion and theological dogma'.[10] In other words, the medieval and still persistent self-image of Islam was the product more of imagination than of reason. This is obvious if we look at some of the points still being emphasized.

One prominent point is that Islam is self-sufficient; it does not owe anything to other religions and cultures (except perhaps philosophy to the Greeks), and it has nothing to learn from other religions and cultures. This is held despite the fact that Muḥammad enjoined his followers to seek knowledge from as far away as China. It is doubtless easier for traditionalist Muslims to hold such a view because they have absolutely no idea of growth or development in the religious sphere. A parallel point is the belief that Islam is superior to Judaism, Christianity and other religions, and of course to Western

[10] *Modern Trends*, 124f.

materialism. It is not surprising, then, that some Muslims reject the whole conception of human rights because it is something Western; but this is balanced by the fact that a number of responsible Muslims have seriously discussed the questions raised by the Universal Declaration of Human Rights of 1948 and have themselves published some documents.[11] The chief hesitations have been over the right to change one's religious allegiance and over the equality of women. Otherwise the rights upheld by the Sharī'a are similar to those in the Universal Declaration.

Another facet of the self-image is the claim that Islam has the final truth for all humanity from now till the end of time. This is doubtless credible if one is thinking in terms of a static universe; but it is inconceivable if one is aware of development. There might even be said to be moral dangers in idealizing the period of Muḥammad's prophethood and the rule of the first four 'rightly-guided' caliphs. It was a rough and in some ways barbaric time in which human life was held cheaply. Civilized people are horrified at the assertion that in some cases the amputation of a hand may be an appropriate punishment for theft and stoning for adultery. The Islamic Repulic of Iran issued a postage stamp glorifying the man who assassinated President Sadat of Egypt. How can such a thing be an ideal for all humanity to the end of time?

Despite this claim of finality and despite the claim that the Sharī'a can be adapted to novel situations little has in fact been done to adapt the Sharī'a to modern conditions. Theoretically there is no difficulty about adaptation; each Qur'ānic rule has an 'illa or ground which is not stated in the Qur'ān but has to be discerned by jurists; but once the 'illa has been discerned it can be applied to fresh situations. Thus the 'illa of the prohibition of

[11] Discussions are described and some documents reproduced in *Islamochristiana*, vol. ix (1983), published in Rome.

wine-drinking is taken to be that it leads to intoxication, and so any other intoxicating beverage is likewise prohibited. The making of a fresh application is described as *ijtihād*, the use by a qualified jurist of his own judgement; and this is what nineteenth-century modernists were wanting when they called for the opening of the gate of *ijtihād*. In some Islamic countries minor adaptations have been made, though not usually by *ijtihād* but by roundabout methods; for example, instead of making a law forbidding the marriage of girls under the age of sixteen a government would discourage such marriages by forbidding courts to deal with matrimonial cases where the wife had been under sixteen at the time of marriage.

It should be noted that the movement of Islamic resurgence has shown little interest in the adaptation of the Sharī'a to the world of today. Its main emphasis has been on those practices which distinguish Muslims from Westerners, in order to strengthen the sense of Muslim identity; in the forefront have been the prohibition of alcohol, the prohibition of usury and the veiling of women. This last may indeed also have the practical aim of making life easier for both young men and young women who are unaccustomed to the free mixing of the sexes and feel threatened by it when suddenly introduced to it. Yet if the Sharī'a is to provide a guide for all humanity, there are many areas where its elaboration is urgently required. What controls should be placed on multinational corporations? What rights should trade unions have? Above all, what guidance does the Sharī'a give to Muslims who have to work in conjunction with non-Muslims on international bodies or in states where Muslims are in a minority?

The second main weakness of Islam in the eyes of Sir Hamilton Gibb was intellectual confusion in the minds of the modernists. Such confusion, however, is also found in the conservative ulema. Part of their image of Islam is a philosophical basis developed in medieval times in response to

247

the Neoplatonism of philosophers like Avicenna. The ulema
have no appreciation of the general philosophical climate of the
West, and have not the competence to argue with Western
philosophers. They want to accept Western science, but fail to
realize that no one can truly be a scientist without having a
scientific mentality, and that this last is bound up with some sort
of Western philosophy. They also fail to appreciate current
Western ideas about historical method and historical
objectivity. The most serious lack of all is probably the failure to
appreciate the concept of development and to abandon their
concept of a static universe and a static humanity. It was because
within the Bible some development is implicit that when the
Christian Reformers adopted the principle of 'back to the Bible'
they did not go back to crude barbarities like the murder of
Sisera by Jael.[12]

It is hardly too much to say that the conservative traditionalist
ulema are shutting themselves and the masses who follow them
into a ghetto of their own where they are not open to what is
happening in the rest of the world. In the long run this state of
affairs must lead to disaster. There are so many weaknesses and
contradictions, however, in the traditionalist Islamic self-image
that sooner or later there is bound to be a great revulsion of
feeling against those who are maintaining the image. For the
moment none of the modernizing movements or individuals
appears to have a programme capable of attracting the masses
and wooing them away from the ulema. In so far, however, as
the ulema fail to deal with actual pressing problems of Muslim
groups—other than the problem of threatened identity, which
is of course a real problem—there will be a rising tide of
discontent with their leadership. What is to be hoped for is that
some new leader will arise, who will be a *mujaddid* or renewer of
religion for the present age, and will channel this discontent to

[12] *Judges* 4.17–22—a parallel to the assassination of Sadat?

248

the achievement of positive ends. It is almost certain, however, that only after much struggle and suffering will the medieval self-image be replaced by a truer one and the power of the conservative ulema broken.

Bibliography

Ahmad, Khurshid (ed.), *Islam, its Meaning and Message*; London: Islamic Council of Europe, 1976.

——, and Z. I. Ansari (eds.) *Islamic Perspectives: Studies in Honour of Sayyid Mawlāna Abul A'lā Mawdūdī*; London: The Islamic Foundation, 1979.

Arkoun, Mohammed, *Lectures du Coran*; Paris: Maisonneuve et Larose, 1982.

——, *Pour une critique de la raison islamique*; Paris: Maisonneuve et Larose, 1984.

——, *Essais sur la pensée islamique* (third edition); Paris: Maisonneuve et Larose, 1984.

Ayoub, Mahmoud, *Redemptive Suffering in Islam: A Study of the Devotional Aspects of 'Āshurā' in Twelver Shī'ism*; The Hague: Mouton, 1978.

Azad, Mawlana Abul Kalam, *The Tarjumān al-Qur'ān*; London: Asia Publications, vol. 1, 1962; vol. 2, 1967.

Cragg, Kenneth, *Counsels in Contemporary Islam*; Edinburgh: Edinburgh University Press, 1965.

Gibb, H. A. R., *Modern Trends in Islam*; Chicago: University of Chicago Press, 1947.

Imam (monthly), London: Embassy of the Islamic Republic if Iran.

Keddie, Nikki R., *Roots of Revolution: an Interpretive History of Modern Iran*; New Haven: Yale University Press, 1981.

Khomeini, Imam, *Selected Messages and Speeches*; Tehran: Ministry of National Guidance, n.d. (1980).

Laroui, Abdallah, *The Crisis of the Arab Intellectual: Traditionalism or Historicism?*; Berkeley: University of California Press, 1976.

Maududi, Abul A'la, *Towards Understanding Islam*; 6th edition, Lahore: Islamic Publications, 1960.

——, *Islamic Way of Life*; 3rd edition, Lahore: Islamic Publications, 1965.

Risalat al-Jihad (monthly), Tripoli (Libya): The Islamic Call Society.

Ruthven, Malise, *Islam in the World*; Harmondsworth: Penguin Books, 1984.

Sadat, Anwar, *In Search of Identity: an Autobiography*; London: Collins, 1978.

Watt, W. Montgomery, 'A Contemporary Muslim Thinker', *Scottish Journal of Religious Studies*, vi (1985), 5–10.

Zafrulla Khan, Muhammad, *Islam, its Meaning for Modern Man*; New York: Harper & Row, 1962.

9

PRIMAL RELIGIOUS TRADITIONS IN TODAY'S WORLD

Andrew Walls

(Aberdeen and Edinburgh)

Immense difficulties lie in the way of any attempt at a comprehensive statement on the primal religions.[1] The sheer scale of the exercise: the vast number[2] of diverse peoples, cultures and environments, from the tundra to the rain forests, subject to the most widely different external influences; the absence of central authority or universally recognized texts or traditions; the bewildering variety of religious structure, the virtual impossibility of establishing even rudimentary statistics, inhibit the sort of account which can be attempted for most of the world's religious systems. The problems of definition are acute. For one thing, primal religions underlie all the other faiths, and often exist in symbiosis with them, continuing (sometimes more, sometimes less transformed) to have an active life within and around cultures and communities influenced by those faiths. What we call for convenience 'religions' are not in any case self-contained, mutually exclusive entities which can be

[1] For a general account and bibliographies see Joseph Epes Brown, B. Colless and P. Donovan, Aylward Shorter and H. W. Turner in J. R. Hinnells (ed.) *A handbook of living religions*, Harmondsworth: Penguin 1984, 392–454. See also H. W. Turner, 'The way forward in the religious study of African primal religions', *Journal of Religion in Africa* 12(1) 1981, 1–15.

[2] G. P. Murdock lists 742 separate peoples in sub-Saharan Africa alone (*Africa: its peoples and their culture history*, New York: McGraw Hill 1959). For a geographical survey with bibliographies see W. Dupré, *Religion in primitive cultures: a study in ethnophilosophy*, The Hague: Mouton 1975, pp. 57–176.

adopted or exchanged at will. From the standpoint of the believer or the community of believers there is bound to be a continuum of perception and experience, even through periods of religious change; new ideas and activities, even the need for new ideas and activities, inevitably emerge in terms of the old. The influence of primal world views thus continues long after adhesion takes place to Christianity or Islam, to Hinduism or Buddhism; but this is not the same as saying that the 'conversion' is superficial or negligible. The major symbolic change may be highly significant, and making a turning point in the religious development of a primal society. And thus, in one sense, in 'primal' religion itself.

It has been the fate of the practitioners of primal religions to be classified and theorized over by others and rarely to be heard with their own story. At an earlier period they were pressed into the service of theories of the origin of religion and the early history of mankind, made the keystone of evolutionary interpretative schemes or the arsenal from which evolutionary schemes were bombarded. The modern controversies are, if anything, still more intense, for they now lie at the heart of questions of cultural identity and authenticity. The debates about them are no longer academic and historical: they affect how whole peoples perceive their present and its relation to their past. In Africa, in North America, and now in Australia new interpretations of the primal religions are arising from local scholars working in international languages, making an appeal to local popular consciousness, insisting that these religions have been misinterpreted through being forced into alien categories.[3] A particularly keen debate goes on between African scholars.[4]

---

[3] An African example is Okot p'Bitek, *African religions in Western scholarship*, Kampala: East African Literature Bureau, n.d. (c. 1971); a Native American example, Vine Deloria, *God is red*, New York: Grosset and Dunlop 1973.

[4] Cf. E. B. Idowu, *African traditional religion: a definition*, London: S.C.M.

We will not be able to escape some reference to this process of re-evaluation, for in a sense it is part of the recent history of the religions themselves; but both this question, and that of the continuing effect of the primal religions within communities whose consciousness is formed by another faith (usually Christianity or Islam, but also Hinduism and Buddhism), lie outside the scope of this essay.

The Meaning of 'Primal'

The very term 'primal religions' is rejected by many. It is used here in the absence of any term which would be more widely acceptable when treating of a worldwide phenomenon, not confined to any one region of the world. How else are we to bring together the religions of circumpolar peoples, of various peoples of Africa, the Indian sub-continent, South East Asia, Inner Asia, North and South America, Australia and the Pacific? Suffice it to say that the word 'primal' is not a euphemism for 'primitive', nor are any evolutionistic undertones intended. The word helpfully underlines two features of the religions of the peoples indicated: their historical anteriority and their basic, elemental status in human experience. All other faiths are subsequent, and represent, as it were, second thoughts; all other believers, and for that matter non-believers, are primalists underneath.

Content and Structure in Primal Religions

That is not to say, of course, that the primal religions reflect a single view of the universe or a common religious practice, nor that they are without history or development. That idea has

1973; J. S. Mbiti, *African religions and philosophy*, London: Heinemann 1969; G. M. Setiloane, *The image of God among the Sothe-Tswana*, Rotterdam: Balkema 1976. See also D. Westerlund, *African religion in African scholarship: a preliminary study of the religious and political background*, Stockholm: Almqvist och Wiksell 1985.

been kept in existence by attempts to reconstruct the religion of particular peoples prior to contact with the West as though that past was a static, timeless entity, and has been reinforced by the common use of the 'ethnographic present' in description. It is the sheer quantity and complexity of the history, not its deficiency, which makes it so hard to trace. Like all other faiths, the primal religions have always known adjustments and alterations, fossilizations and revivals, prophets and reformers, new directions and new institutions.[5] Until recent years, the tendency has been to designate types of religion as characteristic of particular societies. Some have concentrated attention on the phenomena of religion itself, identifying, for instance, a common structure of religion across the African continent and sometimes beyond, usually based on a fourfold pattern of Supreme Being, divinities, ancestors and objects of power.[6] Others have concentrated on the symbol systems of particular

---

[5] The work of Professor Åke Hultkrantz of Stockholm and his students has been particularly fertile in its consideration of the historical aspect of primal religions. See, e.g. A. Hultkrantz, *The religions of the American Indians*, Berkeley: University of California Press 1979; L. Backman and Åke Hultkrantz (eds.), *Saami pre-Christian religion: studies on the oldest traces of religion among the Saamis*, Stockholm: Almqvist och Wiksell 1985; Åke Hultkrantz, 'History of religions in anthropological waters: some reflections against the background of American data', *Temenos* 13, 1977, 81–97.
For a recent study of the history of the religion of an African people, and its continuity into the period of Christian inter-action, cf. Janet Hodgson, *The God of the Xhosa. A study of the origins and development of the traditional concepts of the supreme being*, Cape Town: Oxford University Press 1982. One institution in Africa which has received particular attention from historians is the cult-shrine; see J. M. Schoffeleers (ed.) *Guardians of the land: essays on Central African territorial cults*, Gweru: Mambo Press 1979, and W. M. J. van Binsbergen, *Religious change in Zambia. Exploratory studies*, London: Kegan Paul 1981.

[6] Expounded by Geoffrey Parrinder in *African traditional religion*, London: Hutchinson 1954, on lines laid down in his *West African religion*, London: Epworth 1949. See H. W. Turner, 'Geoffrey Parrinder's contribution to studies of religion in Africa', *Religion* 10(2) 1980, pp. 156–164 and A. F. Walls, 'A bag of needments for the road: Geoffrey Parrinder and the study of religion in Britain', *ibid.* pp. 141–150.

peoples.[7] Others again have concentrated on the functioning of the societies themselves, and the place of ritual and religious specialists in maintaining and cementing relationships;[8] while many, following old precedent, have identified religious types according to environments—religions of hunter-gatherers, of pastoral nomads, of settled agriculturalists, and so on.[9] This is no place to pursue these methods of categorization. Bringing them together, however, reminds us:

(i) The elements of religious life are not the same as the structure of religious life. Most obviously, the tradition of a people may include a Being who, when that people came into contact with a God-centred religious tradition, will be invested with all the characteristics of the Supreme Being; or the tradition may in some other way recognize the ultimate unity of the transcendent world, a single principle underlying life. And yet such a recognition may impinge very little on the life of most members of the community, though ritual acts and words may be of regular occurrence. It may be there in the margins of daily life; it may be locked in the specialist knowledge of the experts in tradition. It is one thing, therefore, to identify across many, perhaps most, primal religions, the fourfold series of elements; the different patterns in which those elements are arranged result not only in different religions, but in different *kinds* of religion. From the classical studies of particular peoples there appear to be God-dominated systems, divinity-dominated systems, ancestor-dominated systems, and systems in which the hypostatization of the transcendent is so slight that objects of

[7] G. Dieterlen, *Essai sur la religion Bambara*, Paris 1951; M. Griaule and Dieterlen, G. 'The Dogon', in D. Forde (ed.) *African worlds. Studies in the cosmological ideas and social values of African peoples* London: Oxford University Press 1954. Cf. E. M. Zuesse, *Ritual cosmos. The sanctification of life in African religions*, Athens, Ohio: Ohio University Press 1979, 135–179.

[8] Cf. comments of B. C. Ray, *African religions. Symbol, ritual and community*, Englewood Cliffs, N.J.: Prentice Hall 1976, chapter 1.

[9] Cf. Zuesse *op cit.*, 17–32.

power, or impersonalized power itself, dominate them. At this latter point the line between religion and magic has become of the thinnest.

In a study of the place of prayer among African peoples, Aylward Shorter distinguishes six distinct types of religion, related to the way in which prayer is directed.[10] He calls the first of these 'strict theism', in which, as with the Meru and the Pygmies of the central rain forest, the Supreme Being is experienced directly in life and worshipped directly in prayer. There is however, a 'relative theism', in which, as with the Nuer and Dinka, worship is rendered through a variety of beings conceived as modes of existence of the Supreme Being, and not as independent entities. Another type is 'symmetrical mediation' in which intermediary spirits (usually ancestral) act as the vehicles of communication to and from the Supreme Being (Kongo, Tumbuka). With 'asymmetrical mediation' the mediators receive prayer and there is little or no formal worship of the Supreme Being but its power and presence are acknowledged in life (Dogon, Shona, Zande). But it is also possible to have 'strict deism' where there is no clear indication of a Supreme Being underlying such cult as exists (Acholi);[11] and very commonly there is 'relative deism' in which neither the concepts of the Supreme Being nor of mediation play any prominent part in a religious life directed towards guardian divinities, cult heroes or ancestors, but where the experience and worship of the Supreme Being are not ruled out (Yoruba, Ngoni, and many others). The same elements of religion appear in at least five of the six models; and yet the models reflect entirely different *structures* of religion.

(ii) As with all religious traditions, there are different levels

[10] A. Shorter, *Prayer in the religious traditions of Africa*, Nairobi: Oxford University Press 1975, pp. 8–13.

[11] Cf. Okot p'Bitek, *Religion of the Central Luo*, Kampala: East African Literature Bureau 1971.

of religious knowledge and experience within the primal community. In thinking of the religious life of a community as a whole it may be necessary to take account of daily pieties, common observances, recognized means of recourse in emergencies, the special knowledge of experts, and the differing types of explanation offered in popular discourse and in the reflection of masters of tradition. The complexity of the African symbol systems elucidated by French anthropologists and the width of their field of reference, can only be explained in terms of a succession of reflective commentators on the seen and unseen world, developing what in another context would be called philosophical method. Quite frequently, different types of divination are found side by side. Wider knowledge now available to outsiders of Ifa divination[12] lays emphasis not on the slight of hand assumed by earlier Western observers, nor on the psychological insight always necessary in the diviner's task, but on the skilled application of a whole encyclopedia of myth covering every possible eventuality. This is essentially the 'word of God' in a surer sense than can be derived from the apparently direct utterance of the spirit medium in trance sought by many ordinary people in need. It comes, as it were, from a deeper source in the divine world.[13]

(iii) If symbol system, religious ritual and social system are interrelated, unassimilated stress in any of these areas will place strains upon the others. Cataclysmic social changes leave an outdated symbol system and useless rituals which have lost their rationale—unless they can be adapted to take account of the new conditions. Additions to or drastic revision of the symbol system or ritual pattern call in question the established social

[12] W. R. Bascom, *Ifa divination. Communication between gods and men in West Africa* Bloomington, Indiana: Indiana University Press 1969.

[13] Cf. Zuesse, *op. cit.*, chapter 11. On divination as a 'cybernetic' system. see V. W. Turner, *The drums of affliction. A study of religious processes among the Ndembu of Zambia*, Oxford: Clarendon Press 1968, pp. 25–51.

order, or certain functions within it. Institutions must adapt to the new pattern, or ignore it and produce a divorce between symbol and order.

(iv) Living religion is likely to relate intimately to the basis of livelihood within a community. This is not to say that it is *determined* by the community's environment; Åke Hultkrantz has indicated how ecological factors give shape to, indeed, 'veil' religion, rather than provide content, which comes from that religion's own history and tradition.[14] Nevertheless, a change in the basis of livelihood either requires a new set of 'veils' or leaves the religion without contact with the basis of the community's living.

Factors in Change in Primal Religions
These generalizations all point to important religious implications of any fundamental change in the society; whether environmental change, caused by migration or drastic alteration in the habitat; new modes of exchange, or anything else which alters the mode of personal relationships and the basis on which status is acknowledged; changes in kinship patterns or the community's order brought about by political or economic change or exposure to new pressures from an alien presence. None of these factors is new, nor a product solely of the conditions of the modern world. Primal societies have been open to such changes from time immemorial, and occasionally one can trace the pattern of change in the society and its religion over centuries. The Navajo, for instance, are descended from hunting peoples reaching northern New Mexico in the fourteenth or fifteenth century, necessarily turning to

---

[14] Åke Hultkrantz, 'An ecological approach to religion', *Ethnos* 31(1–4), 131–150; 'The religio-ecological method in the research on prehistoric religion, *Valcamonica Symposium: Les religions de la préhistoire*, Capo di Ponte: Centro Camuno di Studi Preistorici 1972. The idea of 'veils' is developed in his Gifford Lecture series still to be published.

agriculture, and thereafter acquiring a matrilineal clan system, the use of sheep and a complex mythic system under the influence of their settled agricultural Pueblo neighbours. In their case the new mythic system was superimposed on the rites and values appropriate to a hunting culture.[15] We must therefore proceed to some further generalizations arising from the phenomenon of recurrent change in primal societies.

(i) While models of distinct types of primal religion, such as Shorter's already referred to, are useful, they require certain caveats. In particular we must not assume that any given people's representation of a given model is a static one; the pattern of the elements, and thus the structure, may be in flux, for instance, between his 'relative theism' and 'relative deism', or vice versa. We must in any case be cautious with the use of categories derived from other types of tradition. Geoffrey Parrinder has shown how misleading it can be to use the words 'monotheistic', 'polytheistic' and 'pantheistic' of an African religion: the very same society may produce examples of all three attitudes (or what in Western culture would be so designated) without any sense of the perceptions being incompatible.[16]

(ii) Where change occurs sufficient to disturb the interrelated social, symbol and ritual systems, the 'expert' tradition is most in danger of marginalization. Its prestige, and that of its possessors, may remain high; but its application, or even the recognition of its application to daily life becomes less obvious. Genuinely new questions and situations are beyond its scope: no longer, therefore, does it cover every eventuality. Unless it can be adapted, or supplemented, it may become associated with a small élite; perhaps locked into durable, but occasional practices,

---

[15] See G. H. Cooper, *Development and stress in Navajo religion*, Stockholm: Almqvist och Wiksell 1984, especially chapter 6.

[16] E. G. Parrinder, 'Monotheism and pantheism in Africa', *Journal of Religion in Africa* 3(2) 1970, 81–88.

such as those associated with ruler cult; perhaps the esoteric possession of a learned class. (There have been instances, of which the Maori are perhaps the best known example, of the learned class deliberately choosing not to hand on their tradition.)[17] But popular religious knowledge and attitudes remain, to be reconciled with, or added to, elements derived from the new influences working in the society.

(iii) Such change does not necessarily affect all members of the society equally or in the same way. The society in change thus displays a series of symbolic worlds, which are not mutually exclusive but overlapping.[18]

(iv) There is therefore no inevitability about the nature of symbolic and ritual change under the pressure of social change. All societies tend to be conservative in matters of ritual and liturgy, and the mere *presence* of phenomena alien to a well-established world view does not immediately change it. There are various possible responses other than conservative affirmation. There may be a process of adjustment whereby elements derived from the forces influencing the society are incorporated into the traditional world view and modify its structure. There may be a radical break with that world view at some crucial point, an abandonment of major elements of the tradition. Such a break may occur in relation to 'conversion' to one of the universal faiths, but it may also occur without; and it does not of itself alter all traditional perceptions.

(v) Where the gap between the traditional patterns and the new experience of reality becomes inescapable, or where the traditional religious patterns prove powerless to cope with

[17] James Irwin, *An introduction to Maori religion*, Bedford Park, South Australia: Australian Association for the Study of Religion 1984, 33ff., discusses the historical basis of the pre-contact cult of Io.

[18] This is vividly conveyed in some of the outstanding African post war novels, such as Chinua Achebe's *Things fall apart* and Ngugi wa Thiono's, *The river between*. Cf. the revealing biography of his father by S. D. Okafor, *A Nigerian villager in two worlds* London: Faber 1966.

breakdown in the society, the society may enter a period of disillusionment and re-evaluation which might be described in religious terms as agnosticism. This 'agnostic' condition, in which the traditional ritual pattern may be continued unchanged, may be the prelude to, perhaps is the essential pre-condition for, major religious change.

(vi) Where the gap between tradition and the new experience of reality is less severe, certain symbols or institutions may fall into desuetude, others may be retained largely for customary ceremonial purposes. Unless the traditional system is expanded or adjusted to take account of the new basis of life for most people in the community, this situation leads to effective secularization. The matters most affecting the life of the community have now fallen outside the sphere of religion. The remaining elements are no longer knitted into a *living* tradition, an all-embracing customary pattern for all occasions of life.

The Second World War and after
The period since the Second World War has been peculiarly productive of the factors which characteristically accompany change in primal religions. In many areas it has seen the acceleration of processes of change which were already in operation, and it has brought them to areas where they had been previously unknown.

(i) In one area, the Pacific, the Second World War itself had a dramatic religious effect. The Melanesian peoples in particular found themselves swept into a massive conflict between alien peoples, and suddenly exposed to displays far outside their previous experience. Daily events were on an apocalyptic scale; and Melanesian world views frequently had an eschatological element (return of the culture hero or of the ancestors) which could illustrate or explain.[19]

[19] See especially F. C. Kamma, *Koreri: messianic movements in the Biak-Numfar area*. The Hague: Nijhoff 1972.

(ii) The period since the War has seen the end of the European empires which had previously ruled most of sub-Saharan Africa, the Indian sub-continent, the Pacific and most of South East Asia. In a few cases revitalized or adapted primal religions took part in the process of decolonization. In Irian Jaya, new religious movements, in which Christian elements sharpened the traditional eschatological expectation, helped to break down Dutch wartime rule and prepare the way for postwar independence.[20] In the Solomon Islands the 'Marching Rule' movement, strongly asserting traditional values (though perhaps not rejecting Christian teachings as such) long maintained virtually an alternative administration to the British, and seems to have faded only when its aims had been attained.[21] The religious aspects of the Mau Mau movement in Kenya are complex, but it certainly involved the assertion of Kikuyu traditional ritual as a means of mustering opposition to White rule (and specifically to White land ownership). Generally speaking, however, the leading role in mobilizing the movement for independence in Africa and the Pacific, and in setting up the new states, was taken by people educated on the Western model, usually in mission schools, confessedly influenced by Christian ideas and often identified with the Christian churches.

(iii) The colonial empires have been succeeded by nation states in Africa and the Pacific. These states are, however, colonial constructs, retaining the boundaries of the old colonies, frequently maintaining the inherited administrative system, and adding the idea of a national identity transcending the local and

---

[20] F. Steinbauer, *Melanesian cargo cults: new salvation movements in the South Pacific*, St. Lucia, Queensland: University of Queensland Press 1979, pp. 10–17.

[21] Darrell Whiteman, *Melanesians and missionaries: an ethnohistorical study of social and religious change in the Southwest Pacific*, Pasadena, Calif.: William Carey Library 1983, pp. 250–273.

ethnic identities. The new states have thus been even more effective than the old colonies in encouraging mobility and setting up political, economic and social structures which bring into contact with each other people of different interests and localities. The few exceptions have been states where central government has virtually broken down, and where small scale societies are able to live in certain areas virtually undisturbed by other than local factors. For most peoples, the universe has been permanently enlarged. Religious thinking can no longer be conditioned by purely local and ethnic factors: it must take account of other peoples, and of national, not to say international, factors. It thus cuts across primal religions at the most critical point: the obligation of common custom for a common kin.

(iv) On the other hand, the rise of the new nation states has required African and Pacific peoples to establish identities; and identities can only be found by reference to the past. It has thus been a feature of the past generation to affirm the value and worth of the African and Pacific past, by contrast with the denigration or rejection of it which often marked the colonial period. In consequence a new pride in traditional culture, including its religious aspects, has appeared even among people who were not fully nurtured in it. None of this implies rejection of the new, larger, entities such as the nation state, (indeed, it reinforces still larger identities, such as 'African'); nor of modern education, technology and communication, nor of the use of international languages (English, French, Kiswahili). Nor does it necessarily imply rejection of the universal faiths (Christianity, Islam); the intellectual and religious demands come rather from the need to reconcile past and present.

(v) The rise of the new nation states in Africa and the Pacific has been one factor in raising the consciousness of other peoples who through the centuries of European expansion became ethnic and cultural minorities in the lands which they had long inhabited. Native American and Australian Aboriginal cultural identity has been asserted in recent decades in a way unparalleled since the occupation of their lands. In each case this new confidence has arisen against the background of steady population increase after a period of decline: in each case it has been marked by the reclaiming of traditional religious institutions long in decline or even disuse. Once again the appeal to the past, through a quest for roots, appeals less to stricter local and narrowly ethnic considerations than to the larger identity as Native Americans or Aboriginals, over against White majority culture; and again it implies no rejection of the modern world as such; indeed, part of the motive for the revival is the improvement of the temporal lot of their peoples.

(vi) Another factor accelerating religious change has been the adoption by virtually all states of economic development models, centrally conceived and administered in relation to national considerations. The nature of the models differ; some have been explicitly capitalist, others explicitly socialist, some pragmatic and eclectic; but even those (such as Tanzania's 'African socialism') which have claimed inspiration from indigenous tradition have led to the weakening of the traditional links of religion and society. Cash economy, production of surpluses for sale, mechanized exploitation of minerals, a degree of industrialization, large movements of population, the break of the ancestral link with the land; these are features of virtually all modern nations, and the path deliberately chosen, however imperfectly realized, by most of them. Traditional value systems must adapt, wither, or be supplanted. Nor are the new nations the only ones affected; the rain forest areas of Latin America have seen massive penetration leading to development and clearing for cash crops and exploitation of minerals since the Second World War, and altering the basis of life for many forest peoples in Brazil, Colombia, Venezuela and Central America.

(vii) Associated with the pressures for economic development, but not solely caused by them, are major environmental changes. The world's tropical forest area has sharply declined since 1945. This is due partly to the clearance for cash crops (or in the case of Central America, grazing), partly through modern technologically based warfare with its use of defoliants (notably in South East Asia), partly to the steady increase of population taking more and more land for food and fuel. All this involves a change in the basis of life to which religion must relate. A series of droughts across Central Africa, complicated in some parts by regional warfare, has altered the basis of life for many Sahel peoples, uprooting some from their land, and eroding the basis of life of many nomadic and semi-nomadic pastoralists. Above all there is the factor of urbanization. Millions of people whose religious world, or whose parents' religious world, was formed in small agricultural communities recognizing common origin have been brought into vast modern cities of diverse population and subject to stresses, problems and alienation lying far outside the scope of the traditional religious conception and its apparatus. This can apply even to cities which are in world terms quite small concentrations, such as Port Moresby in Papua New Guinea; but many African cities have reached populations of half a million or more since 1945.[22]

(viii) Finally, political pressures on primal peoples, certainly strongly applied during the colonial period, have been if anything, intensified since the European empires came to an end. In this connexion the legislative sphere has probably been the least important. On the whole the successor states have maintained legislative provisions made by the colonial authorities making certain religious institutions, such as human

[22] D. B. Barrett, *World Christian Encyclopedia* London: Oxford University Press 1982, calculates that Africa has ten cities with a population of over a million and no less than 145 with over 100,000. (p. 780).

sacrifice, illegal; but the religions concerned have long since adapted to the use of surrogates (indeed, it has been argued, were in process of doing so irrespective of legislation).[23] Certain forms of witchcraft detection and prosecution also remain outlawed. The prevalence of witch beliefs is unaffected, the scope for the suspicion of witch activity is probably increased by the stresses of urban life, but the new societies seek new means to cope with such activity.[24] Far more significant for primal peoples has been pressure, sometimes coercive, sometimes informal, to incorporate them into larger entities or recruit them into patriotic movements, or to employ them in conflicts directed by others. Before the independence of Malaysia the forest peoples of the peninsula became caught up in fighting between the British authorities and the communists. Since Independence there have been Government sponsored attempts to bring these pig-rearing peoples within the fold of Islam.[25] The more recent endeavour to bring Irian Jaya and East Timor into closer harmony with the rest of Indonesia, including recently resettlement of Javanese populations in Irian Jaya, is fraught with immense consequences for primal peoples. Over centuries various Indian tribal peoples[26] have assimilated in greater or less

[23] S. O. M. Adebola, *The institution of human sacrifice in Africa and its analogies in Biblical literature*, Ph.D. thesis, University of Aberdeen 1985. See also B. M. Boal in note 26.

[24] Witch beliefs are not integral to primal religions (they appear, for instance, not to exist in Australia); and they can be accommodated within any religious frame. It is in the therapy used that the religious aspects appear. Cf. R. W. Wyllie, 'Ghanaian spiritual and traditional healers' explanations of illness: a preliminary survey', *Journal of Religion in Africa* 14(1) 1983, 46–57.

[25] Mustapa b.Hj. Daud, *The religion of two Negrito peoples: a comparative study of the Semang of Peninsula Malaysia and the Andamanese of Andaman Islands*. M.Litt. dissertation 1979, pp. 29ff.

[26] The oldest cultures in the sub-continent are 'often in a stage of acute atrophy' (Dupré, *op. cit.*, p. 76). Among recent substantial studies of Indian tribal societies with their religion are P. Juliusson, *The Gonds and their religion. A study of the integrative function of religion in a peasant, preliterary, and preindustrial culture in Madhya Pradesh*, India, Stockholm: Acta Universitatis

degree to Hindu influences; but there remains still a sharp distinction between a tribe and a caste.[27] The status of tribal peoples is protected by law, but there are obvious advantages to the state in reducing the sharpness of the separate identity of tribal peoples; an advantage underlined by the potentially disturbing part played by border tribes in periods of tension between India and China. Small tribal groups such as those of Bangladesh are an uncomfortable surd in an essentially Islamic state, and they seem to have been subject to particularly intense pressure.[28] Marxist ideology has been officially adopted by many movements and some states in Africa, and though there is little evidence of any sustained attempt to abolish religion (and, as far as the primal religions are concerned, a good deal to the contrary) mobilization by means of party, military or para-military organization provides yet another solvent for primal peoples with an agricultural basis of life. In Central America Indian peoples have been the worst sufferers in the struggles for power in the various republics which have in various ways maintained the centuries old tradition of seeking to assimilate them to the ways of the majority culture. Both there and in some parts of South America such communities continue (partly primal, though largely Christian) to experience violence and disruption.

All these sources of change pose certain threats to primal religions: they create disturbance of *values*, interfacing with the traditional ways of assessing worth, traditional lines of

Stockholmensis 1974; A. van Exem, *The religious system of the Munda tribe* St. Augustin: Haus Völker und Kulturen 1982; Barbara M. Boal, *The Konds: human sacrifice and religious change*, London: Aris and Phillips 1982. Dr. Boal's earlier more popular work, *Fire is easy: the tribal Christian and his traditional culture*, Manila: Christian Institute for Ethnic Studies in Asia 1973, contains a succinct outline of Kond religious life. The journal *Sevartham* (Ranchi) provides a valuable series of studies of tribal religion in India.

[27] Juliusson, *op. cit.*, pp. 102–107.
[28] See *Inside Asia* 9, July 1986, 28ff.

obligation, of traditional patterns of permission and prohibition. They create disturbance of hierarchy; they weaken the link with the land, and thus with the ancestors; they dissolve the link between traditional status and real power; they open new ways of acquiring status; they frequently obliterate vital distinctions (such as that between men's and women's work). And they create disturbance of *focus*, rendering necessary a vision beyond the local; the community is manifestly part of a total world of events; perceptions of the transcendent world must now take account of this total world.

None of these forms of disturbance is new in itself: the basis of life, and thus of perception, of primal peoples has constantly changed through war, conquest, migration, intermarriage, adaptation from neighbours, epidemic, environmental change. What is new is the extent, intensity and universality of the forces of change.

Forms of Response
There is no sign yet, however, of a common pattern of response to these forces of change. Since the Second World War there have been clear signs of processes which we may call Recession, Absorption, Restatement, Reduction, Invention, Adjustment, Revitalization and Appropriation.

(i) *Recession.* This trend, begun long before 1945, has been the most marked. The disturbance of values, hierarchy and focus induced by the processes of modernization has taken place alongside the presence of universal faiths which manifestly relate to the wider universe demanded by modernization. Large numbers of primal peoples have moved towards Christianity or Islam since 1945. In Africa, this continued a long standing trend for both religions; and though there are signs of inter-conversion between Christians and Muslims,[29] instances of

[29] J. K. Parratt, Religious change in Yoruba society: a test case, *Journal of Religion in Africa* 2(2) 1969, 113–128.

large-scale return to primal religions seem rare. In Melanesia, and among primal peoples in Indonesia, the movement towards Christianity has accelerated since the War. India has seen movements of tribal people towards Christianity and towards Hinduism. In some cases the presence of one of the universal faiths has provided a means of maintaining the identity of a tribal people in the midst of pressures from a majority culture; Christianity, with its ready acceptance of vernaculars and preparedness for the Scriptures and the central acts of worship in the vernaculars, has been particularly attractive to groups which have felt themselves under threat of absorption or domination (some Indian tribals, for instance,[30] and minority peoples on the Nigerian plateau). African peoples who have long resisted Islam and shown little interest in Christian missions in their homelands have divided between church and mosque in the cities when migration has got under way. In Greenland and the Canadian Arctic, where the period of contact has been long, active practice of the primal religions seems to have died out altogether, and its most characteristic institution, shamanism, fallen into disuse.[31]

In some previous periods the move towards Christianity in particular was associated with the desire to participate in the power held by whites; the modernizing process was white-led, and coincided with the activities of white missionaries. (Subsequent disappointment when access to such power was not

[30] Cf. A. Kanjumala, 'Christianization as a legitimate alternative to Sanskritization', *Indian Missiological Review* 6(4) 1984, 307–331.

[31] I. Kleivan and B. Sonne, *Eskimos Greenland and Canada*, Leiden: Brill 1985, p. 2 Cf. D. Merkur, *Becoming half-hidden: shamanism and initiation among the Inuit*, Stockholm: Almqvist och Wiksell 1985 p. v: 'To the knowledge of Western observers, Inuit shamanism is today either extinct or obsolescent. Some few former shamans still live, but no longer practise. It remains to be seen whether a revival of shamanism will occur in the years and decades to come.' In view of Native American experience the latter qualification seems wise.

achieved, has affected both Christian and primal religious practice).[32] Conditions since 1945, and particularly in the last twenty or so years, have progressively weakened such direct association. But Christianity and Islam, with their capacity to link into a wider universe, their provision of alternative codes of behaviour and their demand for symbolic change requiring some sort of act of decision, continue to provide keys to meaning and a means of adjustment to new conditions when a people's traditional lore is no longer able to do so. They are still the commonest refuge when agnosticism has set into a primal society.[33]

(ii) *Absorption.* One product of the process of recession has been the absorption of much of the configuration of primal religions into Christian and Islamic communities. The results of this process properly belong to the study of these faiths, both of which have long historic experience of interpenetration with the primal religions. (Christianity, in particular, has from an early period made by far its greatest impact on primal religions, ancient and modern.) The modifications, and rearrangement of priorities may be considerable, and many, perhaps most, live in overlapping worlds of spiritual perception. From one point of

---

[32] H. W. Turner, 'The hidden power of the Whites: the secret religion withheld from the primal peoples', *Archives de Sciences Sociales des Religions* 46(1) 1978, reprinted in *Religious innovation in Africa: collected essays on new religious movements*, Boston: G. K. Hall 1979, 271–288.

[33] A debate about the nature of African conversion has been initiated by Robin Horton, who stresses the aspect of the expanded universe. Among contributions are R. Horton, 'African conversion', *Africa* 6(2) 1971, 91–112; H. J. Fisher, 'Conversion reconsidered: some historical aspects of religious conversion in Black Africa', *Africa* 43(1) 1973, 27–40; C. Ifeka-Moller, 'White power: social structural factors in conversion to Christianity, Eastern Nigeria, 1921–1966', *Canadian Journal of African Studies* 8(1) 1974, 55–72. See also the comments of L. O. Sanneh, 'The domestication of Islam and Christianity in african societies, *Journal of Religion in Africa* 11(1) 1980, 1–12. For a closely argued case study, see C. C. Okorocha, *Salvation in Igbo religious experience: its influence on Igbo Christianity.* Ph.D. thesis, University of Aberdeen 1982.

view, therefore, it may be proper to think of the primal religions having a continued life within the universal faiths.[34] But in another, more fundamental sense, the primal chapter of religious history has closed in such cases. The charismatic prophet may be the successor of the diviner, dealing with similar situations, perhaps using some of the same techniques; but if he does so in the name of the God of Israel, explaining his activities not from old tradition but from the Scriptures, and demanding rejection of both diviners and traditional objects of power, then historic change has come about.

(iii) *Restatement*. This is the hardest of the responses to identify precisely, and yet it occurs by the very presence of the world faiths. Contact with Christian and Muslim apologists forces on believers reflection and explanation; and this inevitably takes on some of the language of the outside faith, and relates to the themes emerging most strongly in Christian and Muslim preaching and conversation. In the nature of things the topic most likely to occur is the nature of God. C. R. Gaba quotes the response of an Anlo elder commenting on the Christian identification of the God of the Bible with Mawu the Anlo Supreme God:

> ' "My son! Mawu is too big to be put into a small room and worshipped only at that place. In all Anloland, it is only the Christians who do this. How can we put into a room a Being we can never see and who is like the wind blowing everywhere? Our lesser gods we are able to house because they reveal themselves to us to see them and are locally connected with us just as other people also have theirs. Indeed I have my doubts if what you Christians worship in your churches is not the lesser god of the white man!" '[35]

[34] A complex case of inter-penetration and symbiosis is traced by P. B. Steinmetz, *Pipe, Bible and peyote among the Oglala Lakota*, Stockholm: Almqvist och Wiksell 1980.

[35] C. R. Gaba, 'The idea of a Supreme Being among the Anlo people of Ghana', *Journal of Religion in Africa* 2(2) 1969, 64–79.

The elder affirms that Mawu has all the characteristics ascribed by Christians to God: and for that very reason decries the familiarity with him indicated in Christian worship; Christianity must be a cult, the worship of a cult divinity, and a foreign one at that. But his theology of Mawu, while probably containing nothing alien to pre-Christian Anlo tradition, is itself shaped in tension with the Christian presence. The presence of Christianity and Islam with their very positive and explicit affirmations about God must be one of the factors in the ongoing process of reflection and adaptation of myth and new explanation of terms and concepts. Actual conversion carries the process still further, especially among peoples becoming Christians. African Muslims characteristically avoid using vernacular names for Allah; Christians commonly make such identifications, thus strengthening the continuum between the old faith and the new, and in measure 'converting' the past. Contentions common in current academic discussion about the characteristics of the Supreme Being and his place in worship in the pre-contact period of a particular people seem rather secondary; the religious process itself constantly reinterprets the tradition, and necessarily interprets the past.[36]

(iv) *Reduction*. Frequently a primal religion has become reduced or confined in its scope, either by the removal of major institutions, or, conversely, by the institutions being cut from the complex of tradition affecting the whole of life. The form of sacrifice may be kept, but carried out in token form, expensive beasts being only notionally immolated; in practice being presented, cropped in the ears, and returned. Initiation of youths may be too rooted in people's self-consciousness to be

---

[36] Cf. O. Bimwenyi Kweshi, *Discours théologique négro africain: problèmes des fondements*, Paris: Présence Africaine 1981, 615ff; and K. Bediako, 'The African evidence for a Christian theology of religious pluralism', in J. A. Thrower (ed.) *Essays in Religious Studies*, Aberdeen: University of Aberdeen Department of Religious Studies 1986, 44–56.

abandoned; but it must not interfere with education, and so is shortened to fit the school holidays. It must take account of knowledge of hygiene; so the circumcision itself may be carried out clinically.[37] The effect is to secularize an institution formerly at the heart of a body of living religion. Royal and chiefly cult has remained in many societies strongly influenced by the universal faiths (it has not been so readily assumed into Christian convention as it was in Europe); widely respected for historical and ceremonial reasons but no longer related to the main springs of religion. Those closely involved in it have often withstood conversion longer than most of their people simply because the cult (and sometimes the requirement of plural wives) was the last 'irreconcilable' institution in the society.[38] Once again, it will be observed, reduction of scope is a mark of secularization.

H. W. Turner has indicated the way in which Christianity itself has been a secularizing influence in Africa, breaking into the 'ontocratic' nature of a political entity functioning within a sacred universe.[39] But however far the secularization process proceeds, it is unlikely to remove the need for the diviner, the specialist in identifying causation and remedy.

(v) *Invention*. From within the primal religions sometimes come bursts of new creative activity which transpose them into new settings, freely absorbing and adopting elements from other cultures. The most striking examples of this process

---

[37] F. B. Welbourn, 'Keyo initiation', *Journal of Religion in Africa* 1(3) 1968, 212–232. See especially the remarks of D. K. Kiprono, himself an initiate, on latter day events, pp. 230–232.

[38] The case of I. B. Akinyele, Olubadan of Ibadan, a prominent figure in a Nigerian Independent church who was installed in 1955 without the traditional sacrifices marks a turning point in that vast city's history. Cf. H. W. Turner, 'The late Sir Isaac Akinyele, Olubadan of Ibadan', *West African Religion* 4, 1965, 1–14, reprinted in *Religious Innovation*, 129–132.

[39] Cf. H. W. Turner, 'The place of independent religious movements in the modernization of Africa', *Journal of Religion in Africa* 2(1) 1969, 43–63.

developed long before 1945 in Haiti and Brazil.[40] The continuities with living religions in Africa are clear enough but in the translation setting they have taken another dimension. In Brazil in particular Umbanda and other spirit-religions strongly influenced by Africa have become increasingly important, and developed new features in recent decades; but with their large and systematic infusion of popular Catholicism it seems better to take these inventions as new religions rather than primal religions.[41]

Other forms of invention include the systematizing of cult and ritual elements in an attempt to produce a 'universal' religion alternative to Christianity or Islam, often with written liturgy and apologia designed for educated people. Such movements had a certain popularity among the politically conscious in the period leading to Independence, as acceptable nationalistic religion.[42] New forms, such as Afrikania, founded by a former Roman Catholic priest,[43] are directed to appeal to a wider African consciousness.

(vi) *Adjustment*. Attempts to adjust and expand world views to take account of new phenomena continue to be a feature of primal religions. Since 1945 this has been particularly noticeable in Melanesia, where the contact with the new influences has been relatively late and unusually drastic. It has now become

[40] R. Bastide, *The African religions of Brazil*, Baltimore: Johns Hopkins University Press 1978; R. F. Thompson, *Flash of the Spirit, African and Afro-American art and philosophy*, New York: Random House 1984.

[41] A vast bibliography is included in I. Zaretsky and C. Shumbaugh, *Spirit possession and spirit mediumship in Africa and Afro-America. An annotated bibliography* New York: Garland 1978.

[42] For instance, Aruosa, associated with the then Oba of Benin and containing elements of the Benin cult, and the National Church of Nigeria and the Cameroons (paralleling the political party with the same initials) vigorously directed by K. O. K. Onyioha.

[43] H. J. Becken collects and comments on Ghanaian newspaper reports, *Zeitschrift fur Mission* 9, 1983, 233–239; cf. *Exchange* (Leiden) 13 (37–38) 1984, 98–106.

common to describe as 'adjustment movements' the plethora of movements once grouped together as 'cargo' cults;[44] over-emphasis on the cargo element, the most exotic and newsworthy from the Western point of view, can be misleading. But an existing religious framework including belief in the eventual return of the ancestors ushering in a time of health and happiness, may be adjusted and harmonized to incorporate unparalleled new phenomena. The unloading of goods for a Papua New Guinea missionary in 1977 led to deputations to send more white people with cargo; the beginning of oil exploration re-awoke the memory that the ancestors would return through a hole in the ground. The regular use of aircraft by another technologically minded missionary developed myth in a new way: 'Mi Kristus has returned from the skyworld and has landed at Taiyeve. Airplanes are continually landing there, bringing cargo for the people of Taiyeve.'[45] The aspect most often requiring adjustment is scale. It is remarkable how frequently the new movements in the Pacific transcend the old ethnic divisions, even between people long alienated from each other.

(vii) *Revitalization.* Primal religions today are not only adjusting; some have been revitalized. In part this results from the assertion of cultural identity, and the regaining of cultural assurance, on the part of non-Western peoples, with the rejection of European norms as the sole standard. African and

[44] On these movements see P. Worsley, *The trumpet shall sound: a study of 'cargo' cults in Melanesia*, 2 ed., New York: Shocken 1968; K. O. L. Burridge, *Mambu: a Melanesian millennium*, London: Methuen 1960; K. O. L. Burridge, *New heaven, new earth: a study of millenarian activities*, Oxford: Blackwell 1969; J. G. Strelan, *Search for salvation: studies in the history and theology of cargo cults*, Adelaide: Lutheran Publishing House 1977.

[45] J. A. De Vries, 'Cargo expectations among the Kwerba people' in Wendy Flannery (ed.) *Religious Movements in Melanesia today* I, Goroka, PNG: Melanesian Institute 1983, 25–30. 'Mi Kristus' is Indonesian for 'Christ' (The three volumes in this series document many other movements of the last decade).

Afro-American scholars, artists and intellectuals are rediscovering and reaffirming the African cultural heritage. In a few instances, usually for short periods, governments and political movements have used certain traditional rites (characteristically those strenuously rejected by local Christian groups) as tests of loyalty.[46] The most striking expressions of revitalized religion, however, are among Native Americans and Australian Aboriginals, minority peoples permanently deprived by white competition. When Joseph Epes Brown found the Oglala Sioux holy man Black Elk in 1948, he found him 'lamenting the broken hoop of this nation', and 'it was generally believed, even by specialists, to be only a matter of time (very little time in fact) before the Indians with their seemingly archaic and anachronistic cultures would be completely assimilated into a larger American society convinced of its own superiority and the validity of its goals.'[47] Black Elk's mission, which caused him so much suffering, 'to bring to life the flowering tree of his people' may not have been fulfilled in the way that he laboured for; but institutions characteristic of traditional religion, such as the sweat lodge and the vision quest, are reviving where they seemed about to die out.[48] And they are gaining the allegiance of younger people who drive cars and watch television.[49] With this comes a revived consciousness of the richness of the religious tradition and especially of its value and respect for the land. Environmental

[46] E.g. Mau Mau 'oathing'; initiation ceremonies in Chad at one period.

[47] Joseph Epes Brown, preface to *The sacred pipe: Black Elk's account of the seven rites of the Oglala Sioux* Harmondsworth: Penguin 1971, p. xv. Black Elk died in 1950.

[48] Joseph Epes Brown, *The spiritual legacy of the American Indian*, New York: Crossroad 1982, 65ff.

[49] Cf. V. Dusenberry, *The Montana Cree: a study of religious persistence*, Stockholm: Almqvist och Wiksell 1962. For bibliography of Native American movements see H. W. Turner, *Bibliography of New Religious Movements. Volume 2. North America*, Boston: G. K. Hall 1978.

blight and other less desirable features of Euroamerican culture values make assimilation not even desirable. Two features may be identified as especially interesting. First, the movement of revitalization, although a search for roots, is not centred on the consciousness of the narrow ethnic group—if anything, it is pan-Indian.[50] Second, the use of the hallucinatory drug peyote, formerly localized but becoming widespread for cultic purposes through the Native American Church, seems to be in decline. The new movement is not passive, but affirmatory.[51]

The Australian scene has some parallels. A major strand is the question of Aboriginal land rights, and a new political consciousness among Aborigines. The land rights issue is closely interwoven with the sacredness of ancestral sites. The very oppression that Aboriginals suffered in being driven away and forced to move has served in many cases to break the effective link between family and site; but a revival of traditional culture (not necessarily involving explicit rejection of acquired Christianity) has promoted a general Aboriginal awareness of the value of *all* the old sites.[52] Once again new movements in primal religion move them from a locally ethnic to a wider consciousness.

(viii) *Appropriation*. Finally, we should note the phenomenon whereby primal religions are being adopted or recommended by those who historically belong to quite another tradition. The development in the West of the idea of

[50] Brown, *op. cit.*, p. 67 notes the 'double-edged' nature of pan-Indianism. '. . . the stimulus behind many of the movements is a reaction to Euro-American attitudes towards ethnic minorities. . . . The result is a complex of heterogeneous forms and practices that have popular appeal and commercial advantage, but risk sacrificing true spiritual content.' Brown stresses, however, the way in which the rites provide outlets for central personal virtues, and the high personal quality of many of the leaders, including some of the new shamans.

[51] Brown, *op. cit.*, p. 18.

[52] See C. Ahern, *Spiritualities on the land*, M.Litt. dissertation University of Aberdeen.

responsibility for the environment has given a new appreciation of the world view of primal peoples without the sharp divisions of humanity/animals, animate/inanimate, sacred/profane. This (combined, perhaps, with a new quest for meaning among people growing up effectively without religion in post-Christian Western societies) has led to a high valuation for Native American religion in particular, some of it expressed in somewhat bizarre and unrealistic terms. There has also been a lively international interest (expressed through such movements as Survival International) in the protection of small societies from exploitation or from more baleful results of contact with the Western world.[53] This movement sometimes focused attention on Christian missions as responsible for the erosion of the primal world view and for conditioning such societies towards a Western influenced culture and economy.[54] Not only is there a new confidence with the cultures historically associated with primal religions; there is a new self-criticism within cultures which formerly took for granted their own superiority. There is no sign, however, that this will significantly reduce the forces of change at work or the inter-action of primal world views, the universal faiths, and the modern world. It is even taking new forms, for instance, in the pressure of the international women's movement, with women from African and Asian cultures well to the fore, for the abolition of clitoridectomy, a deeply rooted part of initiation to womanhood in many African societies.

All eight types of response have been found in primal religions since 1945; all can be identified today. H. W. Turner

[53] The movement's journal documents these regularly, with special reference to Latin America.

[54] S. Hvalkof and P. Aaby (eds.), *Is God an American? An anthropological perspective on the missionary work of the Summer Institute of Linguistics*, Copenhagen: International Work Group for Indigenous Affairs and London: Survival International 1981. Cf. G. Cano a.o., *Los nuevos conquistadores*, Quito: CEDIS 1981.

has suggested a schema for Melanesian movements which includes the categories 'Neo-primal', (those which seek only to remodel the traditional religions); 'Synthetist', (those which are explicitly seeking to combine the old tradition with the newly perceived Christianity in a religion which differs from both); 'Hebraist' (in which there has been a radical transference from the primal world to allegiance to the God of Israel, but in which Jesus Christ is not the means of salvation); and 'Independent churches' which seek to produce new Christian models.[55] The last named is rare in Melanesia, though the characteristic form of new movement in modern Africa. The model would need expansion to take in relations with Islam, and some of the reducing and secularizing movements we have mentioned. But it is worth noticing that the model allows for both a new situation, brought about by the permanent interconnexion of cultures in this century, and for some fluidity between the categories. It points also to the principal change in primal religions since the Second World War: the search for a universal, not a purely local or ethnic field of reference, a new focus suited to a village all now know to be global.

[55] H. W. Turner in Flannery *op. cit.* pp. 1–6. For another version and an exposition see his 'New religious movements in primal societies' in V. C. Hayes (ed.) *Australian Essays in World Religions*, Bedford Park, S.A.: AASR 1977, 38–48 (also in *Religious innovation* pp. 3–13) and 'A typology for African religious movements', *Journal of Religion in Africa* 1(1) 1967, 1–34 (in *Religious innovation* 79–108).

10

THE RELIGIOUS SITUATION IN THE PEOPLE'S REPUBLIC OF CHINA TODAY A PERSONAL REFLECTION

Tu Wei-Ming

(*Harvard*)

The upsurge of activity in organized religions, notably Buddhism, Taoism, Islam and Christianity, throughout China in the last decade has been widely reported in the mass media. It is too early to assess the full import of this development. For a student of religion, it is both exciting and intriguing to observe that China, which for more than a generation has declared itself the champion of scientific materialism, now seems ready to listen to a different voice. For a student of Chinese intellectual history with particular emphasis on Confucian China and its modern transformation, it is gratifying to see the re-emergence of Confucian studies with a dynamism which is unprecedented since the May Fourth Movement of 1919. Yet, the complexity of the religious situation in China is such that my personal reflection is at best an educated guess. This paper has a dual purpose; I intend to describe in the first part my impression of what seems to be happening: no less than a religious revival by any standards of measurement. The second part, excerpted from a statement published by the Harvard undergraduate magazine *Faith*, addresses the difficult issue, what does it mean by being religious for the overwhelming majority of the Chinese intellectuals who do not belong to any organized religion? The relationship between this mode of questioning and the phenomenological description of what actually happens on the religious scene is subtle, but vitally important. Without an appreciation of the critical ideological issues confronting the intellectual élite and the political leadership, we cannot adequately understand the crucial forces that will determine for years to come the shape of religious consciousness, indeed the quality of life, in the People's Republic of China.

Christianity, Islam, Taoism and Buddhism

The most radical sign of the upsurge of activity in organized religions in China is the apparent tolerance of the political regime towards Christianity. This is remarkable, given that not long ago a conscious attempt was made to label Christian missionary movements in China as a form of cultural imperialism. To be sure, the principle of the three autonomies: self-finance, self-governance and missionary work directed by domestic authorities is still enforced, but the unstated policy of eliminating any signs of a foreign Christian presence at institutes of higher learning seems inoperative. Nowadays, cathedrals and churches are filled to capacity during masses and services, a phenomenon that has received much attention in the West. Missionary movements, either well-coordinated by domestic and foreign groups or initiated by committed individuals, are visible on university campuses. Bible study groups and informal gatherings for singing hymns, often conducted by visiting English-language instructors, have become ordinary weekly affairs at many institutes of higher learning. When I made my most recent trip to China in January 1986, I was surprised to learn that one of the best sellers for college students was *The Stories of the Bible*, an informed source book published by the Chinese Academy of Social Sciences. With the re-opening of the Nanjing Theological Seminary, the effort of the Chinese Christian scholars to enter into an ongoing dialogue with leaders of the internal Christian community will be intensified. This may help researchers in the Institute of World Religions at the Academy of Social Sciences to engage themselves in more systematic work on Christian studies. The increased communication between the Chinese Catholics and the representatives of the Vatican has revived interest in the study of Christian theology as an academic discipline. To be sure, Christianity as a subject of scholarly inquiry is yet to be established in college curricula. Yet, that Christianity is being taught as a course at Peking University is itself significant. Also, at Peking University, religion is offered as a concentration for students in the Department of Philosophy. Presumably, a philosophy student can become a religion major with emphasis on Christianity.

The dynamism in Christianity is symptomatic of a religious awakening shared by Islam, Taoism and Buddhism. Reports of Islamic fundamentalism drawing Muslim party members away from the Communist Party may seem alarming to those who assume that political loyalty rather than religious faith defines the grammar of action in China. However, if we consider the historical, ethnic, cultural, and social as well as the political reasons behind the power of the Islam, the conflict between loyalty and faith is quite understandable. After all, Islam has been an indigenous Chinese religion since the fourteenth century. With a Muslim population of over ten million concentrated in two major areas (the southwest and the northwest), Islam has been noted in Chinese history as an important motive force for rebellions against the central government from Muslim areas.

Despite the sinicization of the Chinese-speaking Muslims (the Huis), their dietary laws, ritual practice, and distinctive attire clearly make them conscious of their difference from the dominant Han Chinese, and also make the Han Chinese acutely aware of their presence. Their social life centered around the mosque, their sense of the holy land symbolized by Mecca, and their personal faith directed toward Allah, further help them to develop a separate cultural identity to which fundamentalist movements abroad may very well strike a sympathetic chord. The non-Chinese speaking Muslims, mainly the Uighurs, with the added complexity of separate ethnic identity are more prone than Huis to express their Pan-Islamic sentiments. The upsurge of Sufi, Shī'ite and Sunnī activities in the Chinese Muslim community has far-reaching political as well as religious implications for the leadership in China. It is also significant for our understanding of China not only as a socialist state but also as a multi-lingual and multi-ethnic civilization.

Sharply contrasted with the explosive nature of Islamic fundamentalism, the upsurge of Taoist activity signifies a quiet revolution. In the long run, however, the Taoist persuasion may potentially be more transformative for the Chinese soul than the zealous missionary movements of Christianity and Islam. The Chinese are already, in a profound sense, Taoistic. The Chinese conception of the cosmos as the great transformation of the vital forces of yin and yang, their belief in the organismic unity of all the modalities of being in the universe and their experience of the body as energy fields make them breathe, eat, drink, work, and rest in ways, consciously or unconsciously, informed by the Taoist art of self-cultivation.

Taiji (shadow boxing), *gigong* (breathing technique), herbal medicine, massage, acupuncture, and leisurely strolls in parks are in vogue throughout China. They may very well be perceived pragmatically as useful ways of preserving one's energy and enhancing one's vitality in terms of physical exercise. However, the cultivation of the inner self, through mental and physical discipline of the vital energy (*qi*) inherent in one's body, predisposes one to lend a sympathetic ear to the Taoist persuasion. As Taoist rituals are being revived on every sacred mountain and famous Taoist temples, notably the White Cloud Monastery in Beijing, are re-opened for training Taoist priests, the Taoist philosophy of life has become articulate for the populace as a whole. Taoist studies abroad have further stimulated Chinese scholars to study their own heritage in a new light. An international effort to launch a systematic textual, philological and interpretive study of the Taoist canon is already under way in Paris.

We may pause a moment here to reflect upon the meaning of this Taoist revival for our understanding of the religious situation in China. If we focus our attention on Taoism as an organized religion, our investigation will naturally be confined to those temples that are large enough to accommodate priests and the lay communities that they are supposed to serve. The number of people who are directly involved in our investigation would naturally be very small and we might conclude that Taoism as a religion in China is insignificant. Indeed, if we inquire about the fate of Taoism with a handful of western-trained sociologists and anthropologists at leading universities, we may also learn that to these septuagenarian social scientists, who have been well-seasoned in dialectic materialism, Taoist religion, to be clearly differentiated from Taoist philosophy, is tantamount to superstition, or to an irrational belief system held by the uneducated peasants. The consensus then is that there is no future for Taoist religion in China.

However, if one personally journeys to sacred mountains such as Taishan, Qingchengshan and Laoshan, one will immediately witness a phenomenon that gives special meaning to these places: pilgrimage disguised as tourism. We see subtle signs of worship every step of the way. Small shrines, sometimes barely visible from the mountain paths, come alive with simple but varied decorations. Major temples are always crowded with devotees and onlookers. Taoist priests are often at the center of attention; the surrounding students who ask them questions are eager to learn about every aspect of the tradition. The demand for introductory texts is so great that publishing large editions of

Taoist precepts by the National Taoist Association has become a profit making enterprise. The potential for growth in the Taoist book market is substantial. The manuals for *taiji* and *gigong* alone are sufficient to sustain good business for some small publishing houses. As the Taoist message spreads through oral transmission as well as the printed work, an increasing number of Chinese will learn to be human through the Taoist way.

Similarly, the upsurge of activity in Buddhism cannot be easily measured by the actual number of people who are 'converted' to Buddhism. The Buddhist *sangha*, sanctioned by the government as an integral part of the socialist economic system, signifies a fundamental change in the public perception of the role and function of this Buddhist institution. One might emphasize that the government subsidises a selected number of Buddhist temples to the extent that they even allow ordained monks to take care of these sacred places because of economic and political considerations: tourism to attract foreign exchange, a diplomatic gesture toward Buddhist countries in Southeast Asia and a 'united front' strategy to rally the support of overseas Chinese Buddhists. However, the obvious unintended consequence is that Buddhist temples attract people from all walks of life including sophisticated intellectuals and members of the People's Liberation Army.

I was struck during my own 'pilgrimage' to the Buddhist holy land honoring the 'Goddess of Mercy', Putuo, in the autumn of 1980 before it was open to tourists, that the rise of the Buddhist *sangha* as a center of learning was on the horizon. The financial support of Chinese from abroad helped to set up the infrastructure for Buddhist education and to recruit novices beyond the quota sponsored by the government there. Yet, the commitment of the old monks who voluntarily returned to teach the *dharma* after more than a decade of personal hardship was the single most important factor for re-introducing the Buddhist way of life to the Chinese youth. After I, together with hundreds of others, attended an evening ceremony of sutra chanting at one of the large temples in Putuo, I discussed the future prospects of Buddhist studies with the head monk. He confided to me that since there were so many requests for instruction from brilliant young minds all over China, he had no doubt that a Buddhist renaissance was in the offing. 'How do you know that a government functionary doing his routine job in a small office in Beijing does not, through his personal devotional effort, set the *dharma* wheel turning?' These were his parting words to me.

In addition to the organized religions—Buddhism, Taoism, Islam and Christianity, folk traditions are also being revived both in rural and urban areas. The reinstitution of temple fairs has attracted much interest in major cities. The Earth Altar fair during the Chinese New Year season in 1985 attracted over thirty thousand enthusiasts despite record cold weather. The lantern festivals in Suzhou in the spring of 1986 turned the ancient city into a colorful fairyland reminiscent of the ancient saying that Su(zhou) and Hang(zhou) are paradise on earth for their enchanting scenery and their elegant taste. Indeed, grave-sweeping ceremonies and dragon boat festivities in the spring, mid-autumn moon festival banquets in the fall, city-god temple markets year round and a variety of forms of ancestral veneration further add vibrant color to the Chinese religious landscape.

Confucianism and the Socialist Ideology
Yet the sound and sight of these apparently religious activities does not mean that the political leadership in the People's Republic of China, by allowing a certain measure of religious freedom is no longer concerned about the Marxist-Leninist stance on ideological purity. For me, the intriguing question is, given that the majority of the Chinese intellectuals do not seek membership in any organized religion, in what sense are they

religious? The Chinese Christians, Muslims, Buddhists and Taoists do not present us with serious theoretical problems. The conceptual apparatus at our disposal can be properly employed to understand comparatively and historically their ways of life in a secular state. The religiosity of the Chinese intellectual who is still profoundly influenced by the spiritual self-definition of the Confucian scholar, presents a serious challenge to us. It impels us to broaden our ordinary notions of being religious and reexamine our deeply held convictions that the secular cannot be sacred.

The common impression that Chinese are eclectic, practical, utilitarian and even worldly in their approach to religion has been enhanced by recent anthropological studies of popular beliefs in Taiwan. A field worker was surprised and somewhat amused to learn that a temple manager of a local cult near Taipei periodically reassigns seats of honor to a host of gods according to their performance. A god who fails to answer legitimate requests after proper prayers have been said and rituals observed is likely to be demoted, and moved from the top shelf to the bottom. This reminds us that in traditional China the earth god could be reprimanded, indeed removed by the magistrate, if he consistently failed to bring seasonable rains to the land. However, the Chinese ritual expert past and present knows that the imposition of human will and judgment on the supernatural order is always a grave matter. One rarely takes such action and when one does, it is accompanied by elaborate expiatory sacrifices. The temple manager, I surmise, knows what he is doing and knows the right way of doing it according to the rules of the local cult. His seemingly frivolous behavior is predicated on a deep-rooted Confucian belief: the human heart-and-mind has privileged access to the biddings of Heaven. By implication, the Confucian also believes that that which is truly human will necessarily be approved by the gods. Since one of the Confucian dicta insists that 'Heaven sees as the people see and Heaven hears as the people hear,' the will of Heaven is not only knowable but can very well be realized through the communal enterprise of human hearts and minds.

Being religious, in this sense, entails both a personal dialogical response to the transcendent and a communal act. The transcendent so conceived can simply mean that which is beyond. Understandably, filial love, social responsibility, party loyalty, and patriotism can all evoke strong 'religious' sentiments in China. The Chinese intellectuals' preoccupation with China's modernization renders the collective endeavor to build a 'modern socialist civilizational state with a Chinese character' a 'sacred' mission. In this perspective, the deification (or demonization) of Chairman Mao during the Cultural Revolution was not simply an historical accident. Nor was the acceptance of Marxist-Leninism as the revolutionary ideology which was deemed particularly fitting for saving China from perpetual backwardness and constant humiliation a simple strategic maneuver of the Chinese Communist Party. The tragic fate of China as a civilizational state and the sufferings of the Chinese people since the Opium War have made 'saving the nation' an 'ultimate concern' of the Chinese intelligentsia. The holocausts that the Chinese have endured have left deep scars on the Chinese soul but they have also engendered a collective consciousness unprecedented in Chinese history.

China has been blessed with the longest continuous cultural heritage in human history, as a good many Chinese scholars on both sides of the Taiwan Straits are fond of reminding their foreign audiences, but her memory of the recent past is painfully short. In the Chinese scheme of things, it is virtually impossible to imagine that a university has continuously operated as long as Harvard for example. They could not imagine that a school which was founded in the Ming dynasty (1368–1644), such as the famous Donglin Academy at Wuxi on the lower Yangzi River, could have survived the collapse of the Ming, the

Manchu conquest, the Opium War, the Taiping Rebellion, the Boxer Uprising, the disintegration of the Qing dynasty, the internecine struggles among the warlords, the Northern Expedition, the Japanese aggression, the conflict between the Communists and the Nationalists, and the Cultural Revolution. The oldest modern institute of higher learning in China today, Peking University, can claim no more than ten years of uninterrupted existence.

Understandably, as the Chinese intellectuals re-emerge from the suffering and humiliation of the Cultural Revolution, their quest for personal dignity, communal participation and universal relevance evokes a new sense of urgency for the establishment of a corporate critical self-awareness which necessarily involves tapping the spiritual resources of their own indigenous traditions. The revival of Confucian studies both as an academic pursuit and as a cultural renaissance is a natural consequence of this collective intellectual concern. A recent bibliography on Confucius alone lists more than five hundred authors who published more than a thousand books and articles on the ancient sage in the last decade.

Ironically, however, an overwhelming sense of the weight of the feudal past still haunts the Chinese intellectual community. The intellectuals (including college students and professionals), the majority of whom are dedicated to reform, often consider the more than two thousand years of political culture in which authority features prominently as the regulator and arbiter of every conceivable arena of life the real enemy of modernization. To them, this old habit of the mind is ubiquitous: statism, bureaucratism, nepotism, conservatism, and uniformism are either its blatant or insidious expressions. The recognition that this aspect of 'feudalism' may have already become an integral part of the 'psycho-cultural' construct of the Chinese has made many intellectuals staunch anti-traditionalists and, by implication, anti-Confucians.

The conflicting image of Confucianism as a humanist tradition that still defines the Chinese intellectual and as the feudal past that cannot be expunged from the collective consciousness of the Chinese people helps us to understand a dimension of Chinese religiosity which is most intriguing to the outside observer.

The vice president of the Chinese Academy of Social Sciences, Zhao Fusan, notes in a recent article, that the ideological scene in China for the next decade will be characterized by three major forces: Marxist-Leninist socialism, bourgeois capitalism and Confucian humanism. He hopes for a happy synthesis of (1) a revitalized Marxist-Leninism which will continue as the ideological foundation for building a socialist civilizational state, (2) the introduction of Western science, technology, market mechanism, industrial management, and even some measures of liberal democratic thought to ensure China's modernity and (3) the continuation of Confucian moral values to provide the modern socialist civilizational state with a distinct Chinese character. Unfortunately, in light of the crisis of faith in China in the post-Mao era, it is extremely difficult to prevent Marxist-Leninism from degenerating into dogmatic formalism. Likewise, Confucian humanism faces overwhelming odds in freeing itself from the perception that it is synonymous with 'feudalism', and Western ideas have a hard time escaping the damnation of being labeled as spiritual pollutants.

The challenge for the Chinese intellectuals is complex indeed. Can they develop a communal critical self-consciousness nourished by the spiritual resources of the past and informed by the practical necessities of the present? The deification of Mao and the unquestioned loyalty to the Party clearly indicate that mass mobilization of energy (the communal act) for serving the state as the embodiment of the people (the transcendent) can be dangerously dehumanizing. An eclectic, practical, utilitarian and worldly approach to nation-building without probing the deep meaning of human existence may help China to be strong and wealthy in the short run but it cannot answer the basic question, for what purpose? Similarly, allowing organized religions limited freedom of expression without fundamentally restructuring the overall pattern of symbolic control, which is still dominated by the rhetoric of class struggle, dictatorship of the proletariat, democratic centralism and continuous revolution, may result in destructive tension between the faith communities and the secular state. In some quarters, such as Tibet and Inner Mongolia, the situation is explosive.

The Chinese belief that Heaven is not capricious or unknowable and that, through the cultivation of one's heart-and-mind, one can realize not only one's human nature but also the will of Heaven suggests a faith in the intrinsic worth of being human individually and communally. To Confucian intellectuals, the human condition here and now provides the basis for ultimate self-transformation. We are engaged, indeed embedded, in our humanness not by default but by choice. To know who we are is not merely to know that we are fated culturally and historically to be human in a particular sense; it is also to act communally and to respond faithfully and dialogically to a calling that is forever beyond our limited conception of humanity. To be fully human, which is tantamount to this Confucian meaning of being religious, is to engage ourselves in ultimate self-transformation as a faithful dialogical response to the transcendent and as a communal act. The question remains: is this enough to safeguard the dignity of the person, the authenticity of the fiduciary community and the truth and reality of the transcendent?

Pluralism and the Common Creed
The upsurge of activity in organized religions is a reflection of China's open-door policy. As this policy continues, pluralism

both as an ideological stance and as an experienced reality seems inevitable. The perceived danger of the vulgarization of culture, the disintegration of society (especially the family) and the destabilizing influence on the political structure, as the result of intensified contact with the outside world, will have an effect on the ability of the reformers to sustain high-level support in the ruling minority as well as among the people. The voice of the intelligentsia (the scholars, writers, journalists and those who are characterized as workers in the theoretical fields who are charged with the responsibility of fixing the superstructure) will be critical in setting up the agenda for and adjudicating unavoidable conflicts in determining the priority of values in China's changing, indeed restless ideological landscape. Whether or not a new common creed will actually emerge, as the result of a confluence of many potentially contradictory streams of thought, the quest for a common creed despite pluralist tendencies will continue. This seems to me profoundly meaningful for students of religion. After all, the necessity for working toward a common creed in this pluralistic world of ours is urgent. The Chinese attempt is at least heuristically suggestive.

11

SECULAR WORLDVIEWS IN TODAY'S WORLD

Ninian Smart
(Santa Barbara and Lancaster)

Since World War II some striking changes have occurred affecting the place of traditional religions and exhibiting ways in which secular ideologies are often substitutes for, and rivals of, older worldviews. The movement towards the universal application of the theory of the nation-state was carried forward with the progressive dismantling of colonial dominations. The Western democracies have intensified their trends towards personal individualism. By contrast forms of Marxism have spread well beyond its older confines—as an official worldview—in the Soviet Union. These trends, of course, have often been in mutual conflict, and they have been both antagonistic towards traditional religion and, often, capable of combining with it. Personalistic motifs have been important in postwar Christian theology, e.g. in the thinking of Bultmann and others. Catholicism and Marxism have partially combined in Liberation Theology. Often traditional religion and nationalism make a heady mixture: as with Buddhism and Sinhalese consciousness in Sri Lanka, Islamic nationalism in Iran, Polish nationalism and Catholicism, etc. At the same time, continuing advances in science and technology reinforce trends towards forms of humanism which exclude the concept of transcendence and rest all knowledge upon science. Such humanistic scientism is an intellectual and self-conscious complement to the unreflective practical atheism (or secularism) of many people, especially in northern Europe, Australia and some other Western countries.

Of all these kinds of worldviews and ideological themes the most powerful has been nationalism. An extreme chauvinistic nationalism was responsible for World War II in the shape of the Nazis. But nationalisms, though not typically expressed in such chauvinistic and racist terms, have been potent since the War, and many of the conflicts in the world have had their source in the struggles of ethnic groups of one sort or another to have their own nation-State. In certain ways, nationalisms are closest in practice to the traditional religions. Thus if we define a religion dimensionally, in terms of its doctrines, myths, ethics, experiences, rituals and institutions, we can see their analogues in the nation. A nation has its myth, namely its history as taught in schools and celebrated in various ways including the contemplation of its heroes (great poets, soldiers, musicians, statespersons, sportspersons, etc.). It has its ethics—those of the good citizen who will pay her or his taxes, help fellow-citizens, be productive for 'society' (shorthand for the national group), etc. It has its feelings and experiences—the love of country, as expressed in its rituals. It has its rites, such as national days, marchpasts, saluting the flag, singing the national anthem and other patriotic songs, tourism around the nation's beauty spots, paying respects to the president or royal family etc. It has its institutions—the State apparatus itself, the teachers who inculcate the myths, the soldiers who perform some of the rituals, and so on. It is often however weak on doctrine, beyond the doctrine that each ethnic group, and ours in particular, ought to have independence (collective freedom—no guarantor of course of individual freedom or of minority rights). So very often nationalism combines with some universal worldview— Marxism, Christianity, Buddhism even—and the result will be reinforced in the new telling of the myths. But it makes a truly formidable blend, because loyalty to the nation is seen as some kind of universal duty and connected to world revolution, or to God or to some other Absolute.

The universal ideological theme, to complicate matters, may be democratic pluralism, so that the loyal citizen will not be expected to accept any one religious or secular worldview. But otherwise we effectively have a modern equivalent of the old post-Reformation principle of *cuius regio eius religio*. So the citizen of Romania will be disadvantaged if he or she does not accept and affirm the official ideology, and while Orthodox Christianity and some other forms of religion are allowed within strict limits, it is a disadvantage to be overtly pious. Thus, ironically, it is above all the Marxist countries that carry on the old Christian traditions, which has however been largely discontinued in the one-time predominantly Christian countries of the West, under the combined influences of radical Protestantism from the Anabaptists onwards, enlightenment liberalism, and modern individualism. The combination of national identity and Marxism, natural enough when 'the people' is equated with the majority ethnic group, has itself led to differences of emphasis in different countries. There has proliferated a variety of official Marxisms: Soviet, Chinese, Albanian, Yugoslav, Romanian, Cuban and so on. The chief point about any differences is that they are tailored to the specific national features of each group. The most notable instance of this is Maoism (or Marxism-Leninism-Mao Zedong Thought). Though it is not now, in 1986, so much regarded in the People's Republic, it was a formative influence on the Chinese Revolution. Mao had taken a non-orthodox view, in relation to the Stalinism of the thirties: he stressed the vital role of the peasantry and argued for a direct approach to socialism, without any intervening capitalist phase, as well as espousing a theory of continuing revolution, which inspired both the Great Leap Forward and the Cultural Revolution. His theory of war was also important in directing the successful campaigns both against the Japanese and the forces of Chiang Kai-shek. The Long March also supplied an important myth of the Revolutionary spirit; his strong voluntarism, moreover, created a special ethos for the new China. A kind of evangelical attitude to conversion to Maoism pervaded the propaganda of Mao's days in power. Thus, in many ways Maoism provided a quasi-religious alternative to the pieties and doctrines of the Chinese tradition.

There have also been, though less fashionably in the period since 1945, right-wing nationalisms which incorporate some Fascist or analogous ideology. Franco's Spain continued its authoritarian tradition till 1975; and Portuguese rightism till 1974. The over-throw of Allende led to Pinochet's regime (1973–   ). In the Third World dictatorships are frequent, though they may not assume any very ideological form.

The drive towards national freedom (from colonial and alien rule) was pushed forward greatly with the dissolution of most of the great empires of the nineteenth century—British, French, Italian, Belgian, etc. This was effectively a consequence of World War II, which not only sapped the power of the imperial nations of Europe, except for the USSR, but created a much stronger climate of favoring national independence, with the creation of the United Nations in 1945. Generally speaking the Asian countries adopted some ideology congruent with their national past, such as Hindu pluralistic democracy in India, Buddhist democracy in Sri Lanka, Islamic democracy in Malaysia, pluralistic democracy in Japan, Islamic socialism in Algeria, etc. But some crafted a variety of national Marxism, as we have seen (South Yemen, China, Cuba, Angola, etc.). In general the African countries have the problem that arbitrary colonial boundaries, usually regarded as extra-sacrosanct precisely because to challenge them would put into the open the ethnic absurdities of African political frontiers, mean that consensus democracy is hard to work. This leads to the typical device of the one-party State and some kind of authoritarian rule and coalition politics.

Usually in ex-colonial lands some formal or real tribute to socialism is paid, partly because it promises greater social cohesion during a period in a country's history when solidarity is important; and partly because colonial rule has become frequently identified with capitalism (with some justification, except that the most successful colonial powers remain Marxist). But though some Islamic nations are socialist in theory (such as the Baath regimes in Iraq and Syria), a more important influence has been the ideal of a revived Islam, which is then incorporated into the law of each country to a greater or lesser degree—e.g. in Malaysia, Bangladesh, Pakistan, Saudi Arabia, Sudan, Algeria, etc.

Because the national ideal is so powerful and realized so imperfectly, there are many ethnic trouble spots which have continued to cause problems in the postcolonial era—the struggle for independence among the Kurds, in West Irian, in the Basque country, in Tibet, for instance; and the tensions among Muslims in the Philippines, the Karen in Burma, the Eritreans in Ethiopia, Turks in Cyprus, Protestants in Northern Ireland, Albanians in Yugoslavia and so on. The largest of these struggles and the most complex is in South Africa. It is significant too that a number of conflicts between national identity and some external controlling power are, as we mentioned, in Marxist empires: so though in theory the USSR gives full recognition to nationalities, there are anti-Russian forms of restiveness among the Moldavians, Estonians, Armenians, Central Asian Muslims and a number of other minorities; as well as in the Soviet-controlled Eastern Europe (so that there have been risings in East Germany, 1953, Hungary, 1956, Czechoslovakia, 1967, and Poland, 1979—in some cases with a combination of national, religious and social-democratic ideological factors coming into play, notably in Poland).

Highly important too is the continuing Buddhist resistance to Marxism in Tibet as a mode of imposing Chinese rule.

Between nationalism and the various religions and ideologies that serve to underpin it at the level of doctrine there are, of course, some contradictions, since loyalty to an ethnic community may interfere with universal loyalty as taught by a universal worldview to the human race, all living beings, etc. National chauvinism can thus only combine in an uneasy way with the wider ideals of its coordinate ideology. We may note that there are a number of transnational institutions which may moderate the impact of nationalism—multinational corporations, churches and other ecumenical movements (Buddhist, Christian, Islamic, etc.), the mode in which minorities exist across national divisions, the United Nations and other international agencies, sports federations and so on.

If nationalism is a vital ideological theme it needs, then, to be seen in conjunction with various worldviews, including modern secular ideologies and ideological themes. Let us now turn to one of these important themes, namely liberalism. This as a theory of pluralism and democracy can take many forms, from right wing laissezfaire economics to social democracy. It derives from different themes which have come to the fore especially since the Enlightenment. Partly because capitalism tends to decentralize decision-making, liberal thinking and institutions are associated with capitalist or mixed economies (but of course capitalism can help to underpin very illiberal regimes also, though it rarely goes with that total regimentation of life which is typical of Marxist regimes). The liberal idea, because it favors pluralism, is not by itself anti-religious. But in so far as it arises within the ambience of modern rationalism, it is often closely associated with that more particular worldview known as scientific humanism. As we have noted it has a less articulate version, in many Western countries, of practical atheism among the masses. This practical atheism is what some scholars refer to as 'secularization', or rather as the consequence thereof. It is a kind of pragmatic secularism—namely the view that we can rely, except perhaps marginally, on technological, scientific and social resources to ameliorate our world, on entertainment, from TV to sport, to give it meaning and on personal relations to give it depth.

Since World War II a variety of scientific humanism has become dominant in English-speaking philosophical circles. It is the typical ideology of philosophers, who try to resolve issues about the nature of reality withuot recourse to religious premises and to found ethics and politics on a rational, but not a transcendental, basis. The most aggressive form of this ideology is Logical Positivism, as expressed in A. J. Ayer's bestselling *Language, Truth and Logic* (1938), the chief influence of which occurred in the immediate postwar period. This introduced a strict notion of meaning: all statements which could not be verified or falsified by sense-experience were declared without meaning or empty. The aim was to confine knowledge to scientific knowledge, in a broad sense. All metaphysical and religious claims were by this stroke declared meaningless, and so could not even rise to the level of being false, let alone true. Naturally, there were problems about this account of meaning (it even failed when applied to science): but the doctrine was influential, because it gave formal shape to a widely prevailing scientism—that is a doctrine that science alone is the source of knowledge. A more moderate view was espoused by Karl Popper, who did not regard unfalsifiability as a ground for dubbing a statement meaningless, but rather as a criterion of what counts as scientific. Popper's was one way to loosen up perceptions of the rigors of science, and this trend has continued in subsequent writings in the history and philosophy of science, ranging from Thomas Kuhn's celebrated *The Structure of Scientific Revolutions* (1962) to the work of such writers as P. K. Feyerabend and Hilary Putnam. However, this loosening-up of our definitional accounts of science merely means that we lessen the gap between the physical and human sciences, and it can still be an integral part of modern scientific humanism. Coupled with such a worldview is sometimes a straight materialist thesis —that brain and mental processes are identical. The ethics associated with this position happen to be mainstream Western in emphasizing love of other human beings, the importance of the individual and freedom of belief, etc. It is opposed to Marxist materialism, as being rather unempirical, as well as oppressive.

This ethos of rational humanism has been diminished, after its heyday in the fifties and sixties. Increased interest in Existentialism and the softer offshoots of Marxism has occurred on the philosophical front, while the sixties and early seventies saw an explosion of non-orthdox religious concerns in the West: for example in Eastern religions, methods of yoga and meditation and various new forms of therapy and religious practice. These interests have produced a new kind of 'depth humanism', namely the addition of depth experiences to the range of valuable states to be promoted in human beings. This is a kind of extension of the utilitarian ethic, so that the concepts of happiness and suffering are given a deeper interpretation and related to certain areas of traditional religious practice. This is the ethos pervading some of the seminal writing of the period, e.g. Alan Watts' *Beyond Theology* (1964). Gradually the countercultural movements of this period have become assimilated, through the work of writers like Theodore Roszak, Jacob Needleman and Frithjof Capra.

One of the attractions of Eastern religions and Buddhism in particular was that you do not have to believe in God. Thus it was that a new God-rejecting humanism was born, adopting more positively the spiritual practices of the East: for there are many who may be skeptical about or hostile to traditional Jewish and Christian religion, but not keen on rejecting religion *per se.*

299

In France and elsewhere on the European mainland, the immediate aftermath of the war saw a strong interest in Existentialism, for example that of Jean-Paul Sartre (1905–80), who gave dramatic, French and idiosyncratic shape in Heidegger's quest for authenticity. Heidegger (1889–1976), though for a time sympathetic to Nazism, emerged from the war as a dominant figure in German philosophy. His Existentialism could be described as atheistic, though he himself saw affinities in his own work to the writing of the Japanese D. T. Suzuki (1870–1966), who gave a Westernizing interpretation of some strands in Mahayana philosophy, primarily Rinzai Zen, with its non-theistic form of spirituality. It is interesting and a little ironic that Protestant Christian theologians of the postwar period and earlier had incorporated so much of Heidegger's Existentialism into their thinking—finding its individualist mysticism easier to accommodate to Christian theology than the more abrasive scientism of the English-speaking philosophers. Of course, this was part of liberal Protestantism's assimilation of what it had been partly responsible for: personalism.

While Marxism as an official doctrine is well institutionalized and so has strong affinities to come of the traditional religions, scientific humanism's much looser placement gives it a rather weaker resemblance to religion. Nevertheless, it does exhibit itself in various dimensions. It has a cosmology (that provided by modern science). Its ethics are personalistic and open-minded. It prefers the democratic institutions of modern open societies, such as the United States or Sweden. It confines experience to sense-experience and the inner life, and places strong emphasis upon aesthetics and education. Its rituals are those of demonstrating for good causes, the performatives of interpersonal discourse and public ceremonies of secular society.

Possibly the greatest exponent of scientific humanism in recent times was Bertrand Russell (1872–1970), whose engagement in social action and protest helped to give his outlook a practical outreach which the humanist societies of the Western world could not have.

Another strand in the anti-establishmentarianism of the early seventies was a revived interest in Marxism in the West. Western Communist movements had suffered serious setbacks with disillusionment over Hungary, Czechoslovakia and eventually, after the death of Mao and subsequent revelations, concerning the Cultural Revolution and other matters in recent history, China. The new Marxian interest was somewhat alienated from all forms of official Marxism, and even the Communist Parties of Europe flirted with what came to be known as Euro-Communism, especially the Italian Party under the leadership of Enrico Berlinguer (1920–1984). In Britain, there was the growth in the seventies of a new left with sectarian, Trotskyist leanings, identified in part with the movement known as Militant Tendency. In the United States, there was the great success, for a time, of the critical Marxism of Herbert Marcuse (1898–1977). In philosophy on both sides of the Atlantic there has also been some interest in the work of the Frankfurt School and in the critical stance of Jurgen Habermas (1928–   )—the net result of whose emancipatory philosophy would be a worldview-free position. This is reminiscent of Buddhist Mādhyamika philosophy, though the parallels have not as yet been drawn out.

The decline of Marxist influence in the West is to some extent matched by a diminution of attractions in Marxism in the Third World. This is partly because of the increasingly splintered character of Marxism—thus parties in South Asia divide into pro-Chinese, pro-Soviet and Trotskyist. It is partly because in Asia the Soviet and Chinese actions in Afghanistan and Tibet have alienated various sections of the religious world. It is partly because the examples of Japan, South Korea, Singapore and in some degree India are impressive reminders of the fecundity of capitalism. But it is also because many cultures are seeking again their roots. There is a desire to combine traditional ideas and modern participation in the tightly-knit global city.

This attempt can take many forms of combination, but it often involves trying to mix scientific humanism with traditional religion. Literally it cannot be done; but it is possible to borrow certain themes and graft them into a revised view of the tradition. This has been done very effectively in the Republic of India, whose pluralistic Hinduism has affinities to liberal democracy, and whose religious presuppositions can be made not to clash with modern science. It is done in other ways in Singapore, which grafts Confucian models onto modern technocratic capitalism and a highly developed welfare state. It can safely be said that every country in the non-Marxist world today is trying out a different way of blending some of the motifs of its main cultural tradition with some of those drawn from science and nationalism. In this connection a very important issue is whether science and technology can in the last resort flourish effectively in a closed society. If Karl Popper's thesis that scientific epistemology demands democratic openness, then this would be a vital finding for those States who wish effectively to modernize (and this idea of 'modernization' and its sisters such as 'economic progress,' 'development' and so forth are virtually *de rigueur* throughout the Third World).

There have however been two or three exceptions to this universal concern to enter the modern, global community. The ideologies of the Khmer Rouge and of the J.V.P. in the Sri Lankan uprising of 1971 were remarkably similar in looking to a revolution in which all foreign capitalism would be removed, in a purified autarkic utopia. Though both used some of the jargon and trappings of Marxism their worldviews were really very different: they sought a rural economy cut off from the rest of the world. They reckoned that the strength and tentacles of the international economic system are so great that anything less than complete self-sufficiency would draw their peoples back into its arms. Hence the destruction, in Kampuchea, of the foreign-educated (which meant in effect all education, for education was a foreign process). A more moderate ideology which addressed itself to a similar end was Burmese socialism. Only recently have the doors into Burma been opened a little. It is as if Theravādin countries opt for a kind of social *nirvāṇa*, beyond the *saṃsāra* of the global economy.

This is a very drastic solution to the problems posed by the quest for national identity in the post-colonial era. We have seen other, less drastic, but still hard, backlashes, such as the Iranian Republic of the Ayatollah Khomeini, and the neo-Islamic socialism of Khaddafi. It is hard, though, not to think that the problems of most societies, increasingly plural in their populations (so that Islam is the third largest denomination in Britain), have to be resolved on a pluralistic basis of some kind. Moreover, the forces of science, of international capitalism and modernization all seem to point to a great pressure for democratic institutions. It is therefore probable that the traditional religions will increasingly take on a denominational character, living together plurally without any one having exceptional privileges. If this be so, then a kind of liberal humanism will be the overall framework within which the traditions will exist. It will involve considerable changes in the way people come to regard religious authority. It also means that liberalism may come to be the vital ingredient in the new worldviews evolved by the religious traditions themselves. In other words, we shall no longer look to pure Catholicism, or pure Theravāda Buddhism, or unadulterated Islam. Of course we never had these traditions neat: they were always blended into the cultural orders through which they passed. But now all religions will share a single culture, more or less; and in this circumstance some theory of pluralism is hard to avoid. This will not apply in the Marxist half of the world in the near future;

but it is likely to be the norm in other countries. In brief, we shall have a new pluralistic global worldview which will be analogous to what I referred to earlier as 'depth humanism'. The depth will be supplied by the transcendental character and experiential depth of the traditional religions. In other words the traditions will present their separate visions of true life, true liberty and true happiness in a common aim of 'life, liberty and the pursuit of happiness'.

This pluralism is already evident in some moves to reform religious education, where in northern Europe particularly there are attempts to make it consciously comparative and plural. But even more important is the growth particularly since the 1960s of programmes in higher education devoted to the study of religion and religions. This is a move away from the old theological models in many Christian (or supposedly Christian) countries. It is an important step in the foundation of a kind of world-cultural approach to matters of the analysis and exploration of worldviews. It owes something to the youth movement of the sixties, but more to the application of liberal-humanist ideas to the curriculum. Those ideas are embodied institutionally in the very idea of the University, even if conservatism also is a very vital force in academia. The study of religions is already having an effect on the religions themselves. The direction of that influence is naturally towards the encouragement of dialogue, itself an irenic stance which fits in with the humanistic pluralism implicit in many of the workings of the global city.

Maybe I have here presented an over-optimistic analysis, for after all there are many reactions which occur, naturally enough, to the softening effects of pluralist ideologies—and some backlashes may be very harsh and abrasive in the fabric of international life. In any case we may suppose that the secular ideologies and ideological themes—of forms of Marxism, humanism, nationalism and liberal pluralism will continue to exist both side by side with, and in blending conjunction with, the traditional religions. The fact that there is both blending and rivalry is warrant enough for us to treat the secular worldviews together with and as important for the traditional and transcendental religions. In this respect, the study of religions is also that wide pursuit known as worldview analysis. If before World War II ideological forces were more sharply and brutally defined, the postwar period has seen some interesting twists and turns in the destinies of the ideologies. We have here touched on the evolution of a variety of Marxisms; official creeds in the pattern of *cuius regio eius ideologia*; scientific humanism; forms of Existentialism; fascisms; and forms of quasi-Marxist autarkisms.

Bibliography

On nationalism as a quasi-religion see Ninian Smart *Worldviews*; New York: Scribner, (1983), and Peter Merkl and Ninian Smart (editors) *Religion and Politics in the Modern World*; New York: Scribner, (1983). On varieties of Marxism, Henri Chambre *From Karl Marx to Mao-Tse-Tung* (English trans., New York: Kenedy, 1963); on positivism Leszek Kolakowski *Positivist Philosophy*; Harmondsworth: Penguin, (1972); on various modern worldviews, John Macquarrie *Twentieth Century Religious Thought*; New York: Scribner (2nd edn., 1981); on existentialisms, H. J. Blackham *Six Existentialist Thinkers*; Boston: Routledge & Kegan, (1961); on types of humanism, H. J. Blackham *Humanism*; Boston: Routledge & Kegan, (1968) and Susan Budd *Varieties of Unbelief*; New York: Holmes & Meier, (1977); on secularization, David Martin *A General Theory of Secularization*; New York: Harper & Row, (1978) and Vernon Pratt *Religion and Secularism*; London: Macmillan, (1970).

12

SPIRITUALITY IN TODAY'S WORLD

Ewart Cousins

(*Fordham*)

One of the major developments of religion in today's world has been an increasing interest in spirituality. The meaning of the term 'spirituality' will be treated at length below. The following can serve for the moment as a preliminary description: Spirituality refers to the experiential dimension of religion in contrast with formal beliefs, external practices, and institutions; it deals with the inner depth of the person that is open to the transcendent; in traditions that affirm the divine, it is concerned with the relation of the person to the divine, the experience of the divine, and the journey of the person to a more intimate relationship with the divine.

After the East and the West had settled from the turmoil of World War II, a new spiritual awakening occurred in the West. This was centered chiefly in the United States, but spread to other areas. By the 1960s a large number had become disillusioned with the materialism of Western culture. For many, especially the younger generation, the churches offered no solution; for they seemed caught up with external observance and unable to touch the spiritual core of religion. Into this setting came spiritual teachers from the East: Hindu swamis and Zen masters, who presented their ancient practices of yoga and meditation in a way that could be assimilated by Westerners. Many flocked to these teachers, becoming devoted followers, practicing a lifestyle of spiritual dedication and discipline. Others, while remaining in their traditional churches, added Eastern meditation to their daily prayers. A host of spiritual terms, such as 'mantra' and 'guru', became commonplace in the English language. By the late 1960s spirituality had become a visible part of Western culture.

Having been awakened to spirituality by the East, Jews and Christians began during the 1970s to search for their spiritual roots in their own traditions. They asked probing questions: Does Judaism or Christianity possess a body of spiritual wisdom comparable to that of Hinduism and Buddhism? Spiritual techniques like those of yoga or Zen meditation? The search for answers to these questions led to a recovery of traditional Western spirituality—through spiritual practice, academic research, and major publishing projects. Meanwhile in the East the classical traditions of spirituality had been drawn increasingly into an encounter with social, political, and economic problems that had taken a more complex form after World War II. Spiritual leaders in Hinduism and Buddhism were drawing resources from their classical traditions to deal with the crucial issues emerging in the secular world. Throughout these decades, from the late 1940s into the 1980s, we can discern a process involving a spiritual awakening, a recovery of tradition, and a transformation of tradition— leading towards what can be called a global spirituality on the eve of the twenty-first century.

In order to explore spirituality in today's world, I will first examine the phenomenon of spirituality over the last several decades, focusing on the awakening of spirituality in the West and the recovery of its classical traditions. Secondly, I will explore some of the issues that have arisen concerning the nature of spirituality, its history, and the relation of spiritual traditions in a pluralistic environment. Thirdly, I will present my own theory on the emergence of global spirituality in today's world.

Awakening of Spirituality

After the complacent mood of the 1950s, the West was awakened to spirituality by teachers who came from the East to the United States, bringing their wisdom and practice to thousands of Americans whose lives had lacked a spiritual dimension. Hindu swamis, Zen masters, Tibetan rinpoches, and Sufi sheiks arrived in the United States, attracted large numbers of followers, and established centers, many of which have continued to operate into the present. For example, in the mid-1960s Swami Satchidananda was invited to New York for a brief visit of three days to present his spiritual message to a small audience. He attracted so many young people that he decided to establish a center in Manhattan called the Integral Yoga Institute. This proved so successful that he opened a second center in Manhattan in Greenwich Village. Around the same time, a Zen master named Eido Tai Shimano Roshi arrived in New York from Japan to teach at a Zen Center not far from the Integral Yoga Institute. As his following increased, he moved to a larger site, a beautifully renovated firehouse on East 67th Street. During this period a Christian monk, Brother David Steindl-Rast, of the Benedictine Monastery of Mount Savior in western New York State, came to New York to study Japanese at Columbia University and Zen meditation under Eido Tai Shimano Roshi. Brother David's West Side apartment became a center where young Christians discovered their own spiritual traditions within the context of the newly imported spirituality of the East.

While each of these spiritual teachers attracted followers to his own path, they remained in close contact among themselves, entered into interreligious dialogue, and held common programs of meditation. Into this circle came Rabbi Joseph H. Gelberman, who had been teaching in New York the Jewish spirituality of the Kabbalah and Hasidism. Together the group formed the Center for Spiritual Studies, which had as its goal the development of a tract of land as a common spiritual center within a two-hour drive of New York. On this land they planned to build individual centers where each of the traditions—Hindu, Buddhist, Jewish, Christian, and Islamic— would pursue its own spiritual path, but in contact with the others. Although this dream never became a reality, it functioned as a symbol of the future, a microcosm of the emerging global spirituality. The individual spiritual teachers began to establish their own centers outside New York City. Swami Satchidananda set up a yoga center north of New York, moving later to Connecticut and then to Virginia. Eido Tai Shimano Roshi built a Zendo in the Catskill Mountains north of New York. Brother David became involved in the House of Prayer movement which developed around the country in Catholic circles, to provide settings for contemplation not only for priests and members of religious orders but for laymen and laywomen as well. Later Brother David established an experimental monastic community in Maine and then a center in Connecticut.

This example of New York is only one of many instances throughout the United States in the 1960s of a spiritual awakening through Eastern wisdom. Oriental spiritual teachers flourished in California, especially in the San Francisco Bay area where, for example, there were founded important centers of Zen and Tibetan Buddhism. Throughout, this was a mixed phenomenon. Inevitably the spirituality of some of the American followers of Eastern teachers was superficial, immature, and even bizarre. Yet many became devotees, deeply dedicated to a lifestyle of spiritual practice and ascetic discipline. A large number had their lives enriched for the first time by the resources of classical spirituality. For culture at large, this phenomenon cracked open the hard crust of materialism, revealing the hunger of the Western psyche for spiritual nourishment which had not been available from its own resources.[1]

The Secular Spiritual Awakening

The spiritual awakening was further stimulated by psychedelic drugs and psychotherapy. Both of these developments came not from the classical spiritual traditions East or West, but from modern secular culture. By the late 1960s psychedelic drugs had become a national problem: they were being taken by young people indiscriminately and irresponsibly. Prior to this, however, important scientific research into altered states of consciousness had been conducted by the use of psychedelic drugs. In 1966 R. E. L. Masters and Jean Houston published the results of their extensive research in their book *The Varieties of Psychedelic Experience*.[2] What this and other research revealed was that the human psyche has an extraordinary range of possible states of consciousness that far exceeds the narrow limits of everyday awareness or the empirical-rational mind-set adopted by Western culture over the last several centuries. In controlled experiments, subjects experienced states of consciousness that were rich in aesthetic, symbolic, mythic, cosmic, and mystical qualities. One of the most striking results of this research was the correlation it revealed between these states of consciousness and those sought by the classical spirituality traditions through techniques of prayer and meditation. The question immediately arose: Can such altered states, produced by chemicals or hypnosis, be legitimately

[1] On the influence of Eastern spiritual teachers in the 1960s, see Jacob Needleman, *The New Religions*, rev. ed. (New York: Pocket Books, 1972).

[2] R. E. L. Masters and Jean Houston *The Varieties of Psychedelic Experience* (New York: Holt, Rinehart and Winston, 1966); see also Stanislav Grof, *Realms of Human Unconscious: Observations from LSD Research* (New York: Viking Press, 1975).

compared to the higher consciousness of the acknowledged mystics of East and West? The debate still continues. However it may be resolved, this much is clear: this research showed that the human psyche possesses a capacity that had not been actualized within the strict canons of Western secular culture. Furthermore, it is this capacity that the classical spiritual traditions have sought to realize. In fact, this research produced the closest thing to a Western psychology of spirituality in the sense that it revealed through a phenomenology of consciousness the broad horizons of consciousness one finds in classical spirituality. It opened a window on the psyche that had been closed by secular scientific culture, and it showed the need for the secular West to turn to the classical spirituality traditions for guidance. During the 1960s many travelled through psychedelic drugs to spirituality. By taking drugs they discovered their untapped psychic potential, but then turned to Eastern spiritual teachers to free them from drugs and to guide them along the spiritual path.

Another movement that flowed from the secular sphere into the spiritual awakening was psychotherapy. Although developed in the reductionist climate of nineteenth-century science, psychotherapy has a natural affinity to spirituality since it deals with the inner realm of the psyche and can touch areas that converge on spirituality. In fact, psychotherapy can be called the characteristic spiritual journey of the modern secular person. In spite of its negative attitudes to religion in its theory, Freudian psychoanalysis in practice has awakened many to the spiritual journey. This is not surprising since psychotherapy, in general, activates a process that parallels the stages of purgation, illumination, and union described in classical spiritual literature. For with the therapist as guide, the client must purge himself of his unconscious defenses that have been blocking the development of his personality. This often requires a humility and courage comparable to that demanded by a spiritual guide

311

at the outset of the spiritual journey. As therapy progresses, the client grows in self-understanding which, like the stage of illumination, is not theoretical but activates the positive forces in his psyche leading to the goal of a unified or integral personality. In this respect, C. G. Jung's psychology has much more explicit resonances with spirituality than Freud's. For Jung's process of individuation can be viewed as a map of the spiritual journey. His concept of the archetypes gives a positive role to the symbolic and mythic imagination. He acknowledges a transcendent dimension in the psyche, which for him is not peripheral but central to the life task. This transcendent dimension is crystallized in the archetype of the Self, the dynamism and goal of the psychic process, and which he refers to in the classical terminology of 'the image of God'. In the late 1960s there emerged a movement called Transpersonal Psychology, which is directly interested in the classical spiritual traditions. As its name indicates, it is primarily concerned with the transpersonal dimension of the psyche, whether this is perceived in theistic, transtheistic, or cosmic terms. This movement has attempted to make direct contact with classical spirituality at the same time that it has applied the techniques of scientific research to higher states of consciousness.[3]

The Search for Roots

The spiritual awakening of the 1960s, stimulated by Eastern teachers and secular psychology, caused Christians and Jews in the 1970s to search for their classical spiritual roots. In searching their past for techniques of prayer, they explored the Kabbalah and Hasidism, on the one hand, and Christian monasticism, on the other. In the Houses of Prayer, mentioned above, Christians

[3] See Charles Tart, ed., *Transpersonal Psychologies* (New York: Harper & Row, 1975; Anthony Sutich, 'Some Considerations Regarding Transpersonal Psychology', Journal of Transpersonal Psychology, 1 (1969), 11–20.

experimented with Eastern meditation, it is true, but they also turned to their own tradition for classical resources of prayer. Under the influence of the Transcendental Meditation of the Maharishi, the Cistercian monks of St. Joseph Abbey, in Spencer, Massachusetts, developed an adaptation of the technique of the Jesus prayer and *The Cloud of Unknowing* which they called Centering Prayer.

An example of the recovery of a classical tradition can be found in the renewal of the Spiritual Exercises of Ignatius of Loyola among the Jesuits. These exercises employ a classical type of meditation on the life of Christ developed in the High Middle Ages and oriented by Ignatius in the sixteenth century towards a transformation of the personality. Although in continuous use, these exercises had been condensed and adapted for presentation to large groups. In the 1970s, at various Jesuit retreat houses in the United States and Canada, the exercises were given by one retreat master to one person in what was called 'a guided retreat'. This was a return to the original method that Ignatius himself had used in giving his exercises. The recovery of this classical method attracted numerous retreatants, including many laymen and laywomen, not only for what had previously been the shortened three-day retreat, but also for the original period of thirty days. Along with the recovery of the exercises came a special interest in Ignatian discernment of spirits and spiritual direction, into which was integrated findings of contemporary psychology. In each of these areas, the spiritual practice was augmented by a considerable amount of academic research into classical texts and the history of spirituality.

In the spirit of the recovery of the classical tradition, academic programs in spirituality began to blossom on university campuses during the 1970s. This was a significant development since from the founding of the universities in Western culture in the twelfth and thirteenth centuries, there has been a tension between the objective perspective of academic studies and the subjective experience of spirituality. At Duquesne University in Pittsburgh, Father Adrian Van Kaam developed first a masters and then a doctoral program in what he called Formative Spirituality. This involved an integration of contemporary psychology with classical spirituality. At Fordham University in New York a masters program was inaugurated which focused on the history of spirituality and dealt with contemporary issues in the light of tradition. It is possible for students to do doctoral studies in spirituality at the Graduate Theological Union in Berkeley, California, and at the Catholic University of America in Washington, D.C.

Major Publishing Projects
Another move towards the recovery of the classical tradition was the development of major publishing projects in the field of spirituality, which drew heavily from the resources of the academic community. In 1975 Richard Payne, then associate editor of the Paulist Press in New York, conceived the idea of creating three series to meet the widespread need for having readily available central works on spirituality. One series would contain 60 volumes of the classics of Western spirituality; a second series would contain an equal number of volumes of the classics of Eastern spirituality; and a third series of over 20 volumes would contain articles written by contemporary scholars covering the entire history of the human spiritual journey. Now over ten years later, the first of these series, The Classics of Western Spirituality, published by Paulist Press beginning in 1978, is nearing completion, with over 50 of the 60 volumes in print. The series was so successful that supplemental volumes are already in progress. The next in order of realization is the history of spirituality under the title World Spirituality: An Encyclopedic History of the Religious Quest, in 25 volumes, being brought out by the Crossroad Publishing

Company. The first of these volumes appeared in 1985, followed by two more in 1986. All of the others are in progress and will appear over the next several years. The third project, the Classics of Eastern Spirituality will be brought out by Amity House, a publishing company founded by Richard Payne in 1983. The initial planning has been completed and several volumes have been commissioned. When completed, these three projects will provide comprehensive resource materials on the entire scope of spirituality. For the Classics of Western Spirituality contains translations of the major spiritual writings of Judaism, Christianity, and Islam, as well as the spirituality of the American Indians. The Classics of Eastern Spirituality will contain the major writings of Hinduism, Buddhism, Taoism, and Confucianism, as well as other Oriental traditions, along with the spirituality of the primal peoples of the East. World Spirituality presents the entire sweep of the history of spirituality from archaic cultures, through the major traditions and into the meeting of traditions in the present and future.[4]

The Classics of Western Spirituality presents an excellent example of the recovery of spirituality which characterized the 1970s and which continues into the 1980s. Before launching such an ambitious project, Paulist Press commissioned extensive market research by a New York advertising firm. The results showed that there was a large prospective audience for such a series, not only among libraries, churches, religious institutions, and the clergy, but among the laity as well. Most significantly, it revealed that there was a large constituency of 'spiritual seekers' who had no formal connection with the churches but were deeply committed to the spiritual quest and who sorely needed the nourishment and guidance that could come from the great

---

[4] The Classics of Western Spirituality, 60 vols. (New York: Paulist Press, 1978–); World Spirituality: An Encyclopedic History of the Religious Quest, 25 vols. (New York: Crossroad Publishing Company, 1985–); The Classics of Eastern Spirituality (Warwick NY: Amity House, in preparation).

spiritual writers of the classical tradition. The predictions of the market research have been confirmed. The series has been very successful. It was marketed both as a series, on the basis of a subscription, and in individual volumes. Both sales were impressive, showing the widespread hunger for spirituality in our times and the seriousness of the readers. In an age of superficial entertainment in television and popular publishing, it is indeed heartening to see such serious interest not merely in contemporary spirituality but in the classics of our heritage. Already the series has had an enormous influence as one of the most effective means for the recovery of classical spirituality in the West. It has been widely read and used for prayer and meditation by individuals and groups. Since it drew upon the highest level of scholarship for its translations and introductions, it has been well received in the academic world. Volumes from the series are being used in numerous college and graduate courses, not only in the field of religion, but in philosophy, history, literature, psychology, and art. In fact, the publication of this series has made certain courses possible, for it has provided translations of classical texts where these were not previously available. There is every reason to think that this series will have a continued influence in making the awareness of spirituality part of our collective memory.

World Spirituality

It is possible to explore a number of issues concerning spirituality through the series World Spirituality: An Encyclopedic History of the Religious Quest. For the series was designed to be a microcosm of the state of spirituality through its long history to the present and into the future. From the outset I have been privileged to be involved in the project, working with Richard Payne in its early planning and development, and serving since 1981 as its general editor. More than in the case of the Classics of Western Spirituality and the

Classics of Eastern Spirituality, this series required considerable analysis of issues since it was largely a constructive enterprise rather than a retrieving through translations of classical works from the past. The purpose of World Spirituality is to present the spiritual wisdom of the human race in its historical unfolding from prehistoric times through the great religious traditions into the present and future. When the series was being designed, the question was raised: Should it focus on the diverse traditions in their historical development, for example, Hinduism, Confucianism, and Islam; or rather on archetypal themes or practices found in most or all religions, such as the journey, sacrifice, and techniques of prayer? For theoretical as well as practical reasons, it was decided to follow the history of the diverse traditions. Critically, this is easier to control since it bases itself on the discrete nature of the historical data rather than making an abstraction at the very outset which involves a major interpretation. In keeping with the recovery of the classical tradition of the 1970s and 1980s, the model of diversity employs the genre of history to retrieve the spiritual wisdom not only of one tradition, but of the various traditions. The fact that all the traditions are presented in a single series already situates the work within a global horizon.

The design of the series, then, was set as follows: five volumes on the spirituality of primal peoples—the archaic spirituality of Asia, Europe, Africa and Oceania, North America, South and Meso-America. These are followed by volumes on the major traditions, usually two per tradition: Hindu, Buddhist, Taoist, Confucian, Jewish, Christian, and Islamic. The series includes also Zoroastrianism, Jainism,and Sikhism, as well as traditions which have not survived as such: for example, the Sumerian and Hittite, Egyptian, Greek, and Roman. To these are added a volume on modern esoteric movements and one on the secular spiritual quest. The last three volumes deal with the interrelation of spiritualities. Volume 23 treats the encounter of spiritualities past to the present and explores those archetypal symbols and practices, mentioned above, which are the basis for a creative encounter. Volume 24 is on the encounter of spiritualities present to the future; it will contain a forum of articles by the volume editors on the present and future state of spirituality as they see it from the standpoint of their traditions and from their own perspectives. Volume 25 is a dictionary of spiritual terms drawn from all the traditions. It is not a mere listing of definitions but a view of world spirituality in its diversity and interrelatedness through its technical vocabulary.

Drawing upon the highest level of scholarship, each volume has an editor or a team of editors, who with consultants have designed the contents of the volume. The editors commission articles on specific topics from contributors who are the leading specialists in the field. These articles are not brief factual accounts, but substantial treatments in depth of aspects of spirituality. The project has created a network of some 500 scholars around the world who are working on the series. Wherever possible, editors and contributors have been chosen who have a religious and cultural grounding in the particular tradition. Such a strategy has advantages, especially in the field of spirituality which is grounded in both personal and collective experience. On the other hand, the planners recognize that there are distinctive values in the perspective of one who stands outside the tradition he studies. Although editors and contributors were drawn from the specific traditions, they were expected to present their studies with a scholarly objectivity that would present their tradition to a larger readership.

Meaning of 'Spirituality'
In order to deal with such a vast amount of material from such diverse perspectives, it was necessary to explore the meaning of the term 'spirituality'. Research has been done on the history of the term in Christian circles by Jean Leclercq and Walter

Principe.[5] The word 'spiritual' is found in Paul in the New Testament, where it is associated with life in the Holy Spirit. The abstract term *spiritualitas* has not been found earlier than the fifth century. Throughout its history it has retained the Pauline meaning while acquiring also the meaning of life according to what is highest in the person. At times the term has suggested a dualistic vision which sharply separates spirit and matter, looking negatively on the latter. This would be viewed by many as a deviation from its authentic meaning and verging on heresy. Since World Spirituality is global in scope, it was necessary to formulate a working description of the term that would be acceptable to all traditions and not merely to the Christian. This was all the more challenging since not all of the traditions have a term that corresponds to 'spirituality'. The following is the formulation which was distributed to the editors at the beginning of the project to serve as a guideline for them and their contributors. Since certain traditions, like the Buddhist, do not speak of the divine, it seemed best to formulate the meaning in terms of the human person:

> The series focuses on that inner dimension of the person called by certain traditions 'the spirit'. This spiritual core is the deepest center of the person. It is here that the person is open to the transcendent dimension; it is here that the person experiences ultimate reality. The series explores the discovery of this core, the dynamics of its development, and its journey to the ultimate goal. It deals with prayer, spiritual direction, the various maps of the spiritual journey, and the methods of advancement in the spiritual ascent.[6]

In addition to this general description, each of the editors was

[5] Jean Leclercq, ' "Spiritualitas," ', *Studi medievali*, 3 (1962), 279–296; Walter Principe, 'Toward Defining Spirituality', *Sciences Religieuses/Studies in Religion*, 12/2 (1983), 127–141.

[6] Ewert Cousins, 'Preface to the Series', in Bernard McGinn and John Meyendorff, eds., *Christian Spirituality I: Origins to the Twelfth Century* (New York: Crossroad Publishing Company, 1985), p. xiii.

asked to formulate the meaning of spirituality for his or her tradition. This was first to be sent to the contributors as a guideline and then incorporated into the editor's introduction to the volume. For example, Bernard McGinn focused on the experiential aspect of spirituality in his introduction to the first Christian volume: 'Throughout its long and complex history Christianity has always insisted upon the primacy of the inner meaning of Christian documents, rituals, and institutions— their spiritual depth.' Noting that the editors of the Christian volumes did not want to impose a single definition of spirituality on their contributors, he cites the following as one understanding of the term which the contributors might use as a guideline:

> Christian spirituality is the lived experience of Christian belief in both its general and more specialized forms. . . . It is possible to distinguish spirituality from doctrine in that it concentrates not on faith itself, but on the reaction that faith arouses in religious consciousness and practice. It can likewise be distinguished from Christian ethics in that it treats not all human actions in their relation to God, but those acts in which the relation to God is immediate and explicit.[7]

McGinn refined his understanding further by the distinction between experience and reflection: 'What is contained in this [volume] . . . is obviously not Christian spirituality in the first instance, the actual lived experience itself, but reflection upon the historical manifestations of this experience, that is Christian spirituality as a discipline.'[8]

In the first of the Jewish volumes the editor, Arthur Green, focused on living in the presence of God as the characteristic of Jewish spirituality: 'Seeing the face of God, striving to live in

[7] Bernard McGinn, 'Introduction', in Bernard McGinn and John Meyendorff, eds., *Christian Spirituality I*, pp. xv–xvi.
[8] Ibid., p. xvi.

His presence and to fashion the life of holiness appropriate to God's presence—these have ever been the core of that religious civilization known to the world as Judaism, the collective religious expression of the people of Israel.' Moving towards a more specified formulation, he stated: 'Life in the presence of God—or the cultivation of a life in the ordinary world bearing the holiness once associated with sacred space and time, with Temple and with holy days—is perhaps as close as one can come to a definition of 'spirituality' that is native to the Jewish tradition and indeed faithful to its Semitic roots.' Green points out that to focus on the inwardness of spirituality would not receive universal acceptance in Judaism: 'Defining spirituality as the cultivation and appreciation of the "inward" religious life, we find both assent and demurral in the sources of Judaism.'[9] The tension between the inner and the outer is a pervasive theme in the spiritualities of Semitic origin, as we will see in the case of Islam.

In his introduction to the first Islamic volume, Seyyed Hossein Nasr cited the equivalent of the term 'spirituality' in Arabic (*rūḥāniyyah*) and in Persian (*ma 'nawiyyat*). Both terms are of Arabic origin, the first being derived from the word *rūḥ* meaning spirit; the second from the word *ma 'nā*, literally 'meaning', which connotes inwardness, 'real' as opposed to 'apparent', and also 'spirit' as this is traditionally understood to pertain to a higher level than the material and psychic, being directly related to God. Nasr summarizes the different meanings of these terms used for 'spirituality' as follows: 'that which is related to the world of the Spirit, is in Divine Proximity, possesses inwardness and interiority, and is identified with the real and therefore also, from the Islamic point of view, permanent and abiding rather than transient and passing aspects

[9] Arthur Green, 'Introduction', in Arthur Green, ed., *Jewish Spirituality I: From the Bible through the Middle Ages* (New York: Crossroad Publishing Company, 1986), pp. xiii–xiv.

321

of beings.' Echoing the issue raised above, Nasr states: 'The spiritual cannot be simply equated with the esoteric as opposed to the exoteric.' It is true that the spiritual is closer to the esoteric dimension of Islam than to any other aspect of the religion. But 'it is also very much concerned with the exoteric acts and the Divine Law as well as theology, philosophy, and the arts and sciences created by Islam and its civilization.'[10]

These definitions of the term 'spirituality', seen from the perspectives of several traditions, underscore the qualities cited at the outset of this chapter: spirituality is concerned with the experiential, with the inner—but not apart from the outer— with the real, the transcendent, the divine. If we examine the articles within the volumes, we will see that traditional spirituality contains an enormous amount of wisdom, guiding one on a journey, through the pursuit of virtues and the exercise of prayer and meditation, towards the goal of spiritual realization.

Spirituality as a Discipline
The preparation of World Spirituality has raised basic questions on the nature of spirituality as a discipline. What is its object? How is it related to other disciplines? Can spirituality be looked upon as one, or are there many different spiritualities? How is spirituality related to other disciplines: to theology and philosophy, to history and anthropology, to psychology and sociology, to the history of religions? McGinn's observation above linked spirituality to a certain kind of experience and described the discipline of spirituality as reflection on the manifestations of this experience. His introduction and those of the other editors attempted to spell out their understanding of this experience in the light of their traditions. I believe that

[10] Seyyed Hossein Nasr, in Seyyed Hossein Nasr, ed. *Islamic Spirituality I: Foundations* (New York: Crossroad Publishing Company, in press).

spirituality is a distinct discipline which can be distinguished from other disciplines by the nature of the religious experience on which it reflects. As indicated in the quotations from the introductions of the volumes of World Spirituality, this experience is not coextensive with the religion as a whole, nor with its theology or philosophy, nor with its historical, sociological, and anthropological dimensions, nor is it psychological in an exclusively modern sense, nor does it encompass all the phenomena studied in the history of religions. Although spirituality must draw from all these disciplines, it must not be swallowed up by them. Perhaps the greatest problem in conceiving and executing the plan of World Spirituality was precisely this: How retain a focus on the experience that is at the core of spirituality? How keep this experience alive when it is submitted to the reflection of academic consciousness? How integrate the dimensions from other disciplines—such as philosophy, the history of religions, and sociology—without so objectifying the experience that the reader loses contact with the heart of the discipline?

Another question has arisen: Is spirituality, as described above, a new discipline? In fact, one of the members of the editorial advisory board, Jaroslav Pelikan, raised the question whether this project was attempting to create a new discipline. If it is not creating a new discipline, I believe that it is at least attempting to transform an ancient discipline. In fact, the systematic transmission of spiritual wisdom may be the oldest discipline in the world, although it had to reach a certain level of reflexive consciousness for it to be considered an academic discipline. Certainly spirituality reached such a level in many traditions. Yet with the development of other disciplines, especially the social sciences, it now has the task of transforming itself by assimilating these disciplines into its own horizon. But it has a further task: to move into a global context. If we can speak of a new discipline of spirituality, surely it is this: global spirituality. Such a discipline would study spirituality not in one tradition alone, isolated from all others, but in a comprehensive geographic and historical context in which it would view the spiritual wisdom of each tradition in relation to that of all the others. It is only by means of the discipline of such a global spirituality that one could begin to resolve the issue of whether there is ultimately one spirituality or many irreducible spiritualities.

The Axial Period

This discipline presupposes the phenomenon of global spirituality. It is this phenomenon that I will address here. What I will present will be my own interpretation and not a common opinion of the editors of World Spirituality. In fact, there was no attempt to arrive at such a common vision. Except for the design of the series and a general acceptance of the realm of spirituality, the editors did not strive to reach a common understanding of either the history of spirituality or its present situation. Although I believe that the data amassed in the series supports my interpretation, it does not necessitate it. Other interpretations are possible, and I have drawn from other sources in arriving at my position.

In order to understand the emergence of global spirituality in our time, we must view it from a long-range historical perspective. In the first millennium B.C., a transformation of consciousness occurred which was decisive for the subsequent history of spirituality. In his book *the Origin and Goal of History*, Karl Jaspers observes that during this period a radical change took place in three geographical regions, apparently without significant influence of one on the other: in China, in India and Persia, and in the eastern Mediterranean including Greece and Israel. Jaspers calls this era the Axial Period because 'it gave birth to everything which, since then, man has been able to be.' He continues: 'It would seem that this axis of history is to be found in the period around 500 B.C., in the spiritual process that occurred between 800 and 200 B.C. It is here that we meet with the most deepcut line in history. Man, as we know him today, came into being. For short we may style this the "Axial Period".[11]

The Axial period ushered in a new form of consciousness which was vastly different from the previous consciousness of archaic, primitive, or tribal peoples. In contrast with the cosmic, mythic, ritualistic consciousness of the archaic peoples, Axial consciousness was self-reflective, abstract, speculative, objective, analytic, critical. The transition from archaic to Axial consciousness did not take place all at once, but was effected gradually, being mediated by the period of the great empires. The actual transition was heralded by teachers such as Socrates, Plato, and Aristotle in Greece; by the prophets in Israel: Elijah, Isaiah, and Jeremiah; by Zoroaster in Persia; by the seers of the Upanishads and the Buddha in India; and by Lao-tze and Confucius in China.

Although this new consciousness has been frequently described as self-reflective and analytic, I believe that underlying these characteristics is a more profound component. What distinguishes Axial from archaic consciousness is, at bottom, individual identity. Among primitive peoples consciousness was cosmic and collective. They experienced themselves at one with nature and with the tribe. This was their primary identity—not as isolated individuals but as part of the whole. They expressed their relation with the cosmos in myths and danced it in rituals. In the Axial Period human beings began to disengage themselves from nature and the tribe. Grounded on a new sense of individuality, the Axial person could stand alone, perceiving reality from a new perspective. No longer immersed

[11] Karl Jaspers, *Vom Ursprung und Ziel der Geschichte* (Zürich: Artemis, 1949); English translation by Michael Bullock, *The Origin and Goal of History* (New Haven CT: Yale University Press, 1953), p. 1.

in the cosmos, he could stand apart from nature, like the Pre-
Socratics, and as a detached observer, seek to understand its
laws. No longer merged with the tribe, he could position
himself over and against the community, criticizing it and
calling judgment upon it. Like Socrates, he ran the risk of being
condemned by a community that did not understand him. With
his consciousness no longer embedded in myth, the Axial person
could think abstractly, judge critically, and like Plato and
Aristotle, cultivate speculative reason. With the clarity of their
new consciousness, Axial thinkers produced philosophy,
mathematics, natural science, ethics; literary and visual artists
created a new aesthetic vision that found expression in drama,
poetry, art, and architecture.

The Axial Period had an enormous effect on subsequent
history in general and on spirituality in particular. The
consciousness that it produced has become the dominant form
of consciousness in the world. Through a complex history this
consciousness has spread geographically until it has
encompassed the earth. Although archaic consciousness still
exists in pockets of primitive peoples, by far the majority of the
world's population possesses the form of consciousness that took
shape in the Axial Period. 'In this age,' Jaspers observes, 'were
born the fundamental categories within which we still think
today, and the beginnings of the world religions, by which
human beings still live, were created.'[12]

The great religions of the world, through their long history
and as they exist today, are products of the Axial Period. For
example, Hinduism was significantly transformed by the
Upanishads, which brought to the cosmic consciousness of the
Vedas an awareness of the *ātman* at the depths of the individual
self. At the peak of the Axial Period, the Buddha opened a path
to individual enlightenment. In Judaism the prophets awakened

[12] Ibid., p. 2.

a sense of individual morality in contrast to ritual worship. Out of this transformation of Judaism, later came Christianity and Islam. In the Axial Period metaphysical consciousness was awakened, creating eventually the great philosophical schools which played so important a role in the world's religions: for example, the schools of Vedanta in Hinduism and Neoplatonism in Judaism, Christianity, and Islam. It is true that forms of archaic consciousness have survived to this day in the great religions, in creation myths and in rituals rooted in the cosmos and the cycles of nature. In fact, the Pre-Axial archaic level perdures as a substratum under the Axial consciousness of the world's religions, emerging in dreams, visionary mysticism, art, and architecture. Some traditions, like the Hindu, have preserved this level more integrally than others. In contrast, Western Christianity has exerted enormous intellectual energy to demythologize archaic elements from its tradition, which it deemed out of joint with nineteenth-century science.

The Axial Period had a foundational effect on the spiritualities of the world's religions. It released a burst of spiritual energy whose influences are being felt even to this day. When human consciousness emerged from myth, from its fusion with the cosmos and the tribe, the individual spiritual path opened up. The new individual consciousness could look within and find the divine in the depths of the soul. It could follow the light of its own conscience even against the opinions of the many. It could strike out alone on a journey leading to enlightenment or union with the divine. These journeys tended to take the form of an ascent: from the material to the spiritual to the divine. With extraordinary enthusiasm, the Axial spiritual seeker freed himself from the constraints of matter and climbed the lofty mountain of the spirit towards its divine summit.

The most striking example of the new Axial spirituality is found in monasticism. It was in the Axial Period that monasticism came into being. In ancient Hinduism, it is true, forest dwellers lived a kind of proto-monasticism; but it was at the peak of the Axial Period that monasticism emerged as a major spiritual path in Buddhism and Jainism. Monasticism is not found among archaic peoples. Their consciousness is too closely tied to the cosmos and the tribe, and to the fertility cycles of nature to allow for the radical step that the monk takes. For he is the supreme individual. He not only seeks enlightenment through his personal Axial consciousness, but he stands outside the cosmos and the community—through celibacy breaking with the fertility cycles of nature and with the social matrix of the community. Through poverty, he becomes a beggar, disengaging himself from its economic structure. He may follow the lifestyle of a hermit, a wandering beggar, or join a community of monks who have made a similar renunciation. Although united in a community, they nevertheless express their radical individuality by standing apart from the larger community and its way of life. Monasticism alone would be sufficient to establish the significance of the Axial Period for subsequent spirituality since it has played such a powerful role in three of the major religions: Hinduism, Buddhism, and Christianity; and its ideals have filtered into other major traditions.

The series World Spirituality mirrors the great transformation of spirituality wrought in the Axial Period. The first five volumes, which deal with archaic spirituality, reflect the characteristics of archaic consciousness described above. The emergence of Axial consciousness is treated in the volumes dealing with the Hindu, Jain, Buddhist, Confucian, Taoist, Zoroastrian, Jewish, and Greek traditions; and its subsequent development in the Christian and Islamic volumes. These volumes also show the survival of the archaic level in the later traditions. Because of the triumph of Axial over archaic consciousness, the latter could easily have been omitted even in such a series as World Spirituality. Some might have ignored it altogether; others might have deemed it not worthy of being treated in the series, or at least not so extensively. However the planners judged that it is not only necessary for telling the complete story of the human spiritual quest, but that its forms of spirituality—myth, symbol, and ritual—are valuable both in themselves and in their survival into the great world religions. And, as we shall see shortly, archaic spirituality has a special contribution to make to the emerging global spirituality of the future.

The Second Axial Period

At the present time, on the eve of the twenty-first century, I believe that we are in a Second Axial Period.[13] We are caught up in a transformation of consciousness that is as momentous as that of the First Axial Period and that will have comparable far-reaching effects on religion and spirituality. For centuries forces have been at work that are now in the twentieth century producing a global consciousness. What were once isolated tribes, then nations, then regional groups are being drawn into a communication network encircling the earth. Coupled with this has been the increasing world population, which can no longer live in isolation. Rapid means of transportation are bringing peoples together. Westerners are experiencing the sights and sounds of Oriental culture and vice versa. Television is delivering instant information around the globe.

This process is bringing about a major transformation of consciousness. Whereas the First Axial Period produced individual consciousness, the Second Axial Period is producing global consciousness. I believe that this new consciousness is

[13] For further treatment of my concept of the Second Axial Period, see my articles: 'Teilhard and Global Spirituality', *Anima*, 8 (1981), 26–30; 'Interpreting Tradition in a Global Context', in *Interpreting Tradition: The Act of Theological Reflection*, The Annual Publication of the College of Theology Society, Vol. 29, ed., Jane Kopas (Chico CA: Scholars Press, 1984), 95–108.

global in both a horizontal and a vertical sense. On the horizontal level, the peoples of the world are meeting on the surface of the earth. This encounter is enlarging the horizons of their consciousness to encompass much more data and human experience than ever before. In the Second Axial Period no one can live for long totally enclosed in his or her own culture. When their horizons expand, they begin to feel a new sense of relatedness. Many, especially the younger generations, are beginning to feel their primary relatedness not to their nation or culture, but to the human community as a whole. I do not believe that this process is, or must, produce a uniformity of culture, of either the contents or the perspectives of thought. On the contrary, this global consciousness is highly pluralistic, capable of encompassing a broad spectrum of diversity without collapsing it into an abstract unity.

Second Axial consciousness is global also in a vertical sense. Here I am taking the term 'global' to mean the physical earth. This implies that the human community must plunge its consciousness into the earth, into matter and the ecological systems that support life. First Axial consciousness separated itself from the earth, both scientifically and spiritually, abstracting general laws and climbing a spiritual ladder that left the earth behind. The very science and technology that are the offsprings of First Axial consciousness have led to problems that now threaten the future of life on this planet. Nuclear holocaust and ecological disaster threaten our future with apocalyptic destruction. The earth itself has become the prophet of the Second Axial Period, calling not for new technologies but for a new consciousness—an awareness that would include the earth in its sphere of value, that would view reality not divisively but organically. With this new global consciousness the human race could courageously and creatively seek solutions to its problems, which from within the limits of First Axial consciousness have already become overwhelming.

From a dynamic point of view, the Second Axial Period represents the peaking of a process of recovery. I believe that consciousness—both individual and collective—develops by way of recapitulation. We can, then, view the emergence of global consciousness as a recapitulation of the dimensions of archaic consciousness, the very dimensions which were submerged at the birth of Axial consciousness. Authentic recapitulation should never be a nostalgic return to a romanticized past. On the contrary, it should involve a recovery, a transformation, and a re-integration. Thus the cosmic and collective dimensions of archaic consciousness must be retrieved without losing the distinctive qualities of the individual consciousness of the First Axial Period. The bringing of these archaic dimensions into the future requires a deep transformation. For example, although archaic peoples had a profound sense of relatedness to the tribe, this usually did not extend to other tribes. This deep relatedness must now be freed from its tribal boundaries and extended beyond national and regional groups to the human community as a whole.

Second Axial Spirituality
What is the spirituality of the Second Axial Period? It must be global in the two senses described above. On the horizontal level it must expand its horizons to include the spiritualities of the entire human community. This has been taking place in today's world in a very visible way since the 1960s. The awakening of spirituality in the West was simultaneously a discovery of Eastern spirituality. Interreligious dialogue has advanced this process, as has the academic study of religions and of world spirituality. However, this encounter must take place on the spiritual level and not merely from a detached observer's standpoint. The participants in the dialogue must by means of empathy 'pass over', as John Dunne states, into the other traditions and share their distinct values—their experience and

331

spiritual wisdom—and return enriched to their own traditions.[14] This has been the experience of many from the East and West who engaged in the dialogue.

This may seem to be an optimistic, idealized picture at a time when tensions and even warfare abound on the international scene. I am not presenting the Second Axial Period as a utopia any more than the First Axial Period was. On the contrary, I am sketching the global context in which both old and new problems will appear. In fact, these problems will become greater by the fact that they are global. My point is that these problems, affecting nations and spirituality as well, must be seen in a global context. In this respect, we must take cognizance of the widespread phenomenon of retrenchment in today's world, which has taken the form of religious fundamentalism and political conservatism. Does this suggest that we are not moving towards global consciousness? On the contrary, I believe that it is due to the very shift into global consciousness. For many feel, consciously or unconsciously, that their identity is being threatened by the move into the Second Axial Period. From a long-range view of history, however, I believe that the forces producing Second Axial consciousness are immeasurably stronger than those causing the conservative reaction.

Second Axial spirituality must be global also on the vertical level. Even if the great religions were mutually enriched by their diverse spiritual heritages, they would not by that very fact have moved into the Second Axial Period. For, as indicated above, they are the products of the First Axial Period, containing its distinctive consciousness. In fact, it was precisely the turn away from matter and the earth that constituted the characteristic thrust of First Axial spirituality, which involved loss as well as gain. In disengaging themselves from nature,

[14] John Dunne, *The Way of All the Earth* (New York: Macmillan, 1972), p. ix.

Axial persons could discover its abstract laws, but in so doing, they alienated themselves from nature. Their eagerness to climb the spiritual ladder left them detached and unconcerned about the material aspects of life. Now, however, the classical spiritual traditions must respond to the prophetic call of the earth and recover those dimensions lost at the transition into First Axial consciousness. Of course, this means not merely a recovery of the sense of cosmic sacrality of archaic peoples, but the awakening of the spiritual significance of the material, biological, and cosmic dimensions of human existence as these express themselves in the political, social, and economic problems of our time. In other words, it is a spirituality that must recover its rootedness in the earth, in matter, in biology, discovering the spiritual significance of the total fabric of human life—as this has become vastly more complex in the Second Axial Period.

The recovery and transformation of these lost dimensions of spirituality offers a great challenge to all the traditions. For it is a creative task, to which each tradition must brings its distinctive resources, but which must at the same time be shared by all the traditions. We can already observe this process taking place. In the West many have turned to the archaic tribes which survive, such as the American Indians, to draw from their wisdom in resolving our ecological crisis. The women's movement which began in the West but is now spreading around the world, can be seen as a sign of the re-emergence of the feminine principle and feminine consciousness which had been suppressed by the patriarchial consciousness of the First Axial Period. Since the last century Neo-Hindu movements have been attempting to relate classical Hindu spirituality to the social, political, and economic problems. This was true of the Ramakrishna movement, in its social and educational concern, and in a striking way of Gandhi and his followers. Although many have looked upon this development as an assimilation by the East of Western social

333

concerns, it can be viewed—in the larger context of the Second Axial Period—as a recovery into the realm of spirituality of the material dimensions of human existence. More recently within Christianity, liberation theology has dramatically drawn attention to the spiritual significance of the political, social, and economic dimensions of life. As this process continues, the future of the human race will largely depend on the success of the world's religions to develop an adequate spirituality of the Second Axial Period.

The concept of the Second Axial Period, then, draws into a much deeper level the process we described in the first part of our presentation. The awakening of spirituality in the West in the 1960s was only an anticipation of the more profound awakening to the horizontal and vertical dimensions of Second Axial spirituality. The recovery of the classical tradition in the 1970s suggests the need to retrieve the earlier archaic dimensions of spirituality, to assimilate these into Axial consciousness, and to transform them into the new global consciousness of the Second Axial Period. This is not an individual but a collective task. There is reason to think that the creative development of global spirituality, through interreligious dialogue, is the distinctive spiritual journey of our time.

13

THE STUDY OF RELIGION IN TODAY'S WORLD

Jacques Waardenburg
(*Utrecht*)

1 *Introductory: some externals*

(a) Fifty years ago

Any observer cannot but be struck by some remarkable differences between the study of religion before the Second World War, say fifty years ago, and the way in which religions are studied nowadays. Half a century ago the scene was dominated by history of religions, which was philologically oriented and concentrated on the religions of Antiquity, and the comparative study of religions and religion of which an offshoot in the Netherlands was phenomenology of religion. This comparative study was also concerned with 'primitive' religion and was sometimes connected with specific philosophical or theological assumptions and implications. Such connections gave a 'spiritual' orientation to the study of religion. The heritage of the giants Emile Durkheim and Max Weber on the one hand, and Wilhelm Schmidt and Bronislaw Malinowski on the other, overshadowed the social sciences of religion. In psychology the heritage of William James and his American colleagues could be set against that of Wilhelm Wundt and his circle; Carl Gustav Jung was still in the midst of his research career.

It is no accident that the study of religion at the time could be linked to the names of some great individuals. It was a branch of study for a certain élite representing the quintessence of the intellectual climate at the time. There were only a few university posts available and a small number of students were working in this field. Work was concentrated round scholars in the great university centres of western and eastern Europe who published in various languages, and several lines linked the study of religion with philosophy and theology, problems discussed in the latter disciples making themselves palpable for instance in certain formulations and evaluations in the former. In congresses of history of religions it was possible to meet most scholars who were prominent in their fields and to keep abreast of the scholarly production as a whole. That was the time when the study of religion was part of a particular culture looking beyond its geographical and spiritual borders. There were still colonial empires then and the West saw itself as having cultural supremacy and absolute religious truth. It was the time when Gerardus van der Leeuw reached his peak and when Mircea Eliade was still a young man.

(b) The IAHR congress in Sydney 1985

Nowadays the scene is very different. Those 450 researchers from the whole world, for instance, who attended the 15th congress of the International Association of the History of Religions in Sydney in August 1985 moved around between a plethora of sections where the Ancient Near East and the Classics had only a minor place and where Comparative Studies and Phenomenology of Religion constituted only one of the nearly twenty different sections. The very theme of the congress, 'Religion and Identity', would have sounded either incomprehensible or revolutionary to scholars fifty years earlier.

At the congress just mentioned there were sections devoted to the religions of special regions and continents, for instance African studies. Besides history of religions in the narrower sense of the word there were new disciplines like anthropology, psychology and sociology of religion. The opening lecture of the congress was given not by a historian but by a sociologist of religion. There were heavily specialised sections where an interested 'generalist' in the study of religion could scarcely understand the points being made and might even have difficulty in recognising where the subject-matter fitted in at all within the general field of the study of religion. And there was also a central 'think tank': the section on methodology and hermeneutics. This was devoted to problems of method and theory in the study and interpretation of religion and would have been unimaginable fifty years ago. Notwithstanding its central place, even here the interested 'generalist' would have difficulty in grasping and following not only the content of some papers expressed in various kinds of private language but also in seizing at all the relevance of the various views expressed in the discussion. Naive people might say that it sounded chaotic: it rather reflected the complexity of the field at the present time and an urgent need for communication.

There were certainly some top scholars at the Sydney congress but bringing them together was not the congress' main function. In fact, a number of specialists working in the various disciplines of the study of religion would not come to such a general congress but prefer to work at home or attend specialised conferences of Buddhologists, Assyriologists and the like. The number of these specialists may now run into thousands and their scholarly production can only be followed by means of computerized bibliographies. Indeed, most of the participants were not top but middle men in status and there were quite a few participants under thirty. More important perhaps was the relatively small number of European participants (partly due to the distance) so that the majority consisted of researchers from North America, Asia, especially Japan, and also Africa. There were no participants from Latin

337

America, practically none from Muslim countries, and significantly no participants stemming from the 'aboriginal' cultures of Australia and elsewhere, though the stage of illiteracy has now basically been passed in the tribal religions. Apart from a delegation from Peking there were no participants from socialist countries, where history of religions is largely interpreted as the history of the decline and demise of religion. And last but not least, English had become practically the only language used at the congress.

A congress like this one shows how much the emancipation of the study of religion from theology, missiology and also philosophy has become a fact, and how worldwide this field has become, in spite of problems of organisation and communication. Most important in my view is that the present-day study of religion is no longer a European affair, as it was fifty years ago, but is now pursued against the background of the many cultures of our planet which differ not only in cultural and religious expression but also in matters of infrastructure including technology and its impact on society. At the congress Ursula King made a fervent call for the role of women both in religion and in the study of religion to receive more attention: this and the calls for more study of the religions of oppressed people and minorities would never have been voiced in those historic times before the Second World War.

It is important to supplement this description with some observations which Frank Whaling has made in the Introduction to the first Volume of his *Contemporary Approaches to the Study of Religion* (1984) about the contrast between the study of religion in the 'classical' and the contemporary period. He too stresses the increasing diversification of approaches which has occurrerd in this field, hinting at the much greater research involvement of the social sciences and the humanities in it. Improved communications make the data of a living religion anywhere in the world more easily accessible; the data themselves can now be stored in much more advanced ways than was the case in the card systems of earlier times. The shift in emphasis from the study of data of primal religions to those of the major living religions and contemporary religions in general he also links with a shift of approaches and theories, especially in America and Great Britain where, as he sees it, the contemporary scene enjoys more attention than in continental European scholarship. Moreover the increased teaching of the world religions at the college and university level, in particular in North America, has given a boost to the study of religion.

Whaling pays attention to ideological factors as well. At present, he suggests, people are realising how much religious research has been carried out with western assumptions and in a way implicitly centered on Christianity. The implications of this fact are still difficult to realise but reactions are already forthcoming. And one of the reasons why present-day scholars ought to be aware of the global context of the study of religion nowadays is so as to avoid any parochialism in pursuing research and communicating its findings, parochialisms in the past having already given rise to vehement responses and reactions from authors like Edward W. Said. Whaling also rightly points to the greater involvement at present of different ideologies in the contemporary study of religion, ranging from Marxism to interfaith understanding and dialogue, and from different forms of scientism to the search for and rediscovery of cultural and religious roots and heritage.

Such are some of the external features of the present-day scene in the study of religion. It will be more difficult to grasp some important internal changes in the field. But let us first see what kind of books are now available, comprehensively treating the present state not of one religion but of several.

339

2 From the Book Table: Some comprehensive publications

In making a short inventory of the publications in which contemporary developments of religions and religion as a whole are treated (apart from books dealing with recent developments of a particular religion or anthropological monographs on a particular people), it soon becomes surprisingly evident that notwithstanding a host of scholarly publications on religions in general and the history of one or more religions in particular, there is a cruel lack of factual studies treating recent developments of various religions at the same time. Most handbooks of the history of religions treat the recent development of each living religion only summarily. Only Trevor Ling[1] gives a comprehensive view when, in his last chapter (7), 'Religion and Industrial Society', of his book *A History of Religion East and West* (1968), he passes in review successively Religion in the West, Hinduism, Islam and Buddhism in the modern period, roughly the 19th and 20th centuries.

It is unfortunate that the yearbooks *The Religious Situation*[2] after the first two years (1968 and 1969) were not continued since they contained much information about the situation of major religions at the present time, including social and ethical issues in which adherents were involved. The *International Yearbook for the Sociology of Religion*,[3] which started in 1965, changed after its 8th volume and stopped after its 11th, and *The*

[1] Trevor Ling, *A History of Religion East and West. An Introduction and Interpretation*. London etc.: Macmillan and New York: St Martin's Press, 1968.

[2] Donald R. Cutler (Ed.), *The Religious Situation: 1968* and ... : *1969*. Boston: Beacon Press, 1968 resp. 1969.

[3] *Internationales Jahrbuch für Religionssoziologie/International Yearbook for the Sociology of Religion*. Opladen: Westdeutscher Verlag, 1965–1973 (8 volumes). This has been continued by the *Internationales Jahrbuch für Wissens-und Religionssoziologie/International Yearbook for the Sociology of Knowledge and Religion*, 1975–1978 (3 volumes).

Annual Review of the Social Sciences of Religion,[4] which started in 1976, was, alas, discontinued in 1982 for financial reasons.

There are, however, two important books offering a *survey* of the state of religion in a number of countries, and it is to be hoped that they will be updated. The first one, edited by Hans Mol,[5] treats religion in those countries where Christianity is the major religion, except Latin America. The second, edited by Carlo Caldarola,[6] treats religion in a number of countries in Asia and the Middle East where Islam, Judaism, Hinduism and Buddhism are the major religions. The countries are treated separately. Together with a short history of the prevailing religions, 19th and 20th century developments are gone into in some detail, and attention is also paid to economic and political developments until the 1970s. The editors of both books are sociologists of religion and they have succeeded in combining historical and sociological information and providing abundant bibliographical references.

Some interesting collective volumes treat religious and other developments in a group of *selected countries*. Robert F. Spencer[7] has edited a book on seven East, Southeastern and South Asian countries. S. N. Eisenstadt[8] has done the same with a volume containing twelve contributions on countries in Asia and Africa in their 'post-traditional' phase. Twenty years ago Robert N. Bellah[9] edited an instructive volume on religion and economic

[4] *The Annual Review of the Social Sciences of Religion*. Amsterdam etc.: Mouton Publishers, 1976–1981 (6 volumes).

[5] Hans Mol (Ed.), *Western Religion. A Country by Country Sociological Inquiry* (Religion and Reason 2). The Hague and Paris: Mouton, 1972.

[6] Carlo Caldarola (Ed.), *Religions and Societies: Asia and the Middle East* (Religion and Society 22). Berlin etc.: Mouton, 1982, pb. 1984.

[7] Robert F. Spencer (Ed.), *Religion and Change in Contemporary Asia*. Minneapolis: University of Minnesota Press, 1971.

[8] S. N. Eisenstadt (Ed.), *Post-Traditional Societies* New York: W. W. Norton, 1972.

[9] Robert N. Bellah (Ed.), *Religion and Progress in Modern Asia*. New York: The Free Press and London: Collier Macmillan, 1965.

development with ten contributions on Asian religions, and himself wrote a number of essays on religion in 'post-traditional' societies including the USA.[10] A volume of studies on religious institutions and modernization in Judaism, Catholicism and Islam has been edited by Kalman H. Silvert.[11] All these editors are social scientists. Political scientists have also published various studies of which two volumes concerning the third world edited by Donald E. Smith together with a recent book edited by Peter H. Merkl and Ninian Smart,[12] deserve mention. Essays on *post-war developments in major religions* have been numerous; we will only mention here a collection edited under the auspices of UNESCO.[13]

A special topic is that of *religious movements* in the 19th and 20th centuries. A 'classic' in this respect is Victor Lanternari's study of religious protest and liberation movements.[14] Important is Harold W. Turner's volume of essays on religious innovation in Africa;[15] several books have appeared on religious

[10] Robert N. Bellah, *Beyond Belief. Essays on Religion in a Post-Traditional World*. New York etc.: Harper and Row, 1970.

[11] Kalman H. Silvert (Ed.), *Churches and States. The Religious Institution and Modernization*. New York: American Universities Field Staff, 1967.

[12] Donald Eugene Smith (Ed.), *Religion, Politics, and Social Change in the Third World. A Sourcebook*. New York: The Free Press and London: Collier Macmillan, 1971. The same (Ed.), *South Asian Politics and Religion*. Princeton: Princeton Univ. Press, 1966, pb. 1969.
Compare Peter H. Merkl and Ninian Smart (Eds.), *Religion and Politics in the Modern World*. New York and London: New York University Press, 1985.

[13] Guy S. Métraux and François Crouzet (Eds.), *Religions and the Promise of the Twentieth Century. Readings in the History of Mankind*. New York and Toronto: Mentor Books, 1965.

[14] Vittorio Lanternari, *The Religions of the Oppressed. A Study of Modern Messianic Cults*. New York: Alfred A. Knopf, 1963 (Mentor Book, 1965).

[15] Harold W. Turner, *Religious Innovation in Africa. Collected Essays on New Religious Movements*. Boston: G. K. Hall, 1979. The author also composed a *Bibliography on New Religious Movements in Primal Societies*, also published by G. K. Hall in Boston (Vol. 1 on Black Africa in 1977, Vol. 2 on North America in 1978).

movements in the USA among them the one edited by Irving I. Zaretsky and Mark P. Leone.[16]

Regional studies on contemporary religion are particularly promising, as is proved by the two-volume proceedings of a conference held in Amsterdam in 1979 on religion on the northern and southern shores of the Mediterranean.[17] In this the formal opposition and contrasts between Islam and Catholicism turned out to be much less rigid when one looks at the various forms of folk religion. A special volume of essays on the theme of official and popular religion in a number of religious traditions including Christianity, edited by P. H. Vrijhof and J. Waardenburg,[18] is also worth mentioning.

Whether or nor *political ideologies* ought to be treated together with other world-views alongside the recognised religions is still an issue under debate. In any case the study of Jean-Pierre Sironneau[19] (in French but with an extensive English summary) on the religious aspects of Nazism and Stalinism is a classic of its kind, as is James Thrower's study on the way in which religion and atheism have been interpreted and studied until recently in the USSR.[20]

[16] Irving I. Zaretsky and Mark P. Leone (Eds.), *Religious Movements in Contemporary America.* Princeton: Princeton Univ. Press, 1977.

[17] The conference was held in Amsterdam in December 1979. The two volumes of the proceedings are *Religion, Power and Protest in Local Communities. The Northern Shore of the Mediterranean* (Ed. by Eric R. Wolf) and *Islamic Dilemmas: Reformers, Nationalists and Industrialization. The Southern Shore of the Mediterranean* (Ed. by Ernest Gellner). The books appeared as vols. 24 and 25 of the series 'Religion and Society'. Berlin etc.: Mouton, 1984 resp. 1985.

[18] Pieter H. Vrijhof and Jacques Waardenburg (Eds.), *Official and Popular Religion. Analysis of a Theme for Religious Studies* (Religion and Society 19). The Hague, etc.: Mouton, 1979.

[19] Jean-Pierre Sironneau, *Sécularisation et religions politiques.* With a Summary in English. (Religion and Society 17) Mouton: The Hague etc., 1982.

[20] James Thrower, *Marxist-Leninist 'Scientific Atheism' and the Study of Religion and Atheism in the USSR* (Religion and Reason 25). Berlin etc.: Mouton, 1983.

Religious change, that is to say the changes occurring in religions and the rise of new religions, has been a theme to which many studies have been devoted. There is, however, a small German volume edited by Gunther Stephenson[21] on contemporary religious change with a selection of very different examples, that may be mentioned here as exemplary.

Whereas a number of studies have been devoted to the self-interpretation of man, his nature and destiny, and the many ways in which such self-interpretations have been expressed in myths, sacred scriptures and forms of oral tradition, only a few studies of quality pay attention to the way in which various religions and religious worldviews concretely view *the human person* at the present time. As examples may be mentioned a book on the vision of man in Judaism, Christianity and Islam, by Kenneth Cragg,[22] and a large volume edited by Charles A. Moore[23] on the vision of man in Eastern and Western religions. One of the first books on the place of *woman* in various religions including Christianity is that by the well-known scholar Friedrich Heiler who lectured on the subject at the University of Marburg from the 1920s on and whose lecture-notes where published posthumously in German.[24]

One special group of publications on contemporary religions and religious developments consists of books for the use of *students*. Two examles may suffice here: the British Shap *Handbook for Teachers* edited by W. Owen Cole,[25] and an

[21] Gunther Stephenson (Ed.), *Der Religionswandel unserer Zeit im Spiegel der Religionswissenschaft*. Darmstadt: Wissenschaftliche Buchgesellschaft, 1976.

[22] Kenneth Cragg, *The Privilege of Man. A Theme in Judaism, Islam and Christianity*. London: The Athlone Press, 1968.

[23] Charles A. Moore (Ed.), *The Status of the Individual in East and West*. Honolulu: University of Hawaii Press, 1968.

[24] Friedrich Heiler, *Die Frau in den Religionen der Menschheit*. Berlin and New York: Walter de Gruyter, 1977.

[25] W. Owen Cole (for the Shap Working Party on World Religions in Education), *World Religions: A Handbook for Teachers*. London: The Commission for Racial Equality, 1977 etc.

344

interesting volume of readings edited in the USA by Jacob Needleman, A. K. Bierman and James A. Gould.[26]

As the reader will appreciate, the items given above are only a random selection of books of various kinds, nearly all of them in English, dealing with aspects of contemporary religion(s). They are, in fact merely a fraction of the total output of books (in English as well as other languages) dealing with the history of religions or of a particular religion, or with religion in general. Many of these books tend to present the religions as entities beyond time and space, as spiritual realities. To describe 20th century developments in the field of religion something else is needed: an acute sense of the present-day realities to which people respond in religious ways. Or is it true that the majority of believers at the present time essentially hold views that could just as well have been held some centuries ago, and do 20th century religious developments in fact only concern a small minority of believers, at least for the time being?

3 Research: refinement

(a) The quest for adequacy

The above listing of publications on contemporary religions could be multiplied nearly indefinitely in view of the continuous production not only of books but also of articles and popularising items. Whether we lament it or not, the development of scholarship implies ever-increasing precision, that is to say, specialization. One way to counter the negative effects of the atomization which specialised research implies is to pay renewed attention to problems of method and theory in scholarly research. Another way is to develop a self-critical attitude towards our research and its adequacy to its subject

[26] Jacob Needleman, A. K. Bierman and James A. Gould (Eds.), *Religion for a New Generation*. New York: Macmillan, 1973.

matter. And in any case, when the specialists have made their findings we need certain minds able to integrate these findings into meaningful knowledge. How now can we find ways to deal in our research most adequately with contemporary religion?

It is precisely at a time when stocktaking is taking place in the study of religion and the way in which research in it is organised at our scholarly institutions that we become sensitive to the role of non-scholarly factors. The study of contemporary religions is not only determined by an intrinsic thirst for knowledge of these religions as they are lived by their respective communities. In the history of the field we can see debates between different research traditions fighting for the virtues they claim to represent. And in the present-day struggle for survival in a time of budget cuts we can see how individual, group and institutional affiliations and interests which have nothing to do with the field prevail. The study of contemporary religions seems to have been handicapped, for instance, on the one hand by the idea of the more 'classical' research traditions that it is in any case hardly possible to arrive at scholarly knowledge of this subject; and on the other hand by a regrettable lack of organising abilities and power inside or outside existing institutions which would enable researchers to work undisturbed on this particular subject.

Out of the discovery of the anomaly of this situation and stimulated by a new interest in the topic itself, a quest for greater adequacy of the subject to the object of enquiry, in other words of the research techniques, theories and concepts used to the subject-matter of contemporary religion has arisen in the last few years. There is a growing intrinsic interest in what really happens in current religious communities, their traditions and movements according to what the available data can tell us. At least this is the case in the study of the recent history of Islam. Not only are data derived from many sources but also the nature

346

of these data is scrutinized together with the kind of light they can throw on the subject, offering as they may straightforward or indirect interpretations, official or alternative versions of what is really happening and what is really meant.

It is no accident that such an interest focusses on the activities, thought and imagination of real people in real situations. It is concerned with the ways in which people respond to reality and it discerns how different people in different situations can interpret the same elements of a religion and even the religion itself in very different ways. It also analyses the various uses that non-religious interpreters can and do make of a religion in order to legitimate or change a given state of affairs. In the same vein this interest concentrates on real encounters between adherents of different religions and tries to assess the way in which the people involved perceive themselves as well as each other.

This search for a new kind of adequacy between the researcher and his or her subject-matter also tries to avoid any ideologization, including that of the field of the study of religion itself. More attention is now paid to the reality of the people concerned, and to the relations between people. In fact, it is slowly dawning upon some of us that the impersonal character of our knowledge of religion, which is the pride of science, constitutes precisely a kind of drawback when it comes to grasping a subject-matter consisting of human realities and relationships, human aspirations and dreams.

(b) The problem of what is meant by 'religion'
The quest for adequacy sketched above has brought to light a problem closely connected with the 'western' nature of much religious research, as Frank Whaling has pointed out. For the essential tool with which religion is identified so as to be studied is the concept of religion as it has been elaborated in the West. As a result it is strongly imbued with normative connotations bearing witness to the debates in the West concerning what was

347

held to be religion, and reflecting both religious and anti-religious concerns. Alternatively, religion has been defined in scholarship as the presence of something that is absent elsewhere (for instance the sacred), or as the presence of certain facts that constitute religion (for instance the belief in spiritual beings).

The problem with both the normative and the factual concepts of religion is quite simply that they prevent us arriving at an adequate perception and consideration of the specific meanings and ethical values, inseparable from emotions and feelings, which contemporary 'religions' convey to the people concerned. By using this kind of concept of religion a researcher may even impose on other peoples' ways of life and basic orientations a concept of religion that prevents him from seeing what those other peoples' religion means to them. In fact it may reify particular representations and ways of behaviour as 'religion', isolating them from closely related data which are intertwined with the 'religious' ones but do not fall under the concept of religion used.

An important refinement of research over the last twenty years, datable to W. Cantwell Smith's *Meaning and End of Religion* of 1963, is our much more careful handling and use of our own concepts when describing 'other' cultures and religions. In our study of contemporary religions we need a new kind of descriptive and open concept of religion, one which would apply not only to what, according to western definitions, is 'real' religion but also to what may constitute a 'working' or 'effective' religion for the people concerned, even if they would perhaps not recognise it as 'religion' themselves because it does not fit into what is considered as 'official' religion in their society.

In these studies the quest for adequacy leads to taking a community's culture as a whole without separating 'religion' from 'non-religion'. The primary task is then to distinguish religious from non-religious meanings, and see where the latter are located. This requires that the researcher communicate openly with the people concerned: and go beyond participant observation.[27]

(c) The problem of religious meaning

Current research in the field of subjective meanings can be used to illustrate a change of perspective that is relevant for the study of living religion. Research on meaning in the field of religion has for a long time been practically identified with etymological research, that is the search for original meaning in lexical terms; original meaning was held to explain later meanings. Likewise, in religious myths and rituals, as well as in religion itself, the original version was held to contain the core or true meaning of the phenomenon which was subsequently to undergo its historical development.

The approach to the problem of meaning was broadened through the notion first of contextual and then of functional meaning. The notion of a contextual meaning suggests that a phenomenon, including a word, derives its meaning not only from its historical origin but also and perhaps more so from the context within which it is used. When this 'context' is taken not only in the sense of the immediate word context but also in the sense of the broader social context within which a particular word or expression is used, we arrive at the notion of a functional meaning. The functional meaning of religious words, expressions and phenomena at large is the meaning which they convey to an audience within a broader social context, for instance when used in a sermon in a church service with reference to particular events known to the audience. A further development in meaning research is that pursued in

[27] On the concept of religion, compare my 'Über die Religion der Religionswissenschaft', *Neue Zeitschrift für Systematische Theologie und Religionsphilosophie*, Vol. 26, No. 3 (1984), pp. 238–255 (with English summary).

structuralism where formal relationships are investigated as to the meaning they convey.

For our purposes—the study of contemporary religions—the notion of contextual meaning can be further developed, thus throwing new light on the problem of meaning both of religious data and of religions. Here it is not the etymological, contextual, functional or structural 'objective' meaning that is the subject of the enquiry but rather the 'subjective' meaning, that is to say the 'objective' meaning as realised by the receiver whether that is a group or a person. What can we know about what particular religious data and even complete religions mean to different people in different circumstances? What does a particular group or person make of particular religious phenomena? Formerly this 'subjective' meaning was generally supposed to lie outside the domain of scientific knowledge; now, however, it has acquired scholarly respectability, since we can analyse subjective meanings through the interpretations to which they give rise.[28]

4 The researcher: awareness

(a) New motivations for the study of contemporary religions

Research on religion as on other subjects is carried out by researchers who have their own motivations in studying it. It has been observed that a better knowledge of such motivations would help us in our assessment of scholarly work in this field.[29]

---

[28] Compare my *Reflections on the Study of Religion, Including an Essay of the Work of Gerardus van der Leeuw* (Religion and Reason 15). The Hague etc.: Mouton, 1978.

[29] See for instance J. G. Platvoet, *Comparing Religions: A Limitative Approach. An Analysis of Akan, Para-Creole, and IFO-Sandanda Rites and Prayers*, Chapter 1: 'Objective Intention and Subjective Involvement' (Religion and Reason 24). The Hague etc.: Mouton, 1982.

In any case, in the study of contemporary religions we can distinguish certain new motivations underlying evaluations of religion in general or of a particular religion which are no longer linked firmly to Christian theology. The principle of *epochē* in classical phenomenology and in the study of religion generally had already shielded the study of religion from theological judgements and evaluations current at the time. But there are other kinds of value judgement too and the present practice in matters of evaluation is very different indeed from that of Rudolf Otto, Gerardus van der Leeuw and Friedrich Heiler where judgements on the phenomenon of religion were mainly made in Christian theological terms. Let us look at some types of evaluation which may be distinguished in present-day research on contemporary religions.

First of all, most researchers from Asia and Africa are engaged in rediscovering what may be called their cultural and religious heritage. Many of them, when focussing on their own religious history, are implicitly searching for the basic values of their societies. In various ways the study of one's own religious heritage can become instrumental in this way to *rediscovering one's roots*.

On the other hand, quite a few western scholars who try to maintain an open attitude to religious expressions from different parts of the world are yet also developing a critical attitude to the *negative role played by religion in history*, both western and non-western. This critical attitude is, in a way, the opposite of the attitude of rediscovering one's roots mentioned above. It can be philosophically and ideologically structured, as with those who appeal in one way or another to Karl Marx' work, and it has been dogmatically fixed and schematized in the doctrine of scientific atheism in the USSR. It can be found in the line of the *Frankfurter Schule*, whose analysts have been keen to ascertain processes of ideologization taking place under the pressure of interest groups with vested interests in ideologization and intellectual fixation.[30] Just as a sharpening of knives took place in the 19th century schools of thorough-going literary and historical criticism of the Old and New Testament, so the critical study of the history of Christianity throughout the centuries has had a sharp eye for all that has been not only human but inhuman and sinful in the history of that religion, judged according to its own standards. Similar critical attitudes are developing among researchers stemming from other cultural and religious traditions when they not so much look for their roots in their religion's past as evaluate the history of their religion by its fruits, using the yardstick of their own generation's perceptions and values.

Third, a number of researchers, some of them exhibiting the critical attitude just sketched, who work on religious movements and are interested, for instance, in the role of prophetical and puritanical, messianic and reform movements in processes of *emancipation and liberation from outside oppression and pressures generally* reveal a new kind of appreciation for the object of their research. Whereas for a long time such religious movements were seen as obstructive to social development, the insight is now gaining ground in some quarters that in the framework of a given historical situation where a certain religious tradition exists, an appeal to the tradition as a starting point for a new religious movement may be the only way to get things moving for people who are profoundly attached and even committed to this religious tradition. Similarly, the role of a religious quest and of particular forms of religious experience tends to be evaluated more positively now in the light of current theorizing about personality development than was the case some decades ago.

In the fourth place, wider notions, in particular the historical

---

[30] See for instance Rudolf J. Siebert, *The Critical Theory of Religion. The Frankfurt School* (Religion and Reason 29). Berlin etc.: Mouton, 1985.

role which religions have played and continue to play in the great civilisations of the world in past and present, are being looked at anew. The historical role of the 'successful' religions has of course always been recognised by historians: the historical existence of a religion has made it *ipso facto* a worthwhile subject of historical research. But it would seem that scholars are more aware now of the particular kind of moral fibre that can be generated by particular styles and forms of religious faith. This leads to even wider enquiries when, instead of historical religions being contrasted with each other on the basis of their particularities, it is *universal elements* in the domain of the various religions, such as precognised in 'universal theologies' of different kinds, which are sought for.[31]

This search for religious universals can go hand-in-hand with a *critical view of the West* which sees it as incarnating a deviating development compared to the general potential of mankind. Depending on the researcher, the West's rationalisation and automatisation through technology, its historicism and the alienation produced by a loss of roots, its materialism and a new kind of dehumanisation arising from a general loss of values that were upheld in former times may be stressed. Such a pessimism, if not disillusionment, with regard to the West, may not always lead to a search for new universals, religious or otherwise. Instead, it may encourage a search for new dimensions of life and experience which have been known in other times and in other, often earlier cultures in the world but have been lost in the present-day West. Alternatively, it may contribute to the emergence of new styles of life and new ethical codes.

We cannot consider here that continuing motive underlying so many studies in the field of religion, though perhaps more in the period before the second World War than after it. This is the

---

[31] For instance Wilfred Cantwell Smith, *Towards a World Theology. Faith and the Comparative History of Religion*. Philadelphia: The Westminster Press, 1981.

interest, simple curiosity or deeper realisation of the significance of what religious people have to say about the ultimate questions concerning the life of mankind and the realities of the human situation through their religion. The view of mankind as a sort of human brotherhood has always encouraged the study of testimonies coming from outside the researcher's own tradition, testimonies which are attentively listened to.

(b) The need for reflection

The study of contemporary religions, then, requires not only technical research abilities but also a good deal of reflection by the researcher. We possess an immense body of knowledge. Tremendous intellectual capital has been invested in learning languages, studying texts, analysing societies and cultures, understanding the ways in which religious traditions are handed over through generations and to other people as well. All of this has led to a growth of the study of religion in terms of our knowledge of data. But too much empirical work has somehow tended to obnubilate some basic questions concerning for instance the choice of an appropriate method, the pondering on a hypothesis to explain certain rules in the occurrence of religion, the device of a theoretical blueprint to account for the variety of religious interpretations of reality and ways of acting towards that reality.

There is something anomalous in this lack of intellectual endeavour and vigour. It seems to me at least that students of art, for instance, are really concerned with what art is like, why there is art when there are human beings, what art's function and task in society could be. Many of them are interested in other forms of art, including contemporary art forms, than those found in the West. Students of religion, on the contrary, tend to be very much concerned with their own religion and much less with different kinds of religious expression whether these are experience, faith or imagination. They seem disinclined to ponder why there has been religion at all in so many human communities, and what the implications of this fact for modern man can be. More than students of art and literature, sociology and anthropology, students of religion seem to be parochial and self-centred. At least they may be said to be still in a pre-reflective stage and this lack of reflection requires an explanation, because it should be remedied if the study of contemporary religions is to attract researchers who are more than scientific technicians. There are several possible answers: (1) Many students of religion have not been schooled technically in philosophical or theological critical thought. This is in part due to the way of specializing at university institutions: one mostly has to opt either for philosophy, taking concepts (language) as a starting point, or for an empirical study, taking empirical data as a starting point. And it is difficult to combine both fruitfully.

(2) Our critical climate, broadly speaking, does not favour investing much intellectual energy in questions of religion, whether 'foreign' or 'home-grown', unless a person has a clear message to preach. Religion has simply become marginal to western society and those who might be able to treat problems of religion critically prefer to study philosophy, social sciences or, sometimes, Oriental studies. As a consequence we face the curious situation that those who would be able to treat religion as an intellectual problem do not find satisfaction in our academic institutions.

(3) The lack of intellectual reflection as distinct from holding private beliefs, opinions and convictions, may also be explained by the popular idea that one must be either a believer or an unbeliever. The contrast between believers and unbelievers may have its social usefulness for groups advocating or combatting a particular belief and looking for adherents, but it is disastrous for sound intellectual pursuits. My guess is that the dichotomy usually supposed between those who believe certain things and

355

others who do not has done a lot of harm to the scholarly study of religion, including contemporary religions, and to the honest intellectual reflection indispensable to it.

It is to encourage genuine reflection in the study of religion, that an interest in methods and theories of research should be promoted. We should train ourselves to be more continuously aware of what we are doing in the study of religion, how we are doing it, and why we are doing it. This cannot fail to contribute to the study of present-day religion anywhere.

There is perhaps another justification of the need of discourse on method and theory in the study of contemporary religions, apart from the technical and pedagogical aspects. What is fascinating in discussions about method and theory in the study of living religion is the tendency such discussions have to open up a reflection on the phenomenon of religion itself. Theories and methods for the study of contemporary religion can in the final analysis be read not only as tools of research but also as intellectual articulations of basic intentions and dispositions on the part of the scholar seen not only as a professional technician but also as a thinker in his own right. The field of method and theory may then be called the very nerve centre of the scholarly study of religion, and be considered here: an authentic intellectual quest aimed at interpreting, understanding and explaining the fact of living religion nowadays.[32]

(c) Responsibilities of researchers

Anyone who is at all sensitive to problems of evaluation will see without difficulty that a most serious problem of responsibility and value judgements arises, not so much in the course of scholarly research on religion, which is largely governed by the norm of impartiality and *epochē*, as before it starts and also when it is over and its results are applied in practical life. What is the

[32] The book series *Religion and Reason*, published by Mouton, has been devoted to this kind of problems.

value, after all, of religion when it is not a personal experience but a subject of enquiry which some people feel urged to spend the best years of their intellectual life studying? What can be said and done by scholars in the face of what seems to be a permanent abuse of norms and truths embedded in religious traditions and their sources? What should be their reaction to appeals to religion which simply express and try to legitimate a refusal to change, over against the better arguments and human insights in favour of change which must somehow have been recognised even by those who make the appeal?

No doubt similar problems with regard to the responsibility of committed researchers exist in the natural and social sciences. What makes the situation so serious in the field of living religion is that we are working here with stocks of energy which, though different from nuclear energy or the psychological forces of collective behaviour, can be mobilised or evoked either to orientate or disorientate human beings. And in the latter case it is not only the individual but also his or her fellow human beings who suffer.

Whereas for a long time scholarly responsibility was held to apply to scholarly truth only, here and there an extension of the concept of scholarly responsibility is taking place. Some scholars at least, see problems of an ethical nature imposing themselves beyond the problems of truth. As is the case in the fields of atomic research and nuclear science, biology and cultural anthropology, an increasing number of scholars in the field of the study of religion (in particular living religion) feel responsibility in the first place for the way in which they collect data and present their findings. In particular they may be confronted by dilemmas if they are obliged to hand over these findings to religious or political bodies that can use them for the pursuit of aims and purposes which are directly opposed to the meaning of the data, the interests of the people concerned and the aims pursued in scholarly research. In former times to work for a missionary society or colonial government may have been a problem. Nowadays one wonders whether one should work for agencies at all if there is no guarantee that the knowledge one assembles will not be used by these agencies against the very interests of the people whose religion has been the subject of enquiry.

The cases of atomic scientists like Leo Oppenheimer and cultural anthropologists advising on matters pertaining to the Vietnam war were extreme and have had no parallels, as far as I know, among scholars of religion. Yet few people realise how much mental 'nuclear' energy is contained in religion, to be used but also misused, in particular when obedience and sacrifices are demanded. Masses can be mobilised by ideological interpretations and applications of religion. Recent events in Northern Ireland, Iran, Lebanon and South Africa have shown the brutal use that can be made of religion for political purposes and the extent to which people can be blinded to the long-term consequences of such use. The present-day rise and official encouragement of civil religion in countries like the USA and Israel is not ony a religious phenomenon but also implies political action.[33] Each state policy towards religion demands expertise which scholars of religion may be able and willing to give. Most politicians have not the faintest idea of the religious forces they may be dealing with. In such a situation experts, scholars of religion, can have a weighty and responsible voice.

5 Towards a more adequate study of contemporary religion[34]

We would like to close this contribution with some suggestions as to how to develop a more adequate study of religion in the

[33] See for instance Robert N. Bellah and Phillip E. Hammond, *Varieties of Civil Religion*. San Francisco etc.: Harper and Row, 1980; Charles S. Liebman and Eliezer Don-Yehiya, *Civil Religion in Israel. Traditional Judaism and Political Culture in the Jewish State*. Berkeley etc.: Univ. of California Press, 1983.

[34] A standard book on different ways of studying religion is Frank Whaling

most recent past and the present time. There is nothing essentially novel in this blueprint; rather it is a consistent continuation of the classical disciplines of the study of religion with an application to modern times. We make a conscious attempt to eliminate that taste for the exotic that has characterized so many romantic descriptions of far-away religious worlds, and also that unavowed tendency to transcendence which gave earlier descriptions of religions at the same time a touch of spiritual elevation and an unmistakable lack of sense of reality. Instead, we apply a scholarly approach, seeking to show the many forms of religion in our time as human expressions both in behaviour and in imagination and ideas. There are four basic approaches then to religion in general which we shall apply to contemporary religion in particular: historical, comparative, contextual and hermeneutical.

(1) In the *historical study* of contemporary religion we are concerned with the diachronical sequence of cause and effect in the history of religious institutions, ideas and ways of acting. In order to understand present-day religion historically we have to see what preceded it and we have to try to explain its forms on the basis of the past. This holds true not only for the official institutionalized forms but also for what may be called traditional ways of acting and thinking. It also applies to new religious movements which have arisen during the last hundred years, and to new religions which were consciously founded or grew so to speak out of a synthesis of elements from different religious traditions. It even applies to the rise of movements which have taken a critical stand towards existing religions or religion in general and which throw a particular light on the

(Ed.), *Contemporary Approaches to the Study of Religion*. Vol. 1: *The Humanities*, Vol. 2: *The Social Sciences*. (Religion and Reason 27 and 28) Berlin etc.: Mouton, 1984 and 1985. For the four ways of studying religion as sketched in this section see Jacques Waardenburg, *Religionen und Religion. Systematische Einführung in die Religionswissenschaft* (Göschen Sammlung) Berlin: W. de Gruyter. 1986.

religious scene in different countries, which is always more complex than our surveys and handbooks suggest.

I am convinced, however, that the real history of religion in modern times comes to the fore only when *religious and non-religious developments* of a particular people are placed, understood and explained *together within the overall social and cultural* history of those people. Only then can we arrive at an adequate historical understanding instead of treating 'religious' history apart from 'real' history.

(2) In the *comparative study* of contemporary religion we are concerned with religious parallels and differences in various religions at the present time. We start out from the fact of a great number of different cultures and civilisations, each with their distinct religious traditions, existing say at the beginning of the nineteenth century. Over the last century and a half a number of developments have taken place within or from these religious traditions and generally speaking these developments have led to greater variety and increasing diversification within them. In nearly every religion, for instance, a distinction is now made between 'modernising' and 'traditional' trends although the terms may be defined differently. It is a valid question of research if we can distinguish certain structural parallels between specific trends in different religious traditions, for instance between modernising Hindu and Buddhist movements, or between liberal Judaism and Islam. One can even go a step further and ask whether we can distinguish within the different religions the development of parallel views of reality and mankind, so that the adherents of these trends somehow come nearer to each other than was possible a century ago. But we also have to ask, then, whether there are also comparable trends in the various religions stressing the superiority, the unique truth of the particular religion of the believer and the inferiority and relative or absolute untruth of other religions and ideologies.

I would like to proceed next to an *explanation* of such parallels and differences in development of the various religions, for instance by concentrating on certain general changes (for instance the diffusion of technology and the spread of a scientific worldview) and then *comparing the different responses that have been given from within the various religious traditions* to such general changes. One can also compare the different ways in which religions have reacted to a competing ideology like Marxism or nationalism, or to the rise of an economic system that has been detrimental to a number of traditional religious institutions, such as modern capitalism.

(3) In the *contextual study* of religion we are concerned with the way in which a religion is conditioned by the social, political and other context in which it occurs and we try to explain certain religious situations and developments out of this context. When the context does not change appreciably, religions will tend to become rather fixed traditions and in fact the seeming immobility of a number of religions in the past may largely be attributed to the lack of fundamental changes of the context within which these religions continued to exist. Applying this starting-point to the study of contemproary religion we can ask, for instance, what has been the impact of certain important developments since the Second World War on religious developments during the same period. We may think of the political independence of the Afro-Asian nations, the rise of nationalist ideologies and of development strategies in these nations and their impact on the many religious traditions existing in Asia and Africa, and the effects of the cold war. We may think of the centralisation of state power in nearly all countries of the world and its impact on the development of various more-or-less official religious ideologies; the more the state appears to be threatened the more it tends to appeal to the resources of religion in order to legitimate and strengthen itself.

Another way of applying the contextual approach to the

study of contemporary religions is to look at the way in which different kinds of religion exist nowadays side-by-side, dependent on social contexts. We may think of the many forms of folk or popular religion existing among those who are not informed about, or interested in, official or normative religion; as soon, however, as a particualr form of religion is proclaimed to be official, this implies the demise of many forms of traditional folk religion. We may think also of the many forms of minority religion, for instance the religion of an ethnic minority, a numerically small religion over against a secular majority, or the religion of a group of immigrants over against the autochthonous majority. In all cases, the forms and development of such a minority religion will be to a large extent conditioned by the fact of being in the minority. In cases such as these and those of civil religions in various countries, or religious forms and practices that are adhered to by women in the first place, for example, the specific forms of religion are largely determined by the context in which the religion occurs.

In such a contextual study of religions at present I would like to suggest that special attention be paid to the current transformations of religious as well as cultural traditions: many elements of religious traditions change: they may be replaced by other elements or they may simply disappear or come into oblivion. Many more elements still remain but undergo a change of role, function and meaning. Through the contextual study we can try to *explain such changes of religious elements and their meaning by contextual changes.*

(4) In the *hermeneutical study* of contemporary religions we focus our attention on the meaning which particular religious data or religions have for the people concerned, and on the interpretations given to them. In modern times there have been considerable changes in the interpretation of traditional religious data and even whole religions. This change of interpretation in itself is nothing new; the interesting fact

nowadays is that radical new interpretations occur in a relatively short time span, and that such new interpretations are given by people and groups who do not necessarily belong to the clergy, or scholars of religious law or theologians. Such new interpretations can be explained, in part, by a context (as shown before), but they can also be seen as religious responses to new situations (which is our hermeneutical approach). Because of technological developments the older traditional meanings of customs and ideas can no longer be maintained. Over against the vacuum of meaning, so to say, which occurs, an intense search for new meaning can take place, leading to sometimes exuberant new interpretations. One way, for instance, is that of rediscovering an older religious and cultural heritage as one's own past and identity. We see this happening in all parts of the world under pressures of various kinds, and it leads to a kind of revival of the given religion. The puritanical forms of such a revitalization of religion, in particular, are interesting since they appear to be able to cope with the need for rationalization given with a modernization process of society.

A particularly fruitful field for hermeneutical research in this sense is to see a number of new interpretations of old-established religions as a kind of *spiritual solution* for problems which otherwise seem to be insoluble and which are of an existential nature. Many newer interpretations focus on the need for unity over against existing diversity, not only politically and economically but also as an attempt to overcome the disunity of religions, hinting at the unity of mankind. Many interpretations focus on the need for peace, not only politically but also spiritually, over against political conflicts and the threat of a nuclear war. Again, a number of current interpretations of religions suggest their readiness to bring about development according to age-old values and encourage exertion over against the prevailing material underdevelopment and poverty in the greater part of the world. In the same vein a number of

363

NOTES ON CONTRIBUTORS

Brian Bocking graduated from Lancaster University with a degree in Religious Studies in 1973, and took his Doctorate from the University of Leeds, his dissertation being on the *chung-lun*, Kumārajīva's Chinese version of the commentary on Nāgārjuna's Middle Stanzas. He has lectured in Japanese Religions at the University of Stirling since 1977; during 1982 he was Visiting Lecturer in Religious Studies at the Institute of Philosophy, University of Tsukuba, Japan. His main book is on *Japanese Religions*, and he has written widely in this field.

Ewart Cousins is a Professor in the Theology Department at Fordham University, and a Visiting Professor at Columbia University and New York University. He is General Editor of the 25-volume series *World Spirituality: An Encyclopedic History of the Religious Quest*. He is Chief Editorial Consultant for the 60-volume series *The Classics of Western Spirituality* and was responsible for the volume in that series on *Bonaventure*. His other books include *Bonaventure and the Coincidence of Opposites*, and *Global Spirituality: Toward the Meeting of Mystical Paths*. He is widely known in the fields of Spirituality and Global Thought.

Phillip Hammond took his undergraduate degrees from Willamette and Columbia Universities, and his Doctorate from Columbia University. He has taught at Columbia and Yale, and the Universities of Wisconsin and Arizona, and is presently Professor of Religious Studies and Sociology, and Chairman of Religious Studies at the University of California, Santa Barbara. He has received a number of academic honours and awards from foundations such as Ford, Danforth, Meyer, Johnson and Lilly, and is presently President of the Society for the Scientific Study of Religion. Among his books are included: *Sociologists at Work*; *Religion in Social Context*; *American Mosaic:*

Social Patterns of Religion in the US; Beyond the Classics? The Scientific Study of Religion; The Structure of Human Society; Varieties of Civil Religion; and *The Sacred in a Secular Age: Toward Revision in the Scientific Study of Religion.*

Louis Jacobs was born in Manchester, UK, and educated at Manchester Central High School and University College, London. He holds BA and PhD degrees from London University. He is Rabbi of the New London Synagogue, Lecturer in Talmud and Jewish Mysticism at Leo Baeck College, London, and President of the London Society for the Study of Religion. His many books include: *Studies in Talmudic Logic and Methodology; Principles of the Jewish Faith; A Jewish Theology; Hasidic Prayer; Theology in the Responsa; Teyku: The Unsolved Problem in the Babylonian Talmud.*

Ninian Smart was educated at the Universities of Glasgow and Oxford where he did his graduate work in the Philosophy of Religion. He has taught Philosophy, Theology, and Religious Studies at various Universities: Wales, London, Birmingham, Lancaster, and since 1976 the University of California, Santa Barbara where he has held a joint appointment with Lancaster. He has written extensively in various areas of the study of World-views. In Philosophy of Religion, his books include *Reasons and Faiths* and *Philosophers and Religious Truth;* in Indian Philosophy and Religion *Doctrine and Argument in Indian Philosophy* and *The Yogi and the Devotee;* in the History of Religions *The Religious Experience of Mankind, The Phenomenon of Christianity,* and *Prophet of a New Hindu Age;* in Politics Mao and (with Peter Merkl) *Religion and Politics in the Modern World;* in Methodology *The Science of Religion* and *The Phenomenon of Religion;* and in Religious Reflection *Beyond Ideology.*

Donald Swearer took his undergraduate degrees from Yale and Princeton, and his Doctorate from Princeton University.

He has taught at Oberlin, the University of Pennsylvania, and Swarthmore College where he Chairs the Department of Religion. He has held Visiting Professorships at Bryn Mawr, Haverford, Princeton, and Harvard, and has received a number of academic awards from foundations such as Rockefeller, Mellon, and Ford. His many books include: *Buddhism in Transition: Southeast Asia*; *A Theology of Dialogue*; *Wat Haripunjaya*; *Buddhism*; *Buddhism and Society in Southeast Asia*; *The Dhammic Socialism of Buddhadasa Bhikkhu*.

Jacques Waardenburg was born in the Netherlands where he was educated at the Universities of Haarlem and Amsterdam. He eventually specialised in Islam and received his Doctorate from Amsterdam University. He has taught at McGill University, Montreal, the University of California, Los Angeles, and the University of Utrecht where he holds the Chair of Islam and Phenomenology. His books include: *Les Universités dans le Monde Arabe Actuel*; *Classical Approaches to the Study of Religion*; *Humaniora Islamica*; *Reflections on the Study of Religion*; *Official and Popular Religion*; *L'Enseignement dans les Pays Arabes*; *Religionen und Religion: Systematische Einführung in die Religionswissenschaft*. As General Editor of *Religion and Reason*, and as Editor of *Religion and Society*, (both series published by Mouton), he has led the way in theoretical discussion of the Study of Religion.

Andrew Finlay Walls was born in Scotland in 1928. He has held appointments in the University of Sierre Leone, the University of Nigeria at Nsukka, and (as Visiting Professor) in the Universities of Botswana, Lesotho, and Swaziland. He was Professor of Religious Studies at Aberdeen University for many years, and in 1982 became the Director of the Centre for the Study of Christianity in the Non-Western World at Aberdeen. After being a Research Fellow at Yale University in 1986–87, he returned to Scotland to become Director of the Centre for the

367

Study of Christianity in the Non-Western World now located at Edinburgh University. He has been Editor of the Journal of Religion in Africa for nineteen years, and has written extensively in the areas of World Christianity and Primal Religions.

William Montgomery Watt was born in Fife, Scotland, and was educated at Oxford and Edinburgh Universities. His PhD is from Edinburgh University, and he has an Honorary Doctorate from Aberdeen University. He lectured in Moral Philosophy at Edinburgh, Islamics in Jerusalem, and Ancient Philosophy at Edinburgh, before becoming Head and later Professor of the Department of Arabic and Islamic Studies at Edinburgh University. He is widely known for his work on Islamics, and his main publications include: *Muhammad at Mecca*; *Muhammad at Medina*; *Islam and the Integration of Society*; *Islamic Philosophy and Theology*; *The Formative Period of Islamic Thought*; and *Islam and Christianity Today*.

Tu Wei-Ming was born at Kunming, China in 1940. He received a BA in Chinese Studies from Tunghai University, Taiwan, in 1961, an MA in East Asian Regional Studies from Harvard in 1963, and a PhD in History and Far Eastern Languages from Harvard in 1968. He taught at Tunghai, Princeton, and Berkeley before taking up his present post as Professor of Chinese History and Philosophy at Harvard in 1981. His research areas are those of Confucian Thought, Chinese Intellectual History, and the Religious Philosophy of East Asia. In addition to his work in Chinese, he has written in English: *Neo-Confucian Thought in Action: Wang Yang-Ming's Youth*; *Centrality and Commonality: An Essay on Chung-Yung*; *Humanity and Self-Cultivation: Essays in Confucian Thought*; and *Traditional China*.

Frank Whaling was born in Yorkshire, UK, and educated at Cambridge University where he took degrees in History and Theology, and at Harvard University where he took a Doctorate in Comparative Religion. He has spearheaded the Religious Studies programme at Edinburgh University since 1973; his academic honours include Fellowships of the Royal Asiatic Society, the International Biographical Association, and the World Literary Academy, and an Associateship of the Research Academy of the American Biographical Institute; he has received academic awards from the British Academy, British Council, Carnegie, Commonwealth Institute, Cook, Farmington, and Fulbright; he has been a British Academy Fellow at the Chinese Academy of Social Sciences, Beijing, a Fulbright Fellow at Harvard, and a Visiting Professor at Calcutta, Dartmouth, and Witwatersrand. His nine books include: *The Rise of the Religious Significance of Rāma*; *An Approach to Dialogue: Hinduism and Christianity*; *John and Charles Wesley* in the *Classics of Western Spirituality*; *Contemporary Approaches to the Study of Religion, Vol 1 (The Humanities)* and *Vol 2 (The Social Sciences)*; *Christian Theology and World Religions: A Global Approach*; and *The World's Religious Traditions: Current Perspectives in Religious Studies*.

INDEX

INDEX